Praise for *Thriving after Trauma*

"*Thriving after Trauma* pulled at my heartstrings, as this author brought such authenticity to life throughout this book. The true stories of her patients, as well as herself, give the reader a deep view into the world of those who struggle after trauma and abuse. The techniques and educational value of this read will be a great help to many people out there who continue to struggle alone. Embrace the journey!"
—Lisa Zarcone, author of *The Unspoken Truth: A Memoir* and Massachusetts National Ambassador for NAASCA

"As the collective understanding and acceptance of the impact of psychological trauma exploded in recent years, Shari Botwin was at the public forefront narrating it in newspapers and television. Now she brings it all together in a series of real-life accounts of despair and how to overcome them. Sharing her gift of translating the language and culture of psychological trauma into plain English, Botwin—a survivor herself—blends her personal anguish with the painful experiences of others she counseled through the years. At its finest points, this book not only informs but opens the soul."
—Bob Stewart, freelance journalist, *New York Daily News*, *Philadelphia Inquirer*, and *Philadelphia Daily News*

"As a survivor of childhood abuse, Shari Botwin brings a deep understanding and empathy to traumatized folks lucky enough to have crossed paths with her—either in her writings, her workshops, her talks, or her individual therapy sessions. I was a domestic abuse victim until she guided me as I worked to become first a domestic abuse survivor and now a domestic abuse thriver. Readers of this book will learn that they are not alone as they meet some of Botwin's patients who have experienced trauma and worked to overcome it. Moreover, each chapter ends with ideas readers can use on their own journey to living a full life unencumbered by the residue of the trauma that has followed them like a shadow through their lives. No matter how long ago the trauma occurred, you can begin today to reclaim your right to happiness and fulfillment."

—Suzanne Dobkin, PhD, domestic abuse warrior

"Botwin's book was a blessing to my survivor life. She immediately drew me in and kept hold of me throughout the entire read. I loved how she so skillfully intertwined her own story with the stories of others and the ways she used her gift of being a helper of the suffering to show us all that any and every emotion can stop to visit trauma survivors and that each one of them is normal. When we speak and are heard, we heal. When we speak and understand our own selves as well as others, we heal. When we give ourselves room to speak our truth, we truly learn how to thrive and not merely survive. It is my honor to know this brilliant, compassionate, talented lady, and I highly recommend this read!"

—Michelle Stolleis Denault, blogger, educator, sexual abuse survivor, and advocate

"Shari Botwin's book is a must-read for trauma survivors. She weaves her expertise as a mental health professional with her personal story of trauma to provide a compelling 'how to' for healing. *Thriving after Trauma* is a powerful testament to the human ability to heal from trauma, however long and difficult the road may be. Botwin's authentic story of reclaiming her life and becoming a fierce advocate for trauma survivors is revealing and empowering."

—Caroline Heldman, PhD, Politics Department, Occidental College, and executive director, the Representation Project

THRIVING AFTER TRAUMA

THRIVING AFTER TRAUMA

Stories of Living and Healing

Shari Botwin

ROWMAN & LITTLEFIELD
Lanham • Boulder • New York • London

Published by Rowman & Littlefield
An imprint of The Rowman & Littlefield Publishing Group, Inc.
4501 Forbes Boulevard, Suite 200, Lanham, Maryland 20706
www.rowman.com

6 Tinworth Street, London SE11 5AL

British Library Cataloguing in Publication Information Available

Library of Congress Cataloging-in-Publication Data

Names: Botwin, Shari, author.
Title: Thriving after trauma : stories of living and healing / Shari Botwin.
Description: Lanham, MD : Rowman & Littlefield Publishing Group, Inc., [2019] | In-
    cludes bibliographical references and index. | Summary: "THRIVING AFTER TRAU-
    MA deals with overcoming trauma including physical and sexual abuse, war-related
    injury, loss due to tragedy or illness, and natural disasters. Real stories and practical
    tools shed light on how to let go of shame, guilt, anger, and despair after a traumatic
    experience. It is possible to grieve, move beyond, and fully live again"—Provided by
    publisher.
Identifiers: LCCN 2019013127 (print) | LCCN 2019980091 (ebook) | ISBN
    9781538125601 (cloth) | ISBN 9781538125618 (ebook)
Subjects: LCSH: Post-traumatic stress disorder. | Stress (Psychology) | Sex crimes. | Natural
    disasters.
Classification: LCC RC552.P67 B67 2019 (print) | LCC RC552.P67 (ebook) | DDC 616.85/
    21—dc23
LC record available at https://lccn.loc.gov/2019013127
LC ebook record available at https://lccn.loc.gov/2019980091

CONTENTS

FOREWORD

Stories of Living and Healing

Dr. Jo Anne White

Trauma comes in many different forms and can haunt us and even debilitate us long after the actual event or events took place. Depending on the type of trauma, it can interfere with our relationships, erode our self-esteem, and even jeopardize our future successes in work and life. Unfortunately, trauma can lead to a premature ending of life if the necessary support isn't in place. A person may take his or her own life as a means to end the pain that's often endured in relentless, tormented silence.

Who is better qualified to write a book about trauma and how to heal and thrive beyond the ordeal than Shari Botwin, a survivor herself of sexual abuse? She knows firsthand the sense of loss, the grief, the pain, and the long journey of coming back home to herself, healed and renewed, and able to help others in their own recovery and personal healing.

Shari's book is a testament, not only to her own strength in coming to terms with what happened to her in her early years, but to the many men and women she's counseled who have experienced a life trauma and to their strength and active commitment in their own recovery. Recovery, as Shari aptly illustrates, isn't overnight. Often people grapple with shame, guilt, and despair and even check out by not remembering the event or by not fully participating in life and experiencing love, joy, or even relief due to what they've relentlessly withstood.

Shari's goal is an admirable one and is realized in this book, whose mission is not just to help the many individuals and families dealing with trauma, but, as she says, "to unite all of us—survivors, family members of survivors, bystanders, and helpers."

How Shari as therapist, witness, supporter, victim, and survivor herself accomplishes this is a compelling blend of true stories from sessions with her patients and strategies to heal from guilt, shame, and the fear of loss. The chapters also highlight behaviors and techniques that foster intimacy, courage, and the ability to reach out to others for help and support, to be loved, valued, and respected without feeling undeserving or not being seen or heard.

Inherent in the recovery process, as Shari so aptly demonstrates, is the often difficult yet rewarding road to finding the way back to self: to the place inside of wholeness and openness to explore life with enthusiasm and joy, the ability to love and be loved, and to dare to pursue their own dreams and reap success and fulfillment in work, love, and relationships. Most important, as Shari and her patients reclaim their lives and thrive, is the development of an ongoing, loving, respectful, and nurturing relationship with oneself.

Self-trust is not always easy to regain and is often eroded in the face of trauma. This is especially true if the mantra in one's head is one of nondeserving or is laden with guilt or remorse. If only I could have done more, or prevented it, or responded differently is a familiar and disturbing repetitive mind dialogue that hounds many survivors, bystanders, and those affected directly or indirectly by trauma.

If-only is illustrated in the case of one of Shari's patients: a soldier who endured posttraumatic stress. At the front lines of Desert Storm, he saw death and violence up close. What tortured him long after the war was the horrific experience of helplessly watching his close friend die right before his eyes. With no recourse to save or help his friend, his own inability to do so plagued him and haunted him for the rest of his life until he faced and confronted the pain and released the self-blame.

Throughout the book are numerous stories of trauma, recovery, relief, and healing from the different people Shari has worked with: a mother coping with the death of her son from a drug overdose, a sibling who witnessed her brother getting run over and the family's loss of connection that followed, a female survivor of domestic violence who freed herself from her abuser after being married to him for twenty-five years, a mother who had a horrific child abuse history that helped her teenage daughter report the abuse she endured to the police, and others' stories that move us deeply.

Shari's account of her own healing sheds light on how one can emerge after devastating sexual assault from a parent whose role is supposed to be one of a protector and nurturer. As an adult, she proactively faced her own misgivings of being a loving mother and a strong role model for her child. One of the beautiful chapters includes testimonials from several individuals who endured trauma. Hearing their heartbreaking stories, as they bare their hearts and their vulnerability, is touching and makes their suffering and their victory palpable and profound.

Thriving after Trauma: Stories of Living and Healing gives us tremendous hope and promise, not only for the people in the book but for ourselves. We emerge stronger and more resilient because of it. I believe another takeaway is that we begin to better understand the depth of trauma and the long road to healing. This offers each of us the opportunity and the ability to feel more compassion and sensitivity to all those individuals confronting trauma or any challenging ordeal, including ourselves. This in itself is a precious gift of Shari's book.

What I find most wonderful throughout the book is how each person fought with tremendous will and persistence to reclaim their lives or to claim their life for the first time. We feel their struggle and their pain, and we are also present for their self-renewal and their victories as though they were our own. We also come away with tools to help us handle our own challenges. And we are better equipped to offer our support to others. By our immersion in this book, we become more humanized by the total experience.

Dr. Jo Anne White is a #1 international best-selling, award-winning author, speaker, certified coach and consultant, and energy master teacher who holistically transforms lives and businesses to success and wellness. Dr. White is also the founder of the Power Your Life Network *and executive host and producer of the* Power Your Life *shows. www.drjoannewhite.com*

ACKNOWLEDGMENTS

This book would not have been possible without the love, bravery, and support of patients and colleagues I have met over the last twenty-two years. I dedicate this book to my son, Andrew Botwin, who has changed my life for the best in many ways. Becoming his mom has made me a braver person. It was not until I stepped into the role of motherhood that I realized I am so much more than a survivor of childhood abuse. He brings me joy and strength, and I have never loved anyone the way I love him. Decades before I started my family, I met the most wonderful therapist in the universe, Dorothy Saynisch, PhD. She traveled down the complicated, dreadful, and empowering path of helping me reclaim my desire to live fully. She is a constant, reliable, empathic, and intelligent woman, and without her help I would not be where I am today.

This book would not be possible without the help of my first editor, Stephanie Susnjara. We began working together from the moment I decided I wanted to write another book. She has taught me how to find words and write about some excruciating events in my life and the lives of my patients. This book would not have come to be without the dedication of my agent, Linda Konner at the Linda Konner Literary Agency, who believed in me and my book. She has been persistent and dedicated to this project. She helped me find a home with Rowman & Littlefield. I am also grateful to the editor assigned to me, Suzanne Staszak-Silva, for all of her guidance and support to make this the best book possible. Thank you Lara Hahn, my production editor, for all your hard work on making this book flow and read so well. I am so glad Rowman & Littlefield sent you my way.

I also met some amazing colleagues early in my work who have served as mentors and guides. I met Jane Shure, PhD, LCSW, and Beth Weinstock, PhD, at a workshop they led on reducing shame at the Renfrew Conference very early in my recovery. Through the years, they have been witnesses to my struggle and pain. They have also been the first ones I reach out to when I accomplish a lifelong goal, such as writing this book. Their wisdom and compassion for people who have lived through horror has inspired me from the moment I met them. I have also been blessed with the friendship of another colleague, Heidi Cooperstein, DO, whom I have worked with in helping many patients through the years. Her dedication to patient care and her ability to be present for anyone involved in her patient's treatment is exceptional. She has also been such a good friend to me. I would not have been able to help half the patients I have counseled without her collaboration and support.

I also want to dedicate this book to the friends I have made over the last several years. Sandy Weston came into my life at such a fragile time. Her spirit, motivation, and passion for life have played a key role in my ability to pursue lifelong dreams. She stood by my side as I gave birth to Andrew, and I will never forget when she danced around the operating room singing, "Oh my gosh, I see a baby!" Sandy is a true example of a warrior who has taken her life adversities and transformed them into triumph. Thank you Karen Eselson Belding, PsyD, for your constant messages of encouragement and support from the moment I started writing this book. You are a wonderful clinician and you have been a great role model for myself and many others when we started in the psychology field.

More recently I have formed special connections with some people I work out with. I call Lifetime KOP my happy place. I can be myself and feel accepted as I am. I have written most of this book while I was dancing or spinning or lifting weights with some amazing friends and instructors. Julie Howard was always the first person I reached out to after finishing another chapter. She took hours of her time to review my work and give me feedback. She has also been one of my biggest cheerleaders when I felt stuck or frustrated with the writing process. I am so grateful for some very special friends at Lifetime KOP: Katie Boyd, Lauren Cuddeback, Kristin Boquist, Sue Capizzi, Dianna Ellis, Joymarie DeFruscio, Janeen Jonak, Jacob Makoyo, Sydney Ruth, Noreen Slamon Geibel, and Meghan Thorburn.

I am truly grateful to the women who took the time to offer testimonials of courage after thriving from trauma. Jennifer Fox, Janice Baker-Kinney, Sally Wark Onesty, Tamie Gangloff, and Karen Finocchio, your words of insight and wisdom have made an impact on so many. I am honored to have featured each of you in this book. As a note, names and details in patient stories have been altered to protect individual privacy.

In the last eight years, I have met some wonderful families after becoming Andrew's mom. I appreciate and love them and the joy they bring into our lives: the Gold family (Michael, Matthew, Jason, Meghan, Michelle, and Owen), the Shkedy family (Amy, Sagi, Guy, and Mia), the Seltzer-Arnold family (Becca, Jackie, Mark, Zack, and Danny), and all the other Belmont Hills Elementary School families. The support of Andrew's school community has also provided me with a sense of belonging and understanding as I parent my almost-eight-year-old son.

I want to acknowledge all the journalists who have helped my voice be heard and have supported me in speaking out and empowering others in coming forward. Here's to Jean Casarez, Alison Gorman, Kate Snow, Marianne Haggerty, Kaci Sokoloff, Bonita Sostre, Tamara Lush, Denise Nakano, and Yitzi Weiner.

Lastly, I want to thank and acknowledge all the patients who have allowed me to help them through their recovery. Every day I learn more about myself as I sit with them and help them work through their darkest memories. I have the utmost respect for them and would never have been able to write this book without the experiences I have had in counseling them. It is truly an honor and a privilege to be a witness as my patients take steps to have a full and meaningful life.

INTRODUCTION

While most kids were skipping around during recess, I was usually standing against the school's brick wall trying to figure out why I felt like such a misfit. I knew something was really wrong but had no words or way to understand my experiences and feelings. From the age of five, I felt depressed and hopeless and could not relate to the smiles and laughter of my young peers. I just remember standing on that playground as a ten-year-old child, telling myself, "Someday you'll find a way to tell the world what is happening to you."

For the first twenty-three years of my life I lived in an abusive family environment. All of this abuse was awful. It took place when I was asleep. I have many memories, which I buried for years, of waking up feeling like something horrible had happened to me the night before. On countless occasions I would sit in front of a mirror with my eyes filled with tears but could not understand why I was crying and in so much emotional agony. I felt ugly, afraid, distrusting, and hopeless.

Starting in kindergarten I looked to food for comfort and relationships outside of my family to feel loved. For years I sat in front of the television watching sitcoms about perfect families, such as *Little House on the Prairie* and *The Brady Bunch*, and dreamed of the happy life I wished I had. I was terrified to go to school. I was built like an athlete or a dancer, and kids would say things like "thunder thighs" or call me "big-butt Botwin." I was constantly being made fun of for "being fat."

I was so vulnerable, a people pleaser, and I had no interest in normal kid-like activities. I was the outsider looking in. When other kids talked about what they did on the weekends, I would listen and try to imagine the kind of parents I wanted to live with. I fantasized about having a mom who would hug me and wipe away my tears and a dad who would protect me and stand up for me when other kids bullied me. When the principal would make an announcement during the school day, I hoped she would call me down to the office and introduce me to my new family. Over and over I was disappointed that this never happened in real life.

Early in my childhood I discovered my love for dance and theater. I began performing onstage when I was nine. What a lifesaver that was! Performing became an outlet for me to express some of my grief and anger. Every time I booked a role in a community musical, I felt hopeful because I proved to myself that if I wanted something and believed in myself, my dreams could come true. I remember playing the role of Frenchie in the show *Grease* at my high school and feeling like, "Oh, this is what my life could be like if I had friends I could trust." I felt safe on that stage because no one could hurt me the way I was being hurt at home.

As I became a teenager, my world became even darker and more full of despair. I was developing into a woman's body, and I began getting more attention from boys. When I walked down the hallways in middle school and high school, I found myself looking at the floor or looking through people versus at them. I was terrified of someone noticing me or making any reference to my blossoming figure. I was also afraid of being raped, but I could not figure out why I was so afraid of something I believed had never happened to me. Rather than look at my fears, I found ways to stay quiet and remain in denial. I would not allow myself to know the truth about what was happening to me at home.

Once I left for college, my depression and symptoms of PTSD worsened. I spent nights feeling hopeless and afraid, and at times I thought about suicide. In the fall of my sophomore year I became ill after having a miscarriage in my dorm room. I was not able to admit that I had lost a baby from an unwanted pregnancy caused by my abuser. I told myself I had a "crazy irregular period," even though I experienced contractions and other symptoms of a miscarriage for hours. And that was not the first unwanted pregnancy caused by my abuser. During my teens and early twenties, I suffered four more unwanted pregnancies that resulted in miscarriages. I never told anyone, not even the gynecologist I was seeing at that time, who would ask me, "Is there any chance you might be pregnant?" I would go see her to find out why I was gaining weight, not having a menstrual cycle, and experiencing nausea, headaches, and other early pregnancy symptoms. Each time she asked me about my sexual activity, I adamantly responded, "I am a virgin!" I was committed to keeping my secret silent. The risk of speaking took over my mind and heart every time I had an opportunity to tell.

As I got older and more independent, I began to recognize my ability to help others. In college I met a couple of young women who suffered from anorexia and bulimia, and I was drawn to them because I was also struggling with similar eating disorder behaviors. Even though I did not start working as a therapist until my midtwenties, I had a long history of counseling others. Around the age of twelve I took on the role of mediator in my family. When fights broke out between others, I intervened and offered ways to restore the peace. I would stand up during dinner and say things like, "Can't we just respect each other?" or, "Please don't say such mean things." In middle school and high school my peers came to me when they felt depressed or taken advantage of sexually, or when they felt like no one liked them. I was like the group cheerleader. I would write letters filled with support to help my friends feel better about themselves. When I lost family members, such as my grandmom and my cousin, I would console anyone who was grieving. I still remember standing up at an extended family Passover seder and reading a letter to honor my aunt who had passed away just weeks before the holiday. I had people in tears, and

some of my cousins came up to me after the seder and told me
how I made them feel comforted and less sad. Teachers, friends,
and family members would constantly praise my ability to show
concern and love for others.

After I graduated from Hofstra University with my bachelor's
in psychology, I started working in the eating disorders field at an
inpatient rehab. From the moment I began working there, I was
struck by all the patients telling stories of how their eating disorder was a reaction to some type of abuse or trauma they suffered
earlier in life. One day I went running to my supervisor at the
clinic and said to her, "These stories are freaking me out. They are
telling stories that I cannot even imagine relating to." She must
have picked up on my pain, and instead of dismissing my concerns
she told me to get a therapist.

For two years I sat in therapy once a week and told my therapist that my life was fine and that my family was supportive. We
talked a lot about my work at the rehab and how I was feeling
lonely and wished I had a boyfriend. On several occasions I would
ask my therapist, "What is wrong with me? Why don't I ever have
a boyfriend?" At the time, she was trying to help me open up more
about the shame and distrust I had in others, but she had no idea
where those feelings were coming from.

One day after a session we had that focused on dating and
intimacy, I began feeling the memories of my sexual abuse in my
body. Hours after the feelings came up, I called my therapist in a
panic. I told her that I remembered how "someone who was supposed to love me went inside of me." The floodgates had opened
and there was no going back. Years of repressed memories and
feelings surfaced. After I broke my silence about my sexual abuse,
I spent three or four days a week in intensive outpatient therapy
for ten years to work through the trauma.

I called my therapist often during the first few years of my
recovery work, saying, "I wish I had never opened my big fat
mouth." I often wanted to take back the truth and not deal with
the upheaval of pain and anger. Yet there was a part of me that
remained determined to plow through the worst of the therapy

because I wanted to live a full life, and I knew that the only way to get there was to come to terms with my past. I was done feeling depressed and worthless, of feeling stranded and living in such isolation. I wanted to experience people loving me, not just be there to support and help others. I wanted to feel confident in my ability to set limits and not just do what others wanted. I wanted to date men. I wanted a family.

Then, in my midthirties, I was hit with another challenge. After being diagnosed and successfully treated for thyroid cancer at the age of thirty-five, I wanted to create a family. After several years of working through the abuse, I felt open to dating and marriage. However, I had to accept that at that point in my life I had not experienced a serious long-term relationship. I knew I was not going to be on earth forever and that it was time to take some risks and be vulnerable with others. My support system grew, and I developed close friendships with colleagues and peers. I allowed myself to explore intimate relationships with men. I was opening up and letting more people know about my abuse and the work I was doing to have a full life, yet I still did not have a romantic partner.

So, after my thirty-eighth birthday, I sought out consultation with a fertility specialist to talk about my options of starting a family as a single working woman. I knew I needed to talk to the fertility doctor about my history of unwanted pregnancies from my abuser. Luckily she listened intently, and she did not question the abuse history I shared and how I had gotten pregnant in my past. She ran a bunch of blood tests, one of which came back showing that I had a genetic clotting disorder. In order to have a healthy pregnancy, she told me, I would need to give myself daily injections of blood thinners to prevent a viable pregnancy from ending prematurely.

Less than a year after I was diagnosed with the clotting disorder, I found out I was pregnant! I will never forget running around my condo shouting at my dog, Chloe, "Guess what! Mommy is going to have a baby!" All my supporters celebrated with me. For almost forty weeks I found a way to love my body and the miracle I referred to as "Baby Botwin" growing inside of me.

Eight years later, my heart leaps with joy when I watch my now second-grade son run around the playground at school. And every day that I have the honor of parenting him, another part of me heals. I have discovered that I am capable of giving love, even after not receiving it during my own childhood. I have found a way to grieve for the part of me that did not have a normal childhood and also to celebrate the safety I can provide for Andrew. I have proven to myself that anything is possible, no matter how bad my abuse left me feeling.

After I gave birth in 2011, the focus of my private practice began to shift. Instead of treating patients who were mainly dealing with eating disorders, almost everyone who came to see me was also reporting some type of trauma. Some were abuse survivors, some had lost loved ones suddenly, and others were survivors of natural disasters, plane crashes, or Desert Storm.

In 2014, after fifteen years of being in private practice I wanted to expand my horizons beyond my office. I wanted to get myself out there publicly to share my story to help others. I had experienced so many moments of hope after parenting Andrew for a couple of years and wanted to share with the world the hope that comes from speaking after childhood sexual abuse. I started writing features for the *Philadelphia Inquirer* on breaking stories related to trauma. After my op-ed on childhood abuse released for the *Philadelphia Inquirer*,[1] I received emails from men and women around the country who were at a loss. They also expressed gratitude and told me that they were inspired and were going to ask for help. My heart leaped every time I got an email from someone in their forties, fifties, or sixties who had suffered in silence for decades. I told them that it was never too late to heal. It is never too late to reclaim "your right to live a full life."

In 2015, I was sitting on my sofa watching the ABC *20/20* interview and *Dateline NBC* interview with thirteen of Bill Cosby's accusers. I could barely breathe as I listened to each of their stories of betrayal and hurt. The next day I sat down and wrote an op-ed for the *Philadelphia Inquirer*.[2] The day that article was released I heard from some of the women who had come forward claiming Bill Cosby had drugged and sexually assaulted them. The time span of these allegations covered thirty years. I also heard from women who had not gone public about their alleged sexual assaults by Bill Cosby. My words regarding trauma and healing were being heard and validated by hundreds of other survivors.

Over the last two years, I have spent hours outside of my office writing and giving commentary to media outlets on the latest sexual abuse scandal, mass shooting, or natural disaster like Hurricanes Harvey and Irma. I attended both Cosby trials[3] and was in the courtroom the day Cosby was sentenced and taken away in handcuffs to state prison for a minimum sentence of thirty-six months.

While all of these stories are different, there are many commonalities. Survivors struggle with the loss. Survivors struggle with feelings of shame and guilt. Survivors grapple with fear of loss. Survivors find themselves feeling despair, and at times some of them want to give up. All of us try to find ways to live with our thoughts and feelings, whether we have been a victim of abuse, a survivor of a mass shooting, or have lost all our property after a hurricane.

My goal for this book is to unite all of us: survivors, family members, bystanders, and helpers. No one walks away from trauma feeling the exact same thing. There are things we have in common and feelings we cannot comprehend. It is not about understanding exactly what someone feels or remembering every detail. It is about hope. It is about acceptance. It is about understanding the impact of our trauma. And it is about fighting for our right to live fully and freely no matter how horrific the trauma or our experiences were. It is about feeling worthy and deserving of becoming parents, having intimate relationships with partners, being successful in business, or whatever other dreams we may have.

I

TRAUMA DEFINED

WHAT IS TRAUMA?

Trauma can take many forms: physical, emotional, or spiritual. According to the American Psychological Association, *trauma* can be defined as "an emotional response to a terrible event such as a car accident, rape or natural disaster." Shock and denial are typical immediately after the event.[1]

One of the worst school shootings in American history occurred at Columbine High School in Littleton, Colorado, on April 20, 1999. Two teens went on a shooting spree, killing thirteen people and injuring at least twenty others before turning the guns on themselves. For about one week after the shooting, images of the shooters, victims, and family members of dead and deceased took over all media outlets. Immediately after the tragedy, schools across the country enacted "zero-tolerance" rules. Bullying or any acts or threats of violence were not tolerated.[2] Days after the horrific shooting, the media stopped covering the story in the front pages or in first stories. Mostly it faded from sight over time. There was some commentary on different news channels about the impact. Very little was said about how all those affected coped as the months and years followed the event.

On September 11, 2001, militants associated with the Islamic extremist group Al-Qaeda hijacked four airplanes and carried out suicide attacks against targets in the United States. It was the deadliest day in history for New York City firefighters—343 of them died that day. Less than fifteen minutes after one of the planes crashed into the World Trade Center, the South Tower collapsed. At 10:30 a.m., the North Tower collapsed. Almost three thousand people lost their lives that day, and over ten thousand were injured.[3]

Everyone was talking about the events that unfolded that day. People were desperate to connect to family members who worked at the World Trade Center and the Pentagon in Washington, DC. Phone lines were down for hours. New York City was on lockdown. Bystanders and witnesses were frantic, as they could not reassure their friends and family they were safe. Life was never going to be the same for American citizens. For weeks there were vigils set up for the pilots and passengers of Flight 93, California bound. Passengers on that flight had learned of the events in New York and Washington via cell phone. A few passengers and flight attendants planned an insurrection. They gave their lives to protect possible targets, including the White House and the U.S. Capitol.

Trauma therapists received an enormous number of phone calls from people asking for help in coping with the aftermath of that deadly attack. For weeks, when people drove into New York City, the skyline had a black cloud hanging over it. There were reminders everywhere. Posters of missing people were plastered all over New York City. Media outlets were interviewing survivors, first responders, and witnesses. On every anniversary of 9/11, schools, offices, and government officials commemorated the event by having a moment of silence during key moments of the attacks. Family members attended different vigils and read the names of their deceased. People around the country and the world had a dialogue about where they were that day and how they would never forget. Occasionally, we heard from wounded police and firefighters about the aftermath of the trauma. They talked about being crippled by posttraumatic stress disorder (PTSD).

PTSD is a psychiatric disorder than can occur in people who have lived through or witnessed a terrorist act, serious accident, natural disaster, rape, or other violent assault. Many of the people directly involved in the 9/11 attacks were writing and giving media interviews in which they were reporting symptoms of severe PTSD. They were having flashbacks, nightmares, insomnia, suicidal thoughts, depression, and panic attacks. First responders were leaving their positions because they could not tolerate the level of anxiety they were experiencing after losing colleagues and watching people jump out of burning buildings. Survivors who had lost friends and family in the attack were leaving their jobs and the city to get away from all the reminders. At that time the media was giving a ton of attention to 9/11. Little was said about what happened to all those people who survived, five, ten, or fifteen years later.

When I started counseling patients around twenty-two years ago, topics like childhood abuse, domestic violence, and sexual assault were taboo. While the research at that time showed that a high percentage of females had lived through some type of assault in their lifetime, there was very little attention given to these people and their stories. Many of these survivors were having similar reactions to their trauma as those who had lived through terrorist attacks like 9/11.

The world was shocked to learn about the report in the *Boston Globe* that over 130 people came forward alleging that former priest John J. Geoghan had raped or fondled them when they were in grammar school. The sex abuse scandal allegedly went on for at least three decades in six Greater Boston parishes.[4] As the priest was facing two criminal trials for his sexual compulsion, many were asking why it took a succession of three cardinals and many bishops thirty-four years to remove the children from Geoghan's reach.

In 2002 the *Boston Globe*'s Spotlight team, which included a team of five investigative journalists, uncovered rampant sexual abuse by the clergy in that district. They also reported that the priests who were accused of abuse were being removed and allowed to work in other parishes. The team's investigation earned them a Pulitzer Prize for public service.[5] In 2015, a Hollywood production company bought the rights to make a film on the Boston Spotlight story, once the movie was made. Before it went into production, the producers and writers of the script were sent walking. No one wanted to buy the rights to a film on such a controversial and unspeakable subject.

In early 2016, the cast and crew, real-life journalists, and survivors of the sex abuse scandal were affirmed, as *Spotlight* won several prestigious awards, including an Oscar for best film in 2015. Several of my patients with an abuse history saw the movie. Many of them told me they were able to have intimate conversations with close family members and partners about the feelings it triggered in them. Several media outlets invited survivors of sexual abuse to share their stories with the public. Finally, victims of abuse in the church were getting the help they needed.

On the other hand were natural disasters, including Hurricane Sandy, and the climate around this story was very different. On the five-year anniversary of the storm, news outlets spoke to survivors. Many of them reported that they were still haunted by the losses and images of the hurricane.[6] One of the survivors reported feeling anxious and fearful and living in a constant state of doom and gloom. He watched the water rush through his home, and he told reporters he could not get the image out of his head. He told reporters he called his disorder "posttraumatic Sandy disorder." He also told journalists that there were hundreds of others suffering with PTSD who were not reaching out for help.[7]

POSTTRAUMATIC STRESS EMERGES

Posttraumatic stress disorder (PTSD) is a mental health condition that is triggered after a terrifying event. In 1980 the American Psychiatric Association added PTSD to the third edition of its

Diagnostic and Statistical Manual of Mental Disorders.[8] Years ago people associated PTSD with combat. In the 1980s veterans were being diagnosed with the disorder after serving in Vietnam. For decades, people thought that only those who have served in the military or been in combat were at risk for developing PTSD. Initially there was some controversy about the inclusion of the diagnosis because it was caused by an outside event rather than a weakness within the individual. Originally the doctors of the original PTSD classification had in mind events like the Holocaust, the atomic bombings of Hiroshima and Nagasaki, and natural disasters. They considered these types of events to be different from living through painful stressors such as divorce, serious illness or injury, sexual assault, and all forms of abuse.

In the latest version of the manual, DSM-5, published in 2013, the criteria for PTSD included exposure to threatened death or injury or a threat to the one's integrity.[9] For example, survivors of rape, child abuse, and domestic violence were considered in the updated classification of the disorder. The DSM-5 also considered those indirectly involved in a life-threatening event to be at risk for developing PTSD. Loved ones of those who lost their lives in 9/11, partners of women who were sexually assaulted, and witnesses or survivors of a natural disaster or deadly car accident were considered as well. Witnesses or close family and friends would report similar symptoms of PTSD as those who had lived through the event.

Anyone who has witnessed a scary or life-threatening experience can develop this mental disorder.[10] People who live through different types of traumatic events, such as childhood abuse, terrorist attacks, natural disasters, sexual assault, or the sudden death of a loved one may temporarily go into a state of shock and denial. Symptoms of PTSD get worse six to eight weeks after the event occurs if there is no psychological intervention or way to process what happened. Over the last couple of years, the term "PTSD" has been used loosely, but there are clear symptoms when someone has the disorder.

PTSD symptoms are grouped into four different types.[11] The first type are *intrusive memories*, which include flashbacks, nightmares, and reliving the event as if it were happening again. For example, if someone has experienced sexual assault, they may have flashbacks of the attack as they are trying to have intimacy with their current partner.

Avoidance occurs when people avoid talking about what happened or stay away from places or activities that remind them of the event. For instance, after 9/11, many survivors left New York City and could not step foot back into their homes or anywhere near where the attacks took place. People who have survived or lost a family member to a car crash may not get back into a car as a passenger or a driver.

Negative changes in thinking and mood may occur. These are commonly described by survivors as feelings of hopelessness for the future, difficulty maintaining close relationships, feeling disconnected from family and friends, and a lack of interest in activities. Some people describe their mood changes by saying they are numb, that they are living life but not feeling like their minds or bodies are in the present. I talked to one patient who was sexually abused as a child, and she told me she could not stay in her body whenever she was around men who were fathers or religious leaders.

Changes in physical and emotional reactions create feelings of hypervigilance, self-destructive behavior such as drinking too much or engaging in eating disorder behavior, poor sleep habits, an inability to concentrate, angry outbursts, and overwhelming feelings of guilt and shame. I worked with one patient who served in combat in Afghanistan for over a year. He struggled for years with moments of rage and at other times could not remember where he was driving because he would get disorientated for no reason when he was having flashbacks of his buddy being killed by enemy shooters.[12]

People diagnosed with this condition struggle with self-blame. It is one thing to live through horror; it is another to admit that there have been long-term effects on one's life. Patients talk about feeling weak when they are having memories or anxiety or are triggered by environmental factors. Some say they should be able to handle these reactions without needing any type of psychological intervention. In the past, people assumed that once diagnosed they would live with PTSD for a lifetime. It was not until recently, when many more people stepped forward about their trauma, that people saw hope in light of being diagnosed or identifying as someone with PTSD.

During the last five years we have become a society that is more accepting of the condition and the challenges that come with recovery. Patients are more willing to accept that they are suffering with the disorder. Earlier in my career, patients would tell me they needed therapy because they had severe depression, anxiety, or related disorders. Once I got to know some of my patients, I realized that they were depressed, suicidal, having panic attacks, or isolating themselves from their connections as a result of what had happened to them.

It is not uncommon for me to meet someone with an eating disorder or addiction who has an underlying trauma buried in their subconscious. PTSD develops over time. The longer someone stays silent, the more likely they will begin displaying PTSD symptoms. Ashwood Recovery, a well-known center for addictions, has found that over eight million people have PTSD.[13] About 75 percent of people checking into Ashwood and other rehab or inpatient facilities for addiction also have a history of trauma. Individuals who have suffered assault or sexual abuse are three times more likely to abuse drugs or alcohol.

Eating disorders are rarely related to issues with food or body image. Most patients entering inpatient or outpatient treatment centers for anorexia, bulimia, or binge eating disorders report an extensive trauma history. Patients who seek help for eating disorders often struggle to get to the root cause of their disorder. They have not been able to make the connection between their symptoms and earlier events that have led to the shame, self-hatred, and despair associated with prior events in their history. Approximately 35 percent of women who develop bulimia have reported symptoms of PTSD over the course of their lifetime.[14]

The flood of emotions and memories that linger in someone's life have led to a wrath of self-destruction. Individuals who have felt out of control or powerless after experiencing trauma react by taking control of what they eat, when they eat, or if they allow themselves to keep the food in their bodies. Others turn to alcohol or drugs to mask their anger or rage toward the person that hurt them or the incident that took the life of someone they loved.

Many trauma survivors describe life after trauma as crazy-making. It is not uncommon for patients to ask me if I think they are insane when they describe how their lives have changed after becoming sick with an eating disorder or addiction. I have spoken to many patients about the outcome of burying memories and feelings associated with their history. Many patients enter treatment years or decades after the trauma occurred. I have talked with patients about how storing all those emotions in their bodies for that length of time can have devastating lifelong effects on their physical and psychological well-being. Addiction and self-harming behaviors become coping strategies when memories or feelings from trauma resurface.

TRAUMA GOES PUBLIC

Five years ago, more and more celebrities and sports stars went public with stories of abuse and domestic violence. In 2014, Lady Gaga announced on *The Howard Stern Show* that she was raped by a record producer when she was a teenager. In 2015, Bill Cosby, once the most loved American dad on television, was arrested and charged with several counts of sexual misconduct. Days after his arrest, dozens of women began sharing stories of their alleged assault on a variety of social media and news outlets. Psychiatrists and other mental health counselors were talking about an insurgence of calls for help for domestic violence and sexual assault after the Cosby arrest went public. Media outlets such as the *Huff-*

ington Post and the *New York Times* began offering blogs and forums to educate our society about the impact of trauma and the aftermath of PTSD.

In 2015 there were 353 mass shootings in the United States.[15] These massacres took place in neighborhoods, schools, bars, restaurants, and churches. On June 12, 2016, fifty people lost their lives to gun violence at a nightclub in Orlando, Florida. More attention was given to this mass slaying, as many of the witnesses, survivors, and family members of the deceased and injured were interviewed by a variety of media outlets. The dialogue continued at the government level, in schools, and in religious organizations. The epidemic of these kinds of killings was not new, but more attention was being paid to the aspect of trauma.

In 2017, three monster hurricanes—Harvey, Irma, and Maria—hit the United States. For months people were talking about what they had witnessed, what they had lost, and how these storms had ruined the lives of so many. While people were not going on media outlets to talk about having PTSD, they were reporting symptoms after experiencing so much devastation. Survivors were talking about losing their entire house in a matter of seconds. First responders were reporting their experiences of rescuing people and pets. Journalists were talking about leaving their jobs as the emotional distress of such a tragedy was interfering in their overall functioning. Numerous celebrities took to the media to raise money to help anyone affected by the storms. Students at different schools around the country sent letters of hope and caring, trying to offer a child a moment of relief from the stress and heartbreak.

Parents bringing children into the world over the last five years are reporting an increase in anxiety. The conversations among educators, medical professionals, and anyone raising children have shifted to fears about safety and mental well-being. While shootings, hurricanes, sexual assault, and childhood abuse have been around for centuries, the attention being paid to these kinds of stories has raised concern and fear. Experts in the mental health field have conducted workshops and led discussions on the impact of mass school shootings on children's mental health. Do kids today worry more about their safety at school than about their English or science homework?[16] A sense of security in children is crucial, especially when they are separated from their families while at school.

When children are exposed to images of shootings or related incidents, they experience many symptoms of PTSD, such as nightmares, resistance to leaving their homes, a decline in academic performance, changes in eating habits, increased anger, hypervigilance, grief, loss, and guilt. I have spoken to a few patients after their children have had mock lockdowns in case a shooter enters their school building. All of these parents have said things to me like, "Maybe I should not have had a child," or, "I feel guilty bringing my children into such a dangerous world."

Schools around the country have been sending mental health professionals into the public to reassure parents and offer strategies for prevention to staff working at schools and universities. While education has been helpful, it has not eased the minds of most people. Trauma survivors are facing more challenges as they bring their own children into the world. Mass shootings affect us all. Days after the massacre at Marjory Stoneman Douglas High School, students directly affected by the tragedy began fighting to change gun laws. They took to all forms of media to let the world know about their hurt, loss, grief, and fear. Some of the students who survived the shooting stood up in front of millions of people so their voices could be heard.

There were conversations happening all around the country. People were processing the fears that the shooting brought up in them. Those with a prior history of combat or loss of a loved one by gun violence were reminded of the events that had led to their PTSD.

As the community around Stoneman Douglas High School prepared to go back to school in the fall of 2018, the Florida Counseling Association hosted a free two-day workshop about communal trauma.[17] The seminar focused on helping students, staff, and parents prepare to walk back into what only months before was the scene of a bloody massacre. Professionals offered strategies and coping mechanisms to help those involved deal with their anxiety, sadness, anger, and fear as they took their first steps to keep on living after such devastation.

Two weeks after the shooting on February 14, 2018, I went on ABC News to offer words of support as the students at Stoneman Douglas High prepared to continue with the school year. I talked about the importance of staff and students returning to school. I also emphasized the hope that came from having a community of witnesses. In most cases, people who live through acts of violence go through it alone. Going back to the place where the shooting happened was an important step in thriving after the trauma.[18]

As the world was being exposed to incidents of senseless killing and natural disasters, celebrities also began raising awareness of sexual assault. Alyssa Milano revived a movement on Twitter with the #MeToo hashtag, a campaign that was started a decade earlier by activist Tarana Burke. There was an insurgence of responses from celebrities and others around the world as Harvey Weinstein faced allegations of sexual assault and harassment. Alyssa wrote, "If all the women who have been sexually harassed or assaulted wrote 'Me too,' as a status, we might give people a sense of the magnitude of the problem."[19] The phrase has been one of the most viral and powerful occurrences in social media history. The hashtag trended in over eighty-five countries, translated into the languages of those countries. Half a million people responded to Milano's tweet in the first twenty-four hours.[20] For months, top stories on news outlets featured men and women coming forward alleging that people in power had assaulted or harassed them. Kevin Spacey, Matt Lauer, Harvey Weinstein, and Fox News's Bill O'Reilly were just a few of the dozens of men accused of some type of abuse in the workplace.

Less than two months after #MeToo went viral, reports of rape jumped 23 percent.[21] More people were seeking justice and getting into psychological treatment. The shame and stigma around all types of abuse dissipated after millions took to social media to share their stories. Trauma experts began commenting on the insurgence of phone calls from current and former patients who revealed that they too had been raped, sexually harassed, or sexually abused.

Around the same time as the #MeToo campaign, the trial of Bill Cosby began. His first trial, which ended in a hung jury, was in June 2017. While the news of a mistrial devastated many, the fight for justice had not ended. Kevin Steele, the current district attorney in Montgomery County, Pennsylvania, announced that they would be staying the course. The witnesses and victims of the alleged sexual misconduct by Bill Cosby were not going to stop the fight. On April 26, 2018, I stood with Gloria Allred and some of Cosby's accusers at the podium minutes after a jury found Cosby guilty of all three counts of sexual misconduct.[22] Cosby was convicted of drugging and sexually assaulting Andrea Constand, a former basketball player who was thirty years old at the time of the alleged incident. Gloria Allred announced, "We are so happy that finally we can say, women are believed, and not only in a hashtag '#MeToo,' but also in a court of law."[23]

After months of appealing and making desperate attempts to stay out of prison, Judge Steven O'Neill sentenced Bill Cosby to three to ten years in state prison. He was also given the label "sexually violent predator" after being interviewed by psychiatrists who specialized in treating sex offenders. Moments after Cosby was sentenced, Montgomery County attorney Kevin Steele said, "For decades, the defendant has been able to hide his true self and hide his crimes using his fame and fortune. Finally, Bill Cosby has been unmasked, and we've seen the real man as he's headed off to prison."[24]

This day in history led to more hope for anyone who had been raped or sexually assaulted. Survivors and advocates took to legislation trying to abolish the statute of limitations. Most states only gave victims of sexual crimes a couple of years from when the crime occurred to press charges criminally or civilly against their accusers. Many of the women alleging that they too were sexually assaulted by Bill Cosby were not going to have their day in court as a result of these laws. Two years before Cosby was marched off in handcuffs to prison, California governor Jerry Brown signed a bill that ended the statute of limitations on prosecuting rape cases.[25] Some of the Cosby accusers spoke publicly to the governor, pleading that the law be ratified.

Over the last couple of years, childhood sexual abuse scandals have also been front and center. Dozens of women alleging that Larry Nassar had sexually abused them confronted him in person as they gave their victim statements. The allegations of abuse committed by him took place over the course of three decades. Nassar was a well-liked, respected doctor who treated hundreds of aspiring athletes. Many of the young women who gave victim statements at Nassar's sentencing were under eighteen.[26] One year after Nassar went to prison, the *Huffington Post* produced a seven-part series commemorating the seven days women stood in Judge Rosemarie Aquilina's Lansing, Michigan, courtroom in January 2018. The hearing forced the world to listen to Nassar's survivors.

Trauma gone public has stirred up conversations all over the world about the impact of childhood abuse, sexual assault, mass shootings, natural disasters, and related incidents. We are becoming a society that can tolerate talking about events that were once taboo. We are becoming a world that accepts the complexities that follow events that are indescribable. People are beginning to understand why victims of trauma stay silent for years or even decades. Experts in the field of psychology are talking about the changes in their private practices and agencies. Men and women are coming forward sooner after they are assaulted. Teenagers and family members of mass shootings are fighting for prevention by challenging gun laws. Combat veterans are becoming more comfortable asking for help when they return to American soil. Survivors of natural disasters are putting themselves in the spotlight, explaining how their lives are forever changed as a result of their loss.

It is in speaking and understanding that people can go from surviving to thriving after trauma. Throughout this book, patient examples will demonstrate the process of digesting and working through trauma. Readers will hear directly from people who have found ways to manage their symptoms of PTSD. Readers will be able to connect with the challenges that come with shame and fear and how they can move to a place of peace. Readers will relate to patients grappling with overwhelming amounts of grief in light of their sudden losses due to death or accident.

Readers will learn about different coping strategies they can implement when facing their deepest losses and experiences. It is impossible to thrive after trauma without having different methods to aid in their recovery. I have been fortunate in my work as a trauma therapist to witness hundreds of people reclaim different parts of their lives after asking for help. I have been a part of births, weddings, job promotions, and other successes as patients stay the course in their fight to keep living. It is possible to live fully, no matter how horrific your trauma. For most people, the hardest part of moving beyond their horror is finding ways to live with whatever happened to them, versus acting like it did not happen. It is not about getting over trauma. It is about thriving after trauma that makes the biggest difference.

2

FACING THE TRAUMA

TELLING YOUR STORY

One of the worst parts of experiencing trauma is the inability to process or find words to describe it while it is happening. Most of the time when I start counseling a new patient, I have no idea what kind of trauma they have lived through. When someone calls me for therapy, they usually say they called me because they knew I specialized in trauma and eating disorders. During the initial call, I do not probe their history. Instead, I encourage them to ask me questions and tell me about their current day-to-day struggles. For instance, prospective patients often tell me about their history of depression, anxiety, and in some instances eating disorders. Everyone has a story. Most people who seek treatment want to feel better, and some call for help because they are on the verge of needing rehab or hospitalization. Sometimes people reach out for outpatient therapy after they have been discharged from some type of treatment center, whether for eating disorders, addictions, or mental disorders.

When I meet a patient for the first or second or third time, I try to meet them where they are. Almost all the patients I have met through the years come to therapy motivated and wanting to live a better life. In the beginning, the most important part of building a therapeutic alliance is building a connection and conveying empathy. I still remember when I met my therapist and what made me want to go back a second, third, and fourth time. As I spoke about more superficial issues, I noticed her ability to listen and convey empathy. She was focused on my words and showed her caring just by being present.

It is scary to call for help. It is terrifying for trauma survivors because it is the first step to telling their story or facing the times in their lives that left them feeling horrified, distrusting, or ashamed.

Samantha's Story: Fighting Her Truth of Childhood Trauma

I started working with one of my patients when she was a junior in high school. I will call her Samantha. Her mom reached out to me after she was discharged from an eating disorders partial hospitalization program. When we started working together, Samantha focused a lot on her body image. For months she walked around in a body she hated. Many times she told me, "I wish I could just jump out of my skin." I tried to find different ways to explore with her what she meant by that. I would ask, "Are you feeling mad or are you feeling scared or guilty or worried?" Samantha was unable to identify what emotion was underlying her self-hatred.

Rather than continue to probe her feelings, our work shifted into concrete behavioral strategies[1] (cognitive behavioral therapy) to help her contain her eating disorder behaviors, mostly restricting and purging. I was concerned about the severity of her symptoms, and we wanted to prevent her from needing to be hospitalized for a second time. The safety and well-being of patients always takes precedence over the trauma work. Cognitive behavioral therapy addresses the specific emotional and mental health needs of trauma survivors in overcoming the destructive effects of trauma that lead to an eating disorder. The strategies of CBT, such as reframing negative reactions and behaviors, help with symptom reduction. The technique was developed in the 1990s by Judith Cohen, Esther Deblinger, and Anthony Mannarino[2] for survivors of severe trauma and abuse.

Samantha and I put together an eating disorder journal, and I asked her to write down what she was thinking before, during, and after she used her eating disorder symptoms. Our goal was to help Samantha identify what she was thinking when she had the urge to use her symptoms so that we could figure out how to name her feelings. We also worked on helping Samantha to reduce her sleep disruption, anxiety, depression, and emotional disconnection.

During the whole first year of our therapy, we worked on stabilizing her symptoms and improving her self-image. As Samantha was getting closer to leaving for college, she began opening up more about her relationship with her mom. She started telling me about times when she felt emotionally abandoned and invalidated by her mom, dad, and brother. There were a few sessions when she would start to tell me about a fight she had with her mom, which usually ended in her sobbing on my sofa while I sat there feeling confused and helpless. The fights she described having were more about curfews, boyfriends, and filling out college applications. Samantha told me she felt guilty about wanting to go away to college, and she talked about incidents when she said her mom was "falling apart" every time the topic came up.

When we sat in session, I would think something did not feel right. I felt like I was sitting in the room with a young woman who was in excruciating pain, but I had no idea why. Samantha made very little eye contact during session, and her affect was flat, with no expression of emotion. There was no indication of any trauma from what I had heard her tell me in words.

As her senior year was winding down, Samantha announced she was going to stop therapy. At the time I felt like the work was not complete, but I also respected her right to make that choice. I challenged her decision and expressed my concern for her in that she was still struggling with her bulimia and self-hatred. I reached out to her parents with her permission and encouraged them to seek treatment for her on her college campus where she would be starting that fall.

In our last session before she left for college, Samantha was guarded and distant. I could feel her pain as we sat together and remember thinking there was something she was still not saying. We left the door open by talking about her right to come back to treatment with me or with someone else at any point. I also encouraged her to stay in touch via email if she felt like that would be helpful.

Years went by before I heard from Samantha again. Toward the end of her senior year in college, she reached out to me. Samantha was tearful and sounded terrified as she told me about her current relationship with her boyfriend. She told me, "I feel so trapped by this guy, and I am terrified that if I break up with him he will kill himself or hurt me badly." Samantha agreed to do phone sessions with me until she graduated from college and then began seeing me every week in my office.

From the onset of her returning to therapy, something felt different. She was more vulnerable and more open. We talked for several sessions about her relationship with Kevin that had lasted two of her four years while she was away at college. She reported several incidents where she felt assaulted and unsafe. Samantha told me that Kevin forced her to take some kind of sedative and then he would force her to have sexual relations. She also brought up times when Kevin became violent when he was mad or wanted to have sex. She told me that the fear of being caught is what kept her quiet. I asked her what her parents thought of Kevin, and she told me, "He was always so polite when he was around other people." Miraculously, Samantha found the courage to leave Kevin without the help of family, friends, or therapy. She told me that between the imminent danger she felt and knowing she was graduating from college and could get away from Kevin, she was able to leave him.

We spent months in therapy talking about this relationship and how her eating disorder had become more serious. She was able to identify that she was using the eating disorder because it was the only thing that made her feel more in control and less alone. We implemented some CBT strategies to quiet the part of her that had so much self-hatred. During a session when Samantha was describing an abusive episode, I asked her, "Did any of what you felt with Kevin feel familiar?" With a lot of apprehension, Samantha admitted that the feelings of shame and fear were not new to her. I told Samantha that we would come back to that idea once she was able to plant her feet and become more in control of the eating disorder and depression.

Once Samantha worked through the fear and shame of being with someone who treated her so poorly, she appeared to be doing better. She reported a decrease in her symptoms, and she told me her depression and anxiety had gotten better. Once again Samantha decided she wanted to terminate therapy, partly because she claimed she was ready and partly due to a job that would take her to another state. When I asked Samantha what she wanted to do with the realization that the feelings during the abusive relationship with Kevin were familiar, she told me, "There is no need to dredge up the past. I am not with Kevin anymore."

A part of me felt worried for Samantha and all the undigested feelings she was still holding on to in her heart. Another part of me remembered that it was not up to me to tell someone else when they needed to tell their story. I had figured out that Samantha was telling her truth in segments, and if that was how she needed to do it, I had to accept that.

Two years went by and I heard nothing from Samantha. One day I received a phone message of her crying and telling me, "I am having a total breakdown." She got in her car, drove over twelve hours to her hometown, and decided to take a short-term leave from her job.

When we started meeting, I felt concerned for her, and I knew she was on the edge of breaking her silence. The anguish I felt when she was in the room was overpowering. Samantha started telling me about all this reading she was doing online, mostly about childhood victims of abuse who repressed their trauma. She asked me, "Do you know what it means to dissociate?" Of course I did, but I wanted her to tell me how she experienced the dissociation in her own words. Samantha described several times over the previous ten years when she felt like her body was floating on the ceiling as she watched herself below. She was not able to identify what triggered her to use this defense mechanism, but she was able to tell me it was happening. During these initial sessions upon her return, I noticed that she would stare at my rug or look at a spot on the wall without even blinking. At times I would say to her, "Are you here with me or are you somewhere else?" Samantha told me she was not in the room but that she could hear my voice. At this point she was not able to tell me what she was remembering or flashing back to.

People who survive some types of abuse or other traumas will leave their bodies to survive the trauma. Some patients describe dissociation as if they are watching themselves being assaulted or abused. According to the DSM-5,[3] dissociation disorders "are characterized by a disruption of and/or discontinuity in the normal integration of consciousness, memory, identity, emotion, perception, body representation, motor control, and behavior. Dissociative symptoms can potentially disrupt every area of psychological functioning."

We talked in session about dissociation and how this coping strategy was not something she had learned as an adult. Christine Courtois is a psychotherapist and has received international recognition for her work on the effects of incest, child sexual abuse, and complex traumatic stress disorders. I told Samantha about her work with adults who were recovering from a variety of childhood abuse traumas and that she could read more about Dr. Courtois's work. Samantha was eager to gain insight and understanding into her dissociative experiences. I explained to Samantha that showing me this part of herself was another step toward healing. Samantha felt safe enough to bring me on this part of her journey.

Dissociation is an unconscious defense mechanism that helps people survive atrocities such as childhood sexual abuse, plane crashes, and different forms of torture. Dr. Bessel van der Kolk,[4] a pioneer in the PTSD research field, has conducted numerous studies on how the brain compartmentalizes and stores memory in the body as a way to live after the horror ends. When Samantha was starting to have her breakdown, she reported many times when she felt like time was passing by with no recollection of what had just occurred. She also described feeling like her body was not her own. Though she was not able to identify when the dissociative symptoms began, she was able to recall times earlier in her childhood when the symptoms had surfaced. For instance, Samantha told me about several times when she was at work before her breakdown and how she felt unable to function.

Sometimes Samantha felt so out of sorts that she had to leave work and put herself in a quiet place where there was no stimulation. The minute she sensed displeasure or anger toward her, Samantha told me, "it was like I became invisible." The sense of danger she felt about the situation did not add up, and as we continued to work in therapy, we explored several instances when she had these familiar feelings. Van der Kolk says that "parts of the brain that have evolved to monitor danger remain overactivated and even the slightest sign of danger, real or misperceived, can trigger an acute stress response accompanied by intense unpleasant emotions and overwhelming sensations." These reactions make it almost impossible for Samantha and others dissociating from their trauma to connect with other people. For years Samantha turned to her eating disorder symptoms to distract from the dissociative features. She told me she was hoping that if she obsessed every minute about what she ate and how she looked she would not have to deal with the layers of pain underneath. Samantha began to understand that she was storing feelings of shame, rage, and fear in her body. However, she had no words attached to the feelings in her body, and she felt disempowered by her inability to hold on to the words and images from her childhood trauma.

When Samantha took her leave from her job, her main goal was to put most of her attention on her PTSD, depression, and eating disorder symptoms. She was determined to piece together the fragmented memories and feelings from her past. Samantha was ready to face her trauma. She wanted to return to her job and work on connecting to others so she did not have to keep living such an isolated life.

Facing trauma is scary, and for some patients it can temporarily disrupt their current functioning. However, for many, fighting the memories of trauma and keeping the memories stored in the body leaves them feeling held hostage by their physical and mental illness. Whenever I meet a patient who is struggling with dissociation and PTSD, part of me wants to push them to speak. Then I look at the research and work done by PTSD researchers and remind myself that it is not up to me to tell someone else when they are ready to speak.

It took me decades to speak in my therapy about my abuse. If I had pushed myself to uncover my experiences before I was ready, I would have fallen apart. For many patients, something will trigger them to begin facing whatever awful events they survived. Sometimes life events, such as getting married, giving birth, or losing a parent or loved one, will be the impetus to working through trauma. The feelings that surface during times of grief or change have pushed many of my patients to take the leap into addressing their past.

STAYING GROUNDED

Trauma recovery is a process. Some patients start therapy with me because they are having a difficult time staying grounded after facing whatever horrible things have happened to them. Unlike Samantha, who dissociated during her trauma, some patients report feeling like they are reliving their abuse, loss, or memories of combat on a daily basis. Abuse survivors have talked in therapy about feeling reactivated when they are talking with bosses or authority figures. Repeatedly I have talked with male and female patients who feel like they are shrinking into a child the second someone of authority shows any sign of disapproval. When I work with patients who have witnessed a parent having a heart attack or have lost a family member in a car crash, they often talk about seeing the image of the corpse multiple times a day. Some report having nightmares about seeing the person they loved get killed. Patients I have met who were in New York City during the 9/11 terrorist attacks talk in therapy about feeling terror throughout their bodies when a plane flies overhead. One of my patients had to move back home after the attack because she was unable to go to class, eat, or sleep. The sounds, sights, and smells after the buildings collapsed right in front of her took over her whole being.

For most patients these feelings come out in physical symptoms, such as nausea, trembling, sudden temperature changes in their body, or tightening of all their muscles. Part of therapy involves teaching patients how to recognize when they are triggered and separate what is about before and what is about the present moment.

Alissa's Story: Dad's Sudden Death in His Forties, Sexual Assault in Her Teens, and an Abusive Boyfriend during Young Adulthood

Alissa reached out to me for therapy after getting her younger sister into intensive counseling for an eating disorder and anxiety. When I met her, she had already lived twenty years of her life storing up emotions from multiple traumas dating back to her prepubescent years. When we began having therapy sessions, Alissa did a lot of talking about her dad's sudden death and then the abusive relationships she had with men after he passed away. During our initial sessions I found myself feeling anxious and overwhelmed. After we met three times, I realized I was experiencing her emotions and could imagine that it felt impossible for her to stay grounded. She had told several people through the years about the things that had happened to her. She talked with her older sister, her aunt, and a couple of friends for years about the anguish she felt about her dad's death. Alissa was not in denial about her survivorship, but she had not digested any of the feelings or developed strategies to stay grounded when she was triggered in the present.

After we had been meeting for a few months, I suggested that we slow down the work by focusing on each of her traumas versus talking about different aspects of her dad's death and abusive past all at once. I wanted to help her sit with whatever emotions she was holding on to and find a way to process her feelings while managing better in her current relationships.

For years Alissa blamed herself for her dad's death. Alissa had a tenuous relationship with her dad going back to early childhood. His approval was important to her, and at times she did whatever she could just to please him. In middle school she found herself "hooking up" with a lot of boys. Alissa wanted to feel accepted and loved, and she told me she was afraid to say no. One day she hooked up with a guy and then regretted it. At that time she did not feel like she could talk to her mom, so she called her dad and left him a voice mail saying some of what had happened. Hours went by, and she never heard from him. At this point in her life, her mom and dad were living in separate homes. Alissa felt worried about him not returning her call, so she decided to walk over to her dad's house. Sadly, she found her dad on the ground, and she told me he was not breathing. A part of her already knew he was gone, but she frantically called 911 hoping they could revive him. When the medics arrived, they told Alissa he was gone and that he had died from a heart attack. Autopsy reports indicated that he had been suffering with a heart condition that was not diagnosed. Alissa's adolescence changed dramatically from that day forward. She found herself in relationships with older men who sexually harassed her and took advantage of her. She was raped by two high school boys during her junior year of high school. She tried to tell her mom what happened. Alissa told me her mom was silent when she told her about the assault. Alissa did not report the rape. She did not have a therapist to help her. She lived in silence as she kept flashing back to the assault. She went to school with these boys and had to face them at times in her classes and in the hallway. Months after she was sexually assaulted she began dating an older man in his midtwenties.

Alissa spent most of her time with him. She knew he was not treating her well and that he was trying to alienate her from her mom and her siblings. At one point her mom kicked her out of her childhood home and told her, "Just go live with your boyfriend and do not bother coming home." Alissa told me she was devastated. She described feeling abandoned twice. "First my dad drops dead, and then my mom practically disowns me." We talked at length about her dad's death and figured out she felt responsible for his death. Even though the doctors told her that her dad had already been sick with a bad heart, Alissa decided that leaving him that phone message about the encounter with the teenage boy pushed him over the edge.

As our therapy continued, Alissa reported multiple incidents where her older boyfriend intimidated, threatened, and physically assaulted her. She knew calling her mom for help was not an option. As the abuse continued with her boyfriend, Alissa assumed that was what she deserved. She was convinced she had killed her dad and blamed herself for the rape during her junior year of high school.

Relationships were virtually impossible for Alissa to maintain. When I asked Alissa what made her leave the abusive boyfriend, she told me she was terrified he would kill her. Alissa went back to her mom's house after an abusive incident and told me she told her mom. Alissa said her mom let her move back home but would not acknowledge any of the abuse Alissa told her about. Alissa had seen her mom being abused by her dad. She knew her mom had never dealt with her own abuse.

I did not start counseling Alissa until she was in her midforties. She spent years of her life living with undigested rage and shame. If someone looked at her with the slightest bit of anger or disapproval, she would lose her temper. As Alissa got more comfortable with me, she brought that part of herself into our relationship. If I said something that triggered her, her initial reaction was to become defensive and angry. She developed this defense mechanism as a way to protect herself from feeling like a victim. The problem with that was that she was reacting to people in her life as if they were all going to leave her or mistreat her.

As we moved further into the recovery work, I talked with Alissa about boundaries and how to help her understand her reactions to people. Jocelyn St. Cyr[5] has been counseling trauma survivors in Massachusetts for over twenty years. She distinguishes between applying relaxation techniques and teaching patients grounding techniques in recovery. She suggests that patients have the most success when she combines talking and building skills. When Alissa came into session feeling like she was going to jump out of her skin, I would not tell her to breathe or calm down. I worked with Alissa on engaging her senses to direct her back to the present. Alissa reported many times when she lashed out at coworkers and friends and said she wanted to live a less turbulent life. When the buttons got pushed, Alissa felt like the impulse to react took over her whole body. St. Cyr suggests that patients turn to art, pets, nature, or yoga and at times reach out for support. When Alissa brought in topics that were emotionally charged, we made space for her to tell me the story.

Rather than just focusing on how mad or sad she was about what had happened, I would ask her if the feelings she had were familiar from her previous traumas. Initially Alissa had a difficult time identifying what was about today and what was coming from her dad's death or other traumas. She would describe feeling like her insides were ripping out of her gut and being frustrated that she could not separate the past from the present.

I explained to Alissa that because she spent so many years in silence about all of her traumas, the feelings would be much more intense. When we had sessions that felt like flooding with feelings, I would suggest that she utilize some of the strategies we set in place. Alissa had a wonderful relationship with her animals and felt comforted by her ability to tend to them. Sometimes after session, she would go home and snuggle on the sofa with them. At times she turned to exercise to release some of the pent-up anxiety. Other times Alissa would keep herself moving by getting engaged in a task that would shift her thinking. She laughed at me when I would tell her, "Wiggle your toes and feel those feet of yours on the ground." I learned this strategy early in my recovery and actually found it to be very helpful.

A turning point occurred in our work after she was verbally attacked by a supervisor at her job. Alissa worked as a psychiatric nurse in the crisis unit at a local hospital. She felt good in her role because she was able to help her patients find safety and inner peace at the times when they felt the most unsafe. One day she was concerned about a patient whom she thought was being discharged prematurely. Without giving it much thought, Alissa approached her supervisor and told him some symptoms the patient was exhibiting that made her feel uncomfortable with the supervisor's decision.

Seconds after he walked away, Alissa told me, he quickly turned his body back toward her and stormed over into her space. "His eyes were glaring as he said to me, 'don't you ever talk to me like that again,'" she said. "You are an embarrassment to this hospital, and you have no idea what you are talking about." Rather than shrink up and shut down, Alissa told me she could feel fire coming out of her body. She said that as her supervisor stood over her, she was flashing back to the look on her abuser's face when he hit her. She told me that she could see the expression on the boys' faces as they raped her. Alissa told me that these images rushed through her mind simultaneously.

I nearly jumped off my seat when she told me she was able to recognize that these were flashbacks and that she made a different choice when the supervisor reprimanded her. Alissa said she waited for him to walk away and immediately turned to her colleague and said, "Did he actually just act like that?" Alissa had several witnesses who affirmed her and told her clearly how inappropriate the supervisor's behavior was. Without a thought, Alissa picked up the phone and reported the incident. She spoke with one of her direct supervisors and was told to go home and take good care of herself. Alissa told me that the ride home was upsetting but that she was able to stay in her body and feel grounded.

There is so much hope that comes from being that triggered and for Alissa to realize that she could deal with life stressors, even when someone treated her similarly to her abuser and her rapist. Alissa walked away from that session knowing that she could stand up for herself, that she could speak and keep herself grounded and not shame herself for someone's else's pathology.

MANAGING FLASHBACKS

Flashbacks can show up in many different forms. Some patients talk about feeling sensations in their bodies after being abused. Other patients who have survived plane crashes or combat describe hearing the sounds of the plane crashing or gunshots being fired at any point during the day. Flashbacks are intrusive and disturbing and lead many to resort to self-destructive behaviors to try to make the auditory and visual images leave their minds.

In *Psychology Today*, Tom Bunn, LCSW,[6] wrote about a Vietnam veteran with PTSD who was driving down the New Jersey Turnpike heading for the airport. A helicopter flew directly over him. Suddenly he slammed his foot on the brakes, pulled his car to the side of the road, jumped out of his car, and hid in the ditch. The unexpected sound of the helicopter took him back to Vietnam under enemy fire. Bunn explained that he was not just remembering the event but reliving it.

Flashbacks from childhood trauma are different. They do not include factual information. Kids under five years old do not have words to store their memories. Rather than remembering sights or sounds, childhood trauma survivors will flash back to feelings they had during their trauma. When I first started talking in therapy about my abuse, I had what I called "feeling memories." When I would sit in Dorothy's office, I would remember feeling the shame and fear I felt during my abuse. I talked a lot in therapy about the feelings I had after the sexual abuse occurred. Those feelings continued to follow me through life anytime I thought someone was mad at me or anytime I felt afraid I was being disbelieved or taken advantage of. The problem with an implicit flashback is that the feelings get directed onto the situation that is happening in the present. This makes it almost impossible for someone with a history of childhood trauma to connect and feel emotionally safe with someone in their present life.

Robin's Story: Gang-Raped First Week of Grad School

I met Robin months after she was sexually assaulted at a college party. Robin was attending grad school for her master's in nursing. Before going to grad school, Robin struggled with feelings of abandonment after her biological mom gave her up for adoption days after she was born. Authorities found her on the steps of an empty apartment building after local neighbors reported a baby left in a bassinet. Robin had a long history of depression and anxiety beginning in her childhood.

When I met Robin for our first session, she looked terrified. She barely looked at me, and her affect was flat. She was also trembling as she sat on the sofa. Her adoptive parents reached out to me to help her recover from the sexual assault. They told me she stopped living and came home from school days after the assault. Robin was living in isolation, and she stopped talking to her family and friends. She did not report the attack to the police, and she did not tell anyone what happened to her at school. Her parents became concerned when they caught her using self-mutilation when she was having flashbacks. Robin decided to tell her parents about the rape after dropping out of the semester and moving back home.

Some people who have extensive trauma or abandonment histories resort to self-harm on different parts of their body as a defense strategy. According to Matthew Tull, PhD,[7] self-mutilation in patients with PTSD deliberately hurt themselves to injure or destroy body tissues. Self-mutilation is not an attempt at suicide, but it can cause severe injury to one's body. Deliberate self-injury provides people with short-term relief from emotional pain.

Some patients cut themselves because they are having flashbacks and they want to get their bodies back to the present. The pain caused from the injury shocks the body back into the here and now, and for some that will end the flashbacks. Cutting, skin carving, severe scratching, head banging, or punching oneself are the most common methods of self-injury.

When Robin and I began having sessions, I felt concerned because she presented so differently than a typical trauma survivor. She was bright, giggly, and could only talk about superficial topics. She was able to acknowledge why she needed treatment, but she was unable to talk about her abandonment history. During our third session, Robin walked into my office, and before she even sat down she started telling me details of her assault. Tears were pouring down her face, and she made no eye contact. At one point she began trembling and lost the ability to speak. I tried to implement some grounding techniques with her. For instance, I told her to try and look around the office and use her fingers to tap on her arm. I knew the flashbacks were intense and that we needed to slow down and help her feel safe.

I never want to tell someone not to speak. However, the safety of patients takes precedence, and at this point in the session Robin was not digesting any of what she was saying. If we had continued to talk about what happened to her, there was a good chance she would not even remember telling me she was raped. When the session ended, I asked her permission to reach out to her psychiatrist. I was concerned she would leave my office and do self-harm. One hour after I spoke with her doctor I received a frantic call from her dad. Robin had inflicted numerous cutting injuries on her body. I advised her dad to take her to a local crisis center.

My heart broke for Robin, and I knew I could not provide her with the support she needed to begin her journey to recovery. When patients come to therapy with little ability to cope with intense emotions, I refer them to programs that offer daily support, such as a day program or partial hospitalization. I spoke with her psychiatrist, and we decided finding a program that offered DBT (dialectical behavior therapy) was the best option. Robin needed to learn how to manage her urges to self-harm before she was going to be in a place to work through her emotions in outpatient psychotherapy.

DBT is a technique that helps people who are struggling to manage their emotions, maintain relationships, and contain impulsivity. Matthew Tull explains that DBT is different from cognitive behavioral therapy in that it emphasizes acceptance of the person's emotions. When Robin was getting in touch with her rage about the sexual assault, she was unable to validate her reaction. Instead of accepting this is an appropriate response, Robin used self-harm to try to get back at her attacker.

When Robin began treatment at the center for DBT, clinicians taught her mindfulness meditation. Rather than stay in the feelings from the flashbacks, meditation helped Robin redirect her feelings into the present moment. When Robin was having urges to self-harm, she went to a quiet place and practiced saying words of comfort to the part of herself that felt so hurt. Many studies done over the last five years by researchers and clinicians show a significant reduction in self-harm when applying DBT techniques, especially early in trauma recovery.

Standard DBT is done in three stages. Stage 1 consists of weekly individual therapy, group skills training, therapist consultation, and between-session coaching. The goal is to help patients achieve control over self-harm urges by using behavioral skills in the area of emotion regulation, distress tolerance, mindfulness, and interpersonal effectiveness. Stage 2 focuses directly on treating PTSD with 90- to 120-minute therapy sessions in addition to group therapy and between-session coaching. Stage 3 is used to address any remaining problems in daily living. The main intent at this level of DBT is to help patients improve their relationships and get involved in more activities at school or work.

Robin continued treatment at the DBT center for one year. She accepted that when we met she was not able to work through her sexual assault and keep herself safe in her present life. Everybody reacts differently to trauma. Robin's prior history of being abandoned as an infant complicated her recovery because she already had issues with self-worth and identity. After the assault occurred, Robin felt like her life meant nothing. While I felt disappointed that I could not provide her with therapy when we met, I was relieved that Robin accepted help from a place that could meet her needs.

I have never met a patient with any type of trauma history who has not experienced a flashback. At times family members of patients with PTSD lack understanding and will say things like, "Why can't you stop dwelling on the past?" or, "You need to stop having those flashbacks." During the early part of my trauma recovery work, I had flashbacks during therapy sessions and between therapy sessions, and I could never predict what would trigger them to surface. One of the most helpful questions my therapist would ask me was, "How does the memory or flashback you are having relate to your life today?" At first I was enraged when she would ask me this because I felt like she was telling me to stop remembering.

Over time I realized that flashbacks were serving a purpose. For example, when Alissa was confronting her supervisor, the memories she was having in her mind and body were reminding her of what she felt like when someone else was abusing or mistreating her. In order for her life to be different, she needed to confront those memories so she could have the choice to change her reaction to people in her life in the present. When Samantha came back to therapy, she was ready to face her childhood trauma. As soon as she left her job due to what she called a "meltdown," she started having flashbacks of how she dissociated during her abuse. In order for Samantha to understand how she buried her trauma, she needed to revisit how her brain protected her from being present during the abuse. Rather than shame herself for not remembering the abuse, Samantha got to the point where she could embrace the power of her mind to keep her sane during experiences that could cause her to be insane. For Robin it was the opposite. Instead of burying the sexual assault, Robin suffered from flashbacks constantly for weeks after the attack. Her earlier issues with being abandoned by her biological mom left her with low self-worth, and the flashbacks reiterated her worst fears. Robin believed that she deserved to be raped and was unconsciously replaying the trauma over and over again to punish herself more. She needed to go to an intensive program so she could work through these feelings and learn how to manage the flashbacks without retraumatizing herself.

HEALING STRATEGIES WHEN FACING YOUR TRAUMA

1. Find a therapist that specializes in treating trauma. Ask people you trust who they have seen or would recommend for treatment.
2. Look after your physical self. Pay attention to changes in your eating or sleeping patterns. If you are not sleeping or want to sleep all the time, or if you stop eating or want to eat every time you talk about what happened to you, consider seeing your primary doctor or psychiatrist for pharmacological support. Also consider seeking nutrition counseling to help moderate your eating or focus on healthy eating patterns.
3. Keep a journal. Write down your long-term goals and how facing your trauma will help you attain them. It is so important to remind yourself, sometimes multiple times a day, why you are facing whatever happened to you. The pain of trauma without constant reminders of hope can lead to despair and hopelessness.
4. Set up support before and after attending therapy sessions. If you get depressed or anxious after you have a session, be mindful of that when setting up appointments. Make sure you have something to keep you focused and the day moving when your session ends.
5. Develop strategies that work for you to manage the anger and sadness that get stirred up as you tell your story. For example, go to yoga or kickboxing, play tennis, play an in-

strument, go for a run with your furry friend, attend art classes, or start knitting or crocheting—any activity that involves focus and a way to stay in your body.

MANAGING FLASHBACKS

1. Work on naming your triggers. Pay attention to changes in your mood or if you are having physical changes in your body. Are you feeling pressure in your chest or suddenly feeling sweaty and hot?
2. Once you understand your triggers, if possible avoid going to those places until you have worked through your feelings. For example, do not go to an air show if sounds of planes flying overhead remind you of the trauma. If having intimacy with a man or woman reminds you of being assaulted, work through those feelings by talking with your partner about ways to help you feel safe.
3. When you are having a flashback, tell yourself, "I am having a flashback. This is not happening today. I am safe!" Return to the present by using your senses. Look around the room. What do you see? Breathe in the air around you and tell yourself what you are smelling. Listen to the sounds around you. Focus on the birds chirping, the wind blowing, the rain hitting the windows. Turn on your favorite kind of music. Sing to the words or imagine the sounds of the music comforting the part of you that feels afraid. Grab something to drink and focus on the flavor. Hold something warm or cold. Take the item and place it on your back or your belly. Focus on what that sensation feels like.
4. Bring a notepad or your journal with you everywhere. Jot down the flashback and reassure yourself that you can talk about it in your next therapy session or with a friend when the time feels right.
5. Don't be afraid to ask for help. Access online support groups or websites that offer different suggestions for stay-

ing sane during your recovery. Flashbacks can make people feel like they are crazy. Tell yourself over and over again, "I am not crazy. What happened is what feels crazy."

3

HOW THE ROAD UNRAVELS WHEN A WITNESS IS PRESENT

LIVING LIFE WITHOUT RE-CREATING TRAUMA

Facing trauma and having a witness present can make the biggest difference once someone has begun to unravel and peel away at the layers underneath their experience. One of the hardest parts of recovery is accepting that there is more work that needs to happen once patients or survivors tell someone what happened to them. It can take my patients months to feel believed by others after they have shared their stories. Often people who have been abused or have lived through a devastating loss of any kind will unconsciously create scenarios where they feel violated, abandoned, disbelieved, and unheard for years to follow.

Denise's Story: Sudden Loss of a Parent

When I first started providing therapy, patients were reporting significant histories of addictions and eating disorders. I still remember my first phone call with a woman I will call Denise, who called me months before she was going to get married. When I asked her what made her want to get help now, she told me, "My eating disorder is out of control. I am using symptoms of bulimia four to five times a day." As we were on the initial call, I was thinking, "How can someone be so sad right before an occasion that should be so happy?"

When Denise entered my office for the first session, I could feel her despair. She was well groomed, but she had dark circles under her eyes and she looked like she had been crying for a year. We jumped right into talking about her eating disorder and her concerns for her health. Denise told me she had developed the eating disorder in her senior year of high school. When we met, she was twenty-nine years old. She had tried numerous inpatient facilities to stabilize her eating disorder and depression and had had periods of temporary remission, but she relapsed every time something in her life changed. Denise told me, "My bulimia came back when I started college, when I graduated college, when I started a new job, when my then fiancé proposed, when I moved into our first apartment, and recently as my wedding approaches." Right away I asked her, "Have you lost anyone due to illness?" Without any emotion, Denise told me the story of her mother's death. At the age of sixteen Denise lost her mom suddenly. She told me, "I left for prom on a Friday in May, and Sunday morning I got a call from my dad that my mom was in the ICU." We talked about her mom's health, and Denise reported that she had no prior history of illness. Denise went on to tell me how the doctors told her and her dad and other family members that it was time to say good-bye. She had suffered a brain aneurysm. The doctors said, "We have tried everything we can, and your mom is unresponsive." Denise explained how her defenses kicked in and that she was numb to any emotions. She told me, "It was like I was watching a movie." She and her family stood vigil by her mom's bedside until she passed away hours later.

As Denise told me the story, I could feel my gut wrenching and heart breaking for her. I explored with her how she went on with life after her mom died. Denise told me she went back to school the following Wednesday and life went on. At the time, Denise did not realize it, but her eating disorder began to show up months after her mom died. She told me that before the symptoms of bulimia arose, she noticed that her relationship with food was different. I asked her, "How did your eating habits change?" Denise told me she began obsessing about "every little thing I ate" and that there was an evident restriction of food intake. Instead of eating three meals a day and snacks in between, Denise was eating maybe a snack at lunch and dinner. No breakfast and no lunch.

During our first several months in therapy, we talked more about how her family was affected by her mom's death and how others were coping with it. She told me, "My dad became a recluse. He would sit in his chair at night and just stare at the television." So in some ways I am thinking, "She lost her dad after she lost her mom." As we talked more about her eating disorder we learned that the bulimic behaviors were more apparent as she got closer to graduating from high school and leaving for college. We talked about her peer relationships, and she discovered by talking in therapy that she distanced herself from her friends after her mom's death. Denise told me, "I did not notice this at the time, but as I went through senior year of high school, I was going out much less, and most of the time when I wasn't in school I was sitting in my bedroom doing not much of anything."

Whenever a patient tells me they are having self-destructive symptoms that are restrictive in nature, I wonder if they are trying to make their feelings go away or to tell people to go away. While Denise had no conscious intent of feeling friendless, at the time that was the only way she could create some sense of stability. Losing a parent so suddenly at such a young age had a devastating impact on her. For years after her mom's death, Denise was re-creating loss by staying disconnected from people.

A lot of our therapy focused on helping Denise process and work through her feelings about her mom's death. She had not talked to anyone after her mom died. She had no siblings. She had no support system. And at that time she felt like she did not have a dad. I explained to Denise that for many, trauma leaves them feeling unraveled and lost. In therapy we talked about fears of abandonment and loss and how that was crippling her ability to make connections with people. Sometimes Denise would tell me, "My bulimia became my mom, my best friend, and my dad." I asked her to explain more of what she meant by that. Denise realized that she was so afraid of someone else dying that she found a way to stay on earth without attaching to people. We were able to connect her eating disorder with the re-creation of feelings from being motherless. For example, when she felt stranded and alone, she resorted to bulimia to get rid of those feelings. Sometimes she would exercise for three or four hours after eating a meal to "purge" away those "horrible" feelings. When she felt angry and scared and yearned to talk to her mom, she would obsess about what she was not going to eat that day to distract herself from the feelings.

It is part of human nature to do the same thing over and over to attain similar outcomes. The problem with trauma and the re-creation of the experience is that it leaves people stuck in the grief and disconnected from others. Facing trauma and telling your story is a crucial step in the healing process. For Denise and many others, learning how to live life without re-creating the same loss over and over again can be a difficult part of the working-through. Once we made the connection between Denise's eating disorder and her mom's sudden death, we were able to work on maintaining connections. We spent months utilizing different strategies to help Denise become aware of her tendency to push her husband and close friends away. Journaling was an integral part of our work moving forward. I asked Denise to write down her thoughts and feelings when the urges to use her eating disorder emerged.

About a month before the anniversary of her mom's death, Denise came into session with pages of entries about her urges to skip meals or get rid of calories through purging or overexercising. In each entry, Denise wrote what she was wanting to accomplish with her symptoms and what she was thinking and feeling before the urges started. In many entries Denise wrote things like, "Stop thinking about Mom" and, "Make the feelings go away. I don't want to feel sad anymore." As we reviewed her entries, we spoke about people she could reach out to when she wanted to talk.

Denise told me she did not even consider telling someone when she felt upset. She had so many memories of trying to talk to her dad after her mom died and repeatedly described feeling shut down by his silence. Her fear of feeling unheard resulted in not wanting to reach out to anyone. Denise and I talked extensively about her dad's reaction to her mom's death and how in some ways she had to grieve for both parents, which at times felt impossible. Her relationship with her dad was more on her mind as she got closer to getting married. On a couple of occasions I suggested that Denise bring her dad to session to do some therapy, and each time she told me, "My dad would never do that." More than anything I wanted Denise to feel connected and loved as she walked down the aisle. Neither of us wanted her to have her eating disorder be the only guest in attendance at her wedding. Actually, during one session we role-played the part where she would be walking down the aisle. We knew her dad would be absent emotionally, so I asked Denise to bring in a list of people she wanted to make eye contact with at the ceremony. She wrote a list of about ten people, mostly friends whom she was excited to see on this life-changing day. Rather than focus on the sadness about her dad's emotional absence, I suggested that Denise find those ten people in attendance and imagine each of them giving her a hug as she walked toward her soon-to-be husband. Her wedding day was an opportunity to not re-create loss by not being present with her guests. At first Denise resisted the idea. After a few more sessions of working on the journal entries and planning for the wedding, Denise decided apprehensively, "Fine, I will give it a shot."

Our first session after her wedding and honeymoon felt like a celebration. Denise spoke about many moments when she wanted to disconnect but instead let herself feel close to her guests. She told me about one moment when she saw her best friend in the aisle and decided to just go over and give her a hug. We both had tears streaming down our faces as she told the story. Later in the book I will talk more about Denise and how she used her relationship with group therapy members to overcome and accept the losses that came with her mom's death.

Combat Survivor: Jonathon's Story

I met Jonathon over fifty years after he served in Vietnam. For decades he struggled with alcoholism and posttraumatic stress disorder. Jonathon reached out to me a week after his marriage dissolved. He told me on the initial phone call that he had an extensive trauma history after surviving combat. When he walked in for the first session, his eyes looked red and worn out, and he seemed very anxious. He looked like he had not slept in days. He barely looked at me when he talked about losing a "buddy" overseas. Unlike Denise, Jonathon was aware that his drinking problem was leading to more loss because his wife had decided she had had enough and had asked him to leave. Jonathon told me, "She gave me a few chances to get help and I refused, and I am sure that is part of the reason why she wants to divorce me."

Owning his addiction to alcohol was admirable and also very sad. By the time he had decided to get therapy, his marriage had little hope. "My wife is done," he told me when I asked him if there was a chance they could reconcile if he got help. When Jonathon started treatment, he had already moved out of his home and was forced to be somewhat disconnected from his toddler-aged son. His drinking habits got worse. He told me he was "downing a whole bottle of wine or a case of beer" hours after he ended his workday. He was living alone, so there was no one who could hold him accountable or even express concern.

As our sessions progressed, we talked about his experience serving in the war. Jonathon was on the front lines and on a daily basis witnessed violence and death. He reported that the day his friend was killed in combat was the day that changed his life. While I never want someone to feel pain or have to revisit horror, I needed to ask Jonathon what happened. It was obvious to me that he had hardly spoken about this loss. It took him several minutes to even begin speaking. We both sat with heavy hearts as he described what happened to his buddy. Jonathon explained, "I watched him bleed to death after being shot, and there was not a damn thing I could do." After his friend was shot, Jonathon was still in enemy territory. He stood by his friend's side and at one point realized that in order to live he had to evacuate the scene. Before he moved forward with his story, I asked Jonathon, "What did you do feel or think as you left the scene and your friend's body?" He told me he felt nothing. He told me that when he got back to his barracks he told his sergeant what had happened. Jonathon was offered brief crisis counseling, which he declined. When I asked what made him turn down the offer, he told me, "Back then it wasn't cool to ask for help, especially counseling." Jonathon served in combat for six more months after he lost his friend and spoke not a word about his buddy. He told me he would imagine the scene of his friend being shot and killed multiple times a day. He reported that the flashbacks from combat kept him awake for hours every night. He also told me that his wife would wake up several times a week to a screaming, inconsolable husband. Jonathon said, "She begged me to get help. She knew I had PTSD. She knew I was using alcohol to numb the pain."

Jonathon had no intention of pushing his wife away. He wanted to be close to her and enjoy his life with his toddler son. After serving in Vietnam, Jonathon worked as a nurse in an emergency room. After I got to understand more about Jonathon's trauma history, I asked him to make a timeline highlighting significant losses he had witnessed working as a nurse. He came to session one day with four or five other examples of watching someone die after being shot or being in a serious car accident.

We took our time talking about his timeline, and we focused on what he noticed about his alcohol dependency during and after his shifts in the emergency room. Jonathon explained that every time he saw someone go into cardiac arrest or lose consciousness, he had flashbacks of his buddy being killed. I asked him, "How did you function in your job as these flashbacks entered your mind?" Jonathon told me he detached from his feelings. He said, "I was doing the motions but literally could feel nothing." Once his shift ended, the anxiety hit him full force. Jonathon described feeling out of control in his body. He said, "My heart would race, my head would pound, and I felt like my blood was boiling." Then Jonathon would go home to his wife and daughter, and he told me he did not even notice they were in the room. On countless nights after work his wife approached him and tried to offer support. I asked Jonathon, "What did you feel when she would do that?" He told me he was so overwhelmed with what happened at work and what that triggered that he made himself disappear. Jonathon went on to explain that he went to the kitchen and grabbed a whole bunch of beer, went into his bedroom, and locked the door. I asked him if there was a part of him that wanted comfort from his wife. Jonathon told me, "A little part of me wanted to go and get a hug from my wife, but I felt too afraid to let myself attach to her." We spent many sessions talking about what it would mean if he let himself depend more on her, especially in times of need. Jonathon realized through talking that he was stuck in his old grief and fear. "The thought of losing someone else I loved scared me so much that I on some level decided to keep to myself." His wife would get angry and hurt, and she did not understand why Jonathon refused to let his guard down. This scenario replayed over and over for a couple of years before she gave up.

As we were working through his trauma, we also spent time in therapy talking about the role of alcohol. He became very good friends with the substance. Unlike people, Jonathon told me, "I never worried alcohol would leave me." There was no risk in his dependency on the substance because he knew it was there for him whenever he wanted it. The problem was that Jonathon was not able to consider how choosing alcohol over his wife would eventually lead to a failed marriage.

Jonathon struggled a lot with his wife's decision to end the marriage. He wanted desperately for her to consider giving it another chance. Unfortunately, after several attempts to have her come to therapy with him, we realized he needed to accept and live with her decision.

From that point forward, our goal in therapy was to help Jonathon not create any more losses. He began seeing a psychiatrist for his anxiety. He began attending Alcoholics Anonymous. He decided he was going to use his relationship with his adult daughter to get him more in the present and not feel like everyone in his world was leaving.

He needed to keep working through his memories in combat to tackle the symptoms associated with traumatic stress. Jonathon and I developed a list of coping and containment strategies to help him stay present. For instance, when Jonathon felt a flashback coming on, I told him to wiggle his toes and look around the room. I told him to write down the memory he was having and tell himself, "I am going to talk more about this with Shari when we have our next session." He began to rely more on physical activity, such as running and yoga, to manage the emotions that at times consumed him. Jonathon had made a choice. He was no longer going to let his past take him away from the people in his present.

After months of healing from the trauma, Jonathon decided not to work as an emergency nurse anymore. He realized that the events he witnessed and played a role in facilitating were too great a reminder of war. He still wanted to work in the medical field, but not in the emergency room. Jonathon transferred into an out-patient surgical center where he could help people and be able to send them home feeling better hours after a procedure.

LEARNING TO TRUST YOURSELF AND OTHERS

An integral part of healing from trauma is finding a way to trust yourself and those around you. When someone is sexually assaulted or abused, in most cases it is by someone they have trusted implicitly. For example, many patients who go to therapy report being raped or severely mistreated by a parent, partner, authority figure, religious leader, or sibling. From the moment the violation begins, victims are left trying to make sense of why someone who was supposed to care about them could hurt them so badly. It is not uncommon for me to learn about someone's abuse history months or even years into the therapy relationship. While being raped is terrible, the worst part is the distrust in others that follows.

According to several abuse organizations, including RAINN (the Rape, Abuse, Incest National Network),[1] most cases of incest are never reported due to the intense level of shame associated with this type of sexual abuse. Most incest survivors are in the very beginning stages of developing their values and trust, so the betrayal that comes with this type of abuse leaves them confused. The pressure to keep the family secret overwhelms most survivors, and they assume no one will believe them even if they begin speaking during their adulthood.

When I meet patients who report extreme depression, anxiety, obsessive-compulsive disorder, or life-threatening eating disorders or addictions, I wonder what pain underlies the behaviors or feelings. I never ask a new patient if they have lived through some type of trauma or abuse. Healing from trauma requires developing trust. It takes time to build a solid connection where there is less fear of rejection or judgment. Sometimes when I meet a patient and they tell me the details of their trauma, they end up not staying in therapy.

Stacy's Story: Incest Survivor

I remember meeting one woman I will call Stacy who entered the first session in tears. We had not even sat down, and the tears were pouring down her face. I could feel her pain in the room and tried to make space to meet her in that spot. I sat quietly as she recounted several episodes of incest done to her by her grandfather. She hardly looked at me the whole session. At different points I tried to stop her and ask her how she was feeling about what she was sharing. Her response was, "I just needed to tell someone." I felt so much admiration for her, but I also felt concerned. I was thinking to myself, "How will she take all this in after the session ends, and why is she trusting me with this information after just meeting me?" I knew I could contain her story, and there was no judgment about what she told me regarding her abuse.

Unfortunately Stacy did not return for another appointment. I reached out to her to let her know she could try again at another time. We did not have the opportunity to talk about what got stirred up as she uncovered so much trauma in a one-hour appointment. Sometimes people are desperate to speak the truth because they have been holding it for such a long time. It is important to remember that walking into a therapist's office is a huge step in recovery. It is okay to attend several sessions and just work on relationship building before disclosing details of trauma. It is okay to let your therapist know you have an extensive history without sharing any specifics in the beginning. Work on just being on the room and ask yourself, "Can I picture that this person can tolerate and accept what I am saying?" It is helpful to write down some memories or feelings and practice asking yourself, "Do I believe my story?" Part of developing trust in a witness, such as a therapist, means finding a way to really believe yourself.

Elyse's Story: Childhood Sexual Harassment and Molestation

I met one patient I will call Elyse, an eighteen-year-old senior in high school with plans to go to college hours from her home. Over our first several months in therapy, she told me about numerous incidents when two older boys cornered her in bathrooms at school and molested her. When I would ask her how she coped with this behavior as it happened, she told me, "I just pretended it wasn't happening." After sitting in the room with Elyse for six months, my gut told me there was some other type of abuse that she might have lived through. I never asked her directly, "Have you ever been assaulted?" Instead I would say things like, "Did the feelings you had when you were being molested by the school boys feel familiar?" Elyse always answered the same way, telling me, "I have been doing that my whole life when something upsets me."

One day Elyse walked into session, sat on my sofa, and said, "I have to tell you something." I could feel the anguish in the room, and I waited for Elyse to finish her story. Tears were falling down her face, and after she stopped talking we sat quietly for a moment. Elyse told me, "My uncle sexually assaulted me in my own home." She went on to tell me, "Sometimes my parents were sitting downstairs when he came into the bathroom while I showered." Before commenting on the specifics of her story, I said, "How do you feel about sharing that with me?" I believed her. I wanted to know if she believed herself. Building that trust with the stories about the boys at school was what she needed to be able to report the abuse by a trusted family member.

Elyse told me she felt doubtful that anyone would ever believe that her uncle could hurt her like that. She believed her parents knew and that they just did not want to accept that "it was happening." I understood why Elyse was so afraid I would disbelieve her. I could not make her know I did not doubt her. That was part of the work we needed to do moving forward.

How do therapists or loved ones help survivors trust again when the trust has been taken in such a horrific way? An integral part to trauma recovery means helping patients or loved ones own their feelings. When Elyse talked about her abuse, we spent a significant amount of time exploring her feelings. When she would talk about what her uncle did to her, I would say things like, "Do you believe what you are saying?" When she would ask me if I believed she was telling me the truth, I would ask her, "What benefit would there be for you or anyone else in your life to make up something this awful?"

During any type of trauma, most people will detach emotionally from the experience. When Elyse was being abused by her uncle, she told me her body went frozen and she imagined it was happening to someone else. That was how she got through the event. When I have talked to survivors of 9/11, they describe a very similar reaction as people's lives were being lost all around them. Humans are born with survival mechanisms that help them get through, no matter how bad it is. The problem with that for so many is that it then requires a lot of processing and talking to understand the coping strategy. Elyse had to keep telling her story in different ways to help her trust her truth.

One of the main reasons people disbelieve themselves is that they do not want their story to be true. Unfortunately the denial that comes with trauma is masked by feelings of shame and guilt.

GOOD-BYE GUILT

How does someone let go of their guilt and sense of responsibility for what happened to them? Common thoughts trauma survivors share are, "I should have stopped him" or, "If I hadn't left, maybe I could have saved her life" or, "Why did I survive when so many others didn't?" Guilt left undigested can lead to years of living an unfulfilled life because it gets in the way of accomplishing one's dreams and goals.

Mark's Story: Sexually Abused Child Silent for Decades

I will never forget meeting my patient whom I will call Mark. From the moment he walked into my office I could feel his guilt. He must have apologized over ten times after he would start to show sadness or say something he thought upset me. When I met Mark, he was in his late forties. He had never done his own individual therapy. He told me that many people, including his daughter, begged him to go to therapy. Mark explained that his depression and anxiety crippled his ability to be engaged at work or at home.

I sensed that Mark was ready to have more in his life. He had career aspirations that were halted as a result of his guilt. For years he felt guilty when success came his way. He wanted to have a closer relationship with his daughter. Sadly, Mark's daughter also battled with depression and anxiety after Mark and her mother divorced when she was in her early teens.

During the first few months of our therapy, Mark talked to me about the sexual abuse he lived through with two different adults as a young teenager. When he was twelve years old, the leader of his youth group assaulted him. When he was fifteen, he was sexually abused by his priest. It was dreadful to witness Mark's despair and guilt as he talked about his abuse.

He told me, "I have not talked about this with anyone." When I explored why he chose to stay silent for so long, he told me, "I did not even know it was sexual abuse." He assumed that because he was a teenager it was his responsibility to say no and stop the abuse. We talked for weeks about the grooming process and how he was a victim of both of these men's pathology. Mark had a difficult time reframing this as something that was done to him.

During the abuse, Mark stayed silent. For decades afterward, Mark did not say a word about it to anyone, including his wife at the time. As we spoke in more sessions about his silence, he realized it was his guilt that kept him quiet. I will never forget when he came to session a few months after he told me he was sexually abused. Mark said to me, "Wait a minute, it really wasn't my fault." I asked Mark to elaborate: "What made you realize that, Mark?" He did a lot of reading between sessions about sexual abuse and the dynamics between a perpetrator and a victim. He learned that part of what makes it abuse is that the adult abuser finds ways to make the victim feel like a willing participant. Mark could remember times when he felt coerced or bribed by both of his perpetrators. At the time, Mark assumed he was the one who was supposed to put a stop to it. Mark spoke about a couple of examples when he blamed himself for "allowing him to hurt me." He told me about one time when he and his youth leader were in the car alone. Mark went on to tell me that as he was being forced to give oral sex, he did not try to fight the man off. I asked Mark, "How would you have done that?" Mark began to understand the fear that came with the abuse and his sense of obligation to someone he looked up to. When he told me about another incident with the priest, he said, "I had an opportunity to leave the room, and I didn't. I should have run away and made him stop." When Mark told me that, I affirmed that a part of him felt that way, but the risk felt too high. Mark had never talked about his abuse, so he never had the opportunity to hear other victims express similar thoughts. Without divulging specifics, I told Mark about some other patients I worked with in therapy who felt the exact same way. In fact I told Mark, "I don't think I have met a sexual abuse survivor who hasn't said 'I should have' or 'I could have' or 'why didn't I?'"

The problem with keeping quiet for so long is that, for Mark and many others, it reinforces such a strong sense of responsibility for things we have no control over. For example, Mark opened up to me more about his daughter's battle with depression and anxiety. A couple of years before we met, he told me his daughter had attempted suicide. Mark was convinced he should have known and could have stopped it. Mark came home from work one day to find his then seventeen-year-old daughter with a pillowcase wrapped tightly around her neck. He said she was barely breathing when he came home from work. He immediately called 911 and took measures to get her back to consciousness. Miraculously she survived. As Mark's daughter recovered in the hospital and then in an inpatient hospital for depression, his PTSD and depression became worse. He told me he hated himself for what had happened to his daughter. Mark was not able to link his history of abuse to his reaction to his daughter's suicide attempt. I pointed out that in both experiences he said very similar things to himself: "I could have stopped it," "I should have known," and "It was all my fault." In sessions with his daughter, the therapist tried to educate Mark about suicidality and how his daughter's inability to voice her despair led her to take such desperate measures. A few times his daughter's therapist said to Mark, "Would you have left her alone if you knew how awful she felt?" Of course he said no. His daughter was masking her depression, and she was unable to tell anyone about her suicidal thoughts.

Mark's daughter slowly began to improve when she came home from the hospital. She continued seeing a therapist and was attending an intensive outpatient program to keep her stable. Mark on the other hand became consumed with his depression. Part of the reason Mark started seeing me was because he knew his daughter's depression and suicide attempt affected him deeply.

Once Mark and I did more work on making sense of his abuse and the role of guilt in stopping him from living fully, we could use more present-day experiences to shift how he reacted. Mark noticed how he felt guilty when anything went wrong. We spent time in session helping Mark question his sense of responsibility or feeling at fault and where it came from.

Working through layers of guilt is one of the toughest parts of the work. Sometimes the best way to manage guilt is to bump it to the side and correctly place it. Guilt is often an induced feeling that comes from feeling responsible, as Mark did during his sexual abuse.

When bad things happen to good people, their initial response is to make it their fault. For instance, survivors of recent shootings in Las Vegas and at Marjory Stoneman Douglas High School have said to the world things like, "Why did I survive when so many others didn't?" People who are sexually assaulted say things like, "Maybe I should have dressed differently," or, "Maybe I should not have gone to that bar." Adults who are abused as kids say things like, "Maybe I caused my parents to hit me," or "Maybe I was the reason they acted so crazy." In a way the guilt serves a purpose. It takes the responsibility off the person doing wrong in cases of abuse and assault. When incomprehensible events take place like 9/11 or the Stoneman Douglas shooting, the guilt survivors feel distracts them from the horror they endured. It takes the focus off the psychopaths who act in such heartless ways.

BANISHING SHAME

One of the biggest challenges to thriving after trauma is working through the feelings of shame. You don't have to be a survivor to identify with this feeling. It is universal. For example, when a parent says things like, "Why would you do that?" or a teacher says, "How could you not know the answer to that question?" it leaves the person feeling small or stupid. Some of the most common phrases I hear when a patient is stuck in shame are, "I am so ugly and disgusting," or, "I do not deserve to have good things," or, "I wish I could make myself disappear." Usually these thoughts follow a negative reaction or anger by someone we admire or look up to as an authority figure.

In instances of abuse or traumatic events, shame is a result of undigested thoughts that get stuck inside someone's body and heart. Most patients who come to therapy with significant eating disorder or addiction histories are using the self-destructive strategy to turn off and numb these feelings. Shame disempowers. Shame can lead to detrimental and life-threatening illnesses when the feelings are left unspoken.

Samantha's Story: Sudden Deaths of Friends by Car Accidents

I met one woman I will call Samantha who came to therapy after surviving multiple traumas. Samantha had an unusually high number of losses by car accidents and was alienated by her family when she refused to leave an abusive relationship as a young adult. She came to therapy because she was tired of having a daily battle with food. Her weight fluctuated from below average to above average because she went through periods of restricting food intake to bingeing on food for months at a time. When I met Samantha, I was not aware of any of her trauma history. During the first few months of therapy, we addressed her disordered eating and the sudden life-threatening illness of her father just months before we met.

Samantha told me she was at her wits' end. We spoke each week about her relationship with food and also about how she was coping with the health scare of her father. Months before we met, her dad had ended up in the intensive care unit after having a sudden heart attack. She told me the doctors warned her several times early in the hospitalization that it was unlikely he would survive. Samantha stood vigil by her dad's bedside after the doctors told her family this. Miraculously, he came through. He spent a couple more months in the hospital once he was stabilized. I asked Samantha to describe her eating patterns during her dad's illness. She told me, "At first I ate nothing. I could not find a space for food because I was so scared about losing my dad." As his health improved and she was able to spend less time at the hospital and go to work, Samantha told me, "I ate like crap. I would skip meals and then come home after work and binge every single night." Over and over she told me, "I hate this eating disorder." Samantha would call herself fat and disgusting and put herself down whenever she had eating disorder symptoms.

Clearly Samantha was deeply affected by her dad's health scare. As we got to know each other more, I was curious to find out why she went into shame when she felt anything about her dad's health. I knew she had a fear of abandonment, but I did not understand why she felt so awful about who she was as a person. She had never hurt anyone, and she had a good relationship with both of her parents. She was in an intimate relationship with a man for over three years and had nothing but good things to say about their connection.

During our sessions I tried to find different ways to decode the darkest parts of her self-worth by asking a variety of questions. One day she walked into session and started talking about her fear of driving and of knowing when others would be traveling far in a car. I had no idea where that was coming from. When I asked her why she was so afraid of driving, she told me she knew three people who were killed in a car accident, she saw a woman get hit by a car and die on the scene, and she was in a serious car accident when she was eighteen years old. We spoke about all of these incidents, but we started with the woman she saw get struck. Samantha told me, "I was just walking down a sidewalk minding my own business and suddenly this woman was hit and lay right in front of me." Samantha remembers calling for help and that there were a number of people on the scene trying to help this severely injured woman. She told me there was a nurse and a doctor who came running over when they realized what had happened.

Samantha said she could barely breathe or remember who she was or where she was as the minutes passed by at the scene. She told me, "I prayed so hard that she would survive. I didn't know what to do." Sadly the woman passed away before the ambulance could get her to the hospital. When I asked Samantha if she talked to anyone about this afterward, she said, "I told my parents, but then I could not ever talk about it again." Samantha reported having flashbacks of the woman's life ending and that she sometimes dreamed about the accident.

After we spent some sessions making sense of this event and how deeply it affected her, she told me about her car accident. She said she was crossing a green light and that a man "blew right through a stop sign" and hit her vehicle so hard that her car was pushed off the side of the road and into a tree. Samantha remembered her life flashing by her in an instant as her vehicle got destroyed. While she was relieved that she had endured little serious injury, she told me she wondered why she survived and the other woman did not.

We spent many sessions talking about the shame she felt about being alive. One day Samantha came to session and started telling me about a horrific binge episode she had a few nights before. She told me she ate so much food that she felt pain in her gut. She said, "A part of me wanted to get rid of the food, but most of me felt like I deserved to feel the pain I caused myself."

When I talk with patients about their self-hatred and shame and they are aware of how these feelings lead to self-destruction, I encourage them to take a moment or two to be in the experience—not to relive the awful feelings that follow the binge episode in Samantha's case, but to help patients talk back to that part of themselves that allows for such punitive choices. Samantha and I used that opportunity to explore her episode and connect it with the part of her that felt undeserving and unworthy of having good things come her way.

We talked about her relationship with her husband and her recent job change, which most of her felt great about. When we talked about the eating disorder symptoms, I was able to ask her, "Are the feelings you have when you binge similar to feelings you have when someone wants to love and care about you?" I also asked her, "Do you notice whether you also feel unworthy of being in a job where the staff and your supervisors are actually looking out for your best interest?" Of course Samantha immediately identified that all these feelings were true.

The layers of shame that Samantha had been carrying in her body and heart from the multiple traumas she witnessed or experienced were preventing her from having a full life. Once we recognized the devastating effects the shame had on her, we were able to have a dialogue about retraining her mind to talk back to the part of her that felt unworthy. For example, I encouraged Samantha to pay close attention to her behaviors and reactions when her husband made gestures of caring and concern. I suggested, "As soon as you feel yourself pulling away from your husband, do the opposite of what feels comfortable." Rather than close herself off and leave those moments, Samantha worked very hard to be present. I would give her homework assignments. I suggested she write down how she felt during these interactions with her husband and how she was able to transform feelings of undeserving to accept the gifts he had to give.

While I try not to judge the feelings patients bring into therapy, I am very familiar with shame from my own history of abuse. I have learned the role it plays and how it cripples trauma survivors from having what they want in their lives. Of all the emotions that follow trauma, I think shame is the most devastating because it disempowers people from having any quality of life.

The last thing someone should have to feel is unworthy when they have suffered any type of trauma. I have learned in my work as a patient and a therapist that shame also becomes the defense to knowing and accepting, no matter the trauma. For example, sexual assault survivors who have been violated by family or loved ones would rather think they caused the abuse than put responsibility on the person who chose to act in such horrific ways. Others would rather feel horrible about themselves than angry about what happened. Survivors of combat and terrorist attacks such as 9/11 have struggled to feel okay about living when they witnessed a death or knew people who died. When I talk to patients who have seen people die in combat or tragic events like fires or car accidents, they report spending years in silence feeling like somehow maybe they caused it. The thoughts that come with shame are not rational. They are illogical, and usually patients working through trauma begin to understand that.

Even though I have been working on my recovery from childhood abuse for over two decades, I still find myself experiencing what I call "shame attacks" when I am triggered. During the last part of the Cosby sentencing,[2] I noticed these feelings come rushing back. I was present for both of the Cosby trials and had heard many stories from women who claimed they were sexually assaulted by him. I watched Cosby during the victims' testimonies, and over and over again I saw him either laughing or looking smug. Part of me felt enraged for the disrespect he showed to all of the alleged victims.

When the time came for Judge O'Neill to issue Cosby's sentence for three counts of indecent aggravated sexual misconduct, I noticed a shift in how I felt. Rather than feeling empowered and relieved, I began to feel a lump the size of a bowling ball in my gut. Then I noticed feeling like I wanted to disappear and like everyone in the courthouse hated me. I realized I was having flashbacks to when I found out my perpetrator was sick with a life-threatening illness. I knew I was reexperiencing emotions that I felt when my perpetrator passed away. For years I believed it was my speaking that caused him to die. It took me countless hours in therapy to shift away from the shame and separate what was about me and what part I had no control over. I found a way to accept that my speaking did not cause him to get sick.

As these feelings took over my awareness during the Cosby sentencing, I wanted to hide. I did not want to see or talk to anyone. I wanted to vanish. I sat in my car for over two hours after the proceedings concluded. I forced myself to pick up my phone and call people. I must have left voice mails for five different friends before one finally picked up. I was not able to share with my friend Karen the agony going on inside of me. I knew I had the choice to stay in the shame or find ways out. I decided as Karen began to commend me and all the other warriors that I was going to work hard to internalize her words. At times when Karen spoke to me I just took some deep breaths. The shame was so loud inside my body, and the tears were streaming out of my eyes. At one point on our phone call I decided to grab a piece of paper and write down what she was saying to me.

I learned through the years that combating shame is crucial to living fully. I learned that the shame was a defense mechanism. If I continued to hate and blame myself, I did not have to feel angry toward my perpetrator and all the bystanders who chose to turn their back on me. While it seemed easier to just hate myself, I learned that self-loathing would mean living an empty, lonely life.

One of the benefits of having a witness present when survivors or patients are in the shame is that it gives them an opportunity to step outside of the feeling and hear how someone else views them. When I was on the phone with my friend Karen after the Cosby sentencing, I was able to put the despair aside and substitute those feelings with the words she was offering me. When I sit with patients and they describe feeling at fault for their abuse or feeling like they could have done more when they saw a friend die in combat, or when they tell me, "If only I had stayed home that night, maybe my mom wouldn't have died," I can talk back to those irrational thoughts. No one has the power to take away someone else's shame. But if people surround themselves with friends, therapists, or anyone who can speak words of comfort, it can help. What I suggest to patients is that they do the opposite of what the shame is telling them. For instance, if a patient feels helpless, I have suggested that they do something that makes them feel empowered. If someone tells me they want to disappear, I have suggested, "Try and do something that makes you feel visible." If someone expresses feelings of unworthiness, I have said,

"Write down all the things you do in life that make you feel worthwhile."

HEALING STRATEGIES TO REBUILD TRUST, REDUCE GUILT, AND ALLEVIATE SHAME

Strategies for Rebuilding Trust in Yourself and Others

1. Have you ever trusted anyone? What does having a trusting relationship mean to you? What keeps you from trusting people?
2. Do you trust yourself? What have you done that makes you feel like you cannot trust yourself and what you feel?
3. Do you find that you trust too easily or not at all? When you trust too easily, do you find that you are reacting to the part of you that feels desperate to be seen or heard?
4. When you hear yourself saying, "I cannot trust this person," have you asked yourself, "What has this person done to show me that I cannot trust him or her?"
5. Do you predict the worst-case scenario during times of change or instability? Is that a way to protect yourself because of the trauma you have already survived? Are you assuming that all will go wrong to protect yourself from the disappointment when something does not go your way?

Guilt-Reducing Strategies

1. Do you feel guilty every time something goes wrong? When you feel guilty, do you isolate? How do you define guilt? It is appropriate to feel guilty when someone does something intentionally to hurt another person?
2. Are you still blaming yourself for the trauma you endured, whether it be from abuse, sudden loss of a friend in combat, or surviving a terror attack while witnessing a friend get

killed? Is there a logical explanation for these feelings, or do you feel guilt to protect yourself from feeling grief or anger? How is it your fault if someone else chose to take action toward you that was abusive or intrusive? How is it your fault if someone in your family passed away suddenly? How is it your fault if you witnessed or were a victim of a shooting or terrorist attack? Did you make the criminal commit the atrocity?

3. Is guilt holding you back from living a full life? Do you stop yourself from having a family or pushing forward in career goals because others you love have not been able to attain their goals? If the answer is yes, how is holding yourself back from having a full life helping others live a better life?

Shame-Reducing Strategies

Thanks to help from two renowned psychotherapists, Jane Shure, PhD, LCSW, and Beth Weinstock, PhD, here are some tips they suggest to consider when combating shame.[3]

1. Know that you are not the only one. Many people struggle to be free of shame. It's a hard process, but with patience you can diminish shame's force and be free of its oppression.
2. Awareness is the first step in any change process. Practice identifying when you are feeling shame.
3. Compassion is the antidote to shame. Work on developing and practicing a compassionate voice that is nonjudgmental, understands you and your experiences, and is kind and encouraging. This voice allows you to be human with all the quirks and wounds and imperfections that make us human.
4. Explore the origins of your shame. Understand how messages from your younger years got internalized. These are the messages that your compassionate new voice needs to counteract.

5. Notice how current behaviors may reinforce your sense of shame. Do you do self-destructive things that reinforce shame? Do you then say, "See? That shows I'm worthless." Plan how you can begin to give up these behaviors and replace them with more self-supportive ones.
6. Learn to focus on your positive attributes, your strengths, gifts, and talents. You are larger than the wounds you carry.
7. Surround yourself with people who treat you well, and stay away from people who cause you to feel bad.
8. Share these tips with someone you trust, your therapist, your partner, your best friend, your life coach, or members of a support group. When we talk to people we trust, rather than isolate, we widen our perspective and promote healing.

Dr. Jane Shure and Dr. Beth Weinstock, cofounders of the Resilience Group, are leadership coaches, psychotherapists, and authors who have been promoting growth and change in individuals, groups, and organizations for the past forty years. They are highly skilled at helping people harness strengths, activate motivation, fortify relationships, and actualize goals. Both teach at the Close School for Entrepreneurship at Drexel University in Philadelphia, the Athena Leadership Lab at Barnard College in New York City, and the Kripalu Center for Yoga & Health in Stockbridge, Massachusetts. They write for the *Huffington Post, Medium, Authority Magazine,* and *ThriveGlobal* and have authored book chapters and articles. See the YouTube of Jane's TEDx talk: "Boost Resilience," TheResilienceGroup.com, or Facebook.com/DevelopingWomenLeaders.

4

CONFRONTING ANGER

HELLO, ANGER

One of the hardest parts of recovering from trauma and managing symptoms of PTSD is addressing the anger and rage. Most people who have been abused or assaulted or who have lived through combat or terrorism associate expressing anger with lack of safety and danger. From the moment a person is the victim of someone else's rage, their sense of safety feels threatened. For example, I have counseled many men and women who report being physically abused in their childhood. I worked with one male patient in his fifties who was beaten by his father at the age of four after breaking a window with a rock. Over the course of treatment, he told this story several times and how at that time he felt threatened for his life. He remembered the force of his dad's hand and the feelings of rage he felt during the incident. He spent decades of his life avoiding any confrontation. Whenever he received an unexpected call from any of his supervisors, he would have anxiety or panic attacks.

I remember many times in my life when the thought of someone being mad at me ruined my entire day. I would ruminate on these thoughts and practically hide from everyone around me. Early in my recovery, my therapist would tell me it was okay to be angry. She also helped me understand that my fears of others being unhappy with me were not based on current situations. All the old feelings that came with being sexually assaulted and disbelieved by others were stirred up. Dorothy taught me that allowing myself to feel my anger was a crucial part of having relationships where I would feel safe and not taken advantage of. She helped me redirect the energy that came with my anger to create change and set limits and boundaries in relationships.

Tammy's Story: Brother Addicted to Heroin, Bullied and Sexually Harassed by Peers

I met Tammy when she was twenty years old. She reached out to me after struggling most of her childhood with bouts of anorexia, binge eating, anxiety, and low self-worth. She was attending a local university, and she told me it was impossible to have connections with her peers. She told me she had two roommates who stole from her and disrupted her daily living. Tammy was having a hard time in her classes and felt unable to reach out to her professors when she began failing some of her classes. Her parents lived two hours from school and showed no interest in helping her or acknowledging her difficulty with the transition of living away from home to attend college.

I still remember our initial call when she asked me if she could come to therapy. Her voice was shaking, and I could barely hear her words. During the first several sessions, we focused on her eating disorder symptoms and her inability to connect with the kids at college. She told me about several incidents when her roommates stole her clothes and food. I asked her many times if she felt angry about how her roommates were acting, and she would look at me as if I was making no sense. Often her response would be, "What is the point of being angry? That will not change anything." I asked Tammy if she learned about setting limits and boundaries in her family, and she said she had no idea what that meant.

As Tammy became more comfortable in therapy, we talked at length about her childhood home experiences. From around the age of seven, Tammy told me about her relationship with food. When she was in elementary school she was bullied by kids for being overweight. At the end of the day, Tammy would come home from school and eat everything in sight. She felt ashamed to eat in front of others, so most days Tammy did not eat lunch. I asked her how it made her feel to be treated so badly by the other kids. I sensed she had some undigested anger, but Tammy was unable to admit feeling angry and would tell me that her feelings were hurt.

When she tried to tell her parents about what was happening at school, their response was, "Tammy, you need to get a thicker skin." When she told me about their reaction, I felt like my blood was boiling. I knew I was feeling some of the emotions that Tammy had pushed away, mostly by bingeing or obsessing about how to skip the next meal. Tammy told me the boys would grab her private parts and mock her, at times right in front of teachers. She said everyone laughed, and the teachers acted like nothing happened. During her childhood, Tammy lived with her stepmom, dad, and older brother, Tim.

I knew Tammy felt disconnected from her brother, but I had no idea that her brother was using her as a pawn to buy drugs. It took a lot of courage for Tammy to talk about her brother's addiction. She was terrified I would call the police or try to get him arrested. When we started therapy, he had already left home and had not been in contact with Tammy or her parents for over a year. Tammy sobbed one day as she spoke about Tim. It was his twenty-sixth birthday, and she had not spoken to him in months.

Tammy told me he started abusing drugs when she was fourteen. No one in her family acknowledged that Tim was having a problem. Tammy said he would come home from school "high as a kite," and her parents never said a word. There were times when Tammy reported feeling angry and scared, but the message she received was don't speak. As Tammy got older and Tim's addiction got worse, he began using her to lure his parents to give her money so he could buy heroin. Their relationship became unsafe for Tammy. When she tried to tell Tim that she did not want to be his pawn, he threatened to hurt her. Sometimes Tammy feared for her life. He forced her to steal money from her parents' wallets, and when they realized the money was missing, Tim forced her say she stole it for food.

During junior and senior year of high school, Tammy resorted to her anorexia to numb the anger and rage she felt at school and at home. She felt powerless and stranded and did not even consider how feeling her anger could help her set boundaries and ask for some help with her brother. Tammy did anything to get the kids to be nice to her. On Christmas of her senior year of high school, she made baskets for almost her entire class of over a hundred kids. She desperately wanted to fit in and be liked.

She repeated similar behavior in college. She let her roommates take advantage of her. She did not speak up when they took her clothes or food. She did not say no when guys were coming on to her sexually. The fear Tammy felt with her brother dictated how she responded in any situation when she wanted to say no. She dated guys who tried to control her. While I knew Tammy was terrified to own her anger, I also knew we had to find a way to help her access and use this emotion to help her better protect herself.

After her second year in college, Tammy moved into her own apartment. She could not handle the stress that came from living with roommates, and she wanted to have space so she could focus on her recovery and her schoolwork. Our work took a turn when she went home to visit her parents for Thanksgiving. The Monday following the holiday, Tammy came into my office and began telling me a story of when she felt like her boundaries were violated. She told me her dad wanted to give her a hug. Tammy said she was very clear in her response. She told her dad that at that moment she did not want any physical contact. Rather than respect her wishes, Tammy said her dad squeezed her tightly and would not let go. At first Tammy did not even realize her anger was surfacing as she told me the story. I sat quietly and listened intently as she went on to say, "How could my parents allow my brother to make me feel afraid for my life? How could my parents hear me tell them about how awful the kids at school treated me and not even try to help me? How could my parents give birth to me and then spend years of life not trying to protect me?" After a few moments I asked Tammy what she was feeling. For the first time since we met, she screamed, "I am so f—ing angry!" I wanted to jump out of my seat and applaud her for owning her anger. Tammy needed to get in touch with this emotion and know it was appropriate.

We spent time in our sessions moving forward, talking about how her anger could help her live a different life. I explained to Tammy that feeling her anger could help her set boundaries. We talked about different situations when she felt afraid to say no and role-played how she could do that—for instance, when Tammy went home for another visit and told her parents that if they could not respect her need for physical space, she was going to get back in her car and go back to her apartment. We talked about dating relationships and how Tammy could set limits and say no. I shared with her a bit about my struggle through recovery to feel and express my anger. I wanted her to know that she was not alone and that it was possible to feel anger, express it, and have a positive result.

Throughout the years of seeing patients, I have found that anger gone unnoticed leads to symptoms of eating disorders, drugs, and other forms of self-destruction. Many people I have met wished they could live life without telling themselves or others they were angry. However, most patients get to a place where they can make the connection between holding on to anger and then hurting themselves. Once people gain awareness of the role of their anger in their symptoms, they usually make the choice to have their anger so they can live life without making themselves sick.

Frank's Story: Sexually Abused as a Young Teen and Later a Combat Veteran

When I met Frank, I sensed right away he was internalizing many emotions from his complicated trauma history. When we talked about his childhood or how awful the kids at school treated him, he could hardly look at me. His voice was soft. I could barely hear him. His sexual abuse began in his teens. He sought out a youth leader to feel less alone in the world. At first Frank said their conversations were meaningful and that he felt like this man cared about him. They spent months together talking and learning about each other before the abuse began. Frank told me that his abuser found a way to make him believe that sexual contact between them could make him feel loved. On an intuitive level, Frank felt that something was very wrong, but at that time he was craving love from a father figure. He decided to trust what his abuser was saying and told me he went along with it.

When Frank talked about the abuse, he would shake and looked visibly sick. He never showed signs of anger. All he could express was the shame and deep sadness he felt for his younger self. Once his abuse ended, he decided to enlist to serve overseas. Frank was looking for a way out and thought fighting in a war would make him feel like a man again. When he left for Desert Storm, he had not told anyone about the abuse. I asked him if he ever thought of telling his mom, but Frank told me he felt his mom would fall apart. She was diagnosed with clinical depression when he was a toddler. Frank told me he spent most of his childhood trying not to upset his mom. Anytime he had a problem or needed help, he looked outside his family for support.

When Frank left for war, he told me he was not doing well. He said he was having bouts of severe depression for weeks at a time. When he applied to serve in the war, he did not answer truthfully about his mental well-being. Frank did not want his depression or abuse to hold him back from serving. We talked extensively about what life was like when he was overseas. Frank described many days when he sat in his barracks barely able to function. He said life was happening around him and that he felt numb. He engaged in some direct combat, but his main purpose was to tend to the wounded soldiers when they came back to the camp. Frank served in Desert Storm for over a year. He saw and heard things that most people will never experience. Men died in his care. Other soldiers had symptoms of psychosis after being hurt so badly in combat. Frank remained calm and did what he needed to do to take care of his fellow men. I asked him a few times what kinds of feelings he felt during his time at war. Not once did he mention the word "anger."

When we talked about his sexual abuse as a teen and Frank became more aware of how his abuser had groomed him, he denied feeling angry. At times he would tell me he felt sad and damaged. But he never seemed mad at his abuser. I understood this phenomenon because it took me years to get mad at the people who hurt me so badly. My therapist would confront me about my anger and try to find different ways to help me get in touch with the emotion. At times I was very irritable toward Dorothy and would pick fights with her. A part of me knew I was furious with others, but at that point I was not ready to direct my anger toward my abuser and his enablers. Sometimes when I left my therapy sessions I would scream and cry and feel pain in my gut. All those emotions then got directed onto me as I went into what I called "shame attacks." I felt hateful toward myself. I wanted to disappear. I will never forget the first time Dorothy asked me, "If you weren't hating yourself or feeling shame, what would you be feeling?" A lightbulb went on inside of me. I told her I would be "pissed as shit." I was able to start expressing in words in my sessions and in my journal entries why I was mad and what I wanted to do with it.

I thought about those sessions when Frank and I were in therapy. One day he came into session furious with a coworker. This particular coworker was the source of a lot of negative energy and served as one of Frank's supervisors. We sat down, and Frank immediately started telling me how triggered he felt as the coworker gave him some feedback. Initially Frank felt shame. He said to me, "I could feel myself shrinking into my four-year-old body when my dad beat the crap out of me." Frank went on to describe other feelings associated with his sexual abuse at the age of sixteen. He was aware of what was happening in his body and that he was experiencing emotional flashbacks from the physical and sexual abuse. He described his body shrinking and felt the fire in his belly simultaneously. Frank worked for months in therapy to be able to identify his triggers and the emotions he would want to have versus the feelings he felt that were more about the past.

As his supervisor was talking, Frank said he was focused on keeping his feet on the ground. He said he wiggled his toes a whole bunch of times and heard himself saying this: "It is okay to be angry! And this dude is not my father or my abuser. He is a supervisor and I am a grown man." As the conversation came to an end, Frank said he was able to address the supervisor's concerns in a calm, firm tone. As Frank told me the story, his voice got louder and louder.

While he felt proud of his ability to contain his anger, he was still walking around with pent-up rage. After we spoke about the old feelings that were stirred up, I asked Frank to say more about his anger. At first he spoke about some other incident when he felt attacked by his supervisor. Then Frank allowed himself to express more of his anger. He got mad at all the people who messed with him. I asked Frank, "Who are you mad at and why?" I wanted to give him the opportunity to share his feelings in a safe, contained space.

At first he looked at me and did not say anything. He got very quiet. I told him, "Frank, it is okay to say how you feel. You have every right to express your anger. It is part of what makes you human." I knew he was terrified to feel his anger. I knew he had rarely said out loud to another human being that he was mad. We sat for another moment, and then off he went. "You want to know who I am mad at? I am mad at all the people in my life who tried to squash me. I am mad at my dad. I hate my abuser. I hate you for turning me into damaged goods."

Suddenly he became quiet again. When I asked him what was going on in his mind, he told me he was worried he was stepping on my boundaries. I asked him why he felt like he had crossed a line, and he said he was afraid the volume and intensity of his anger was going to scare me away. I felt so sad for him, but we focused on the importance of these moments and how his fear was more of a projection from the past. Frank was afraid he was making me feel how he felt when his dad beat him or when his abuser got angry when he tried to get him to stop hurting him.

We spent the last part of the session talking about how he had made a huge jump by allowing himself to express his anger and check in with me about boundaries. We talked about how he could use this experience he had in our session and bring it into his relationship with his wife and friends. Frank was on his way to owning his anger.

When people spend their lives running from this emotion, they usually end up hurting themselves or cutting off from relationships. Trauma survivors often talk about all the relationships gone bad because they are not able to say when they are mad or tolerate others being angry with them. Frank told me he had lost many relationships in his childhood and adulthood because he would keep his anger in and then eventually not want to speak to the person. He also told me that when he thought others were mad at him, he spent his life ducking, doing anything to avoid that person. Eventually Frank quit jobs or broke up with former girlfriends because he associated them being mad at him as a threat. Rather than check it out or learn that he was not the cause of another person's feelings, Frank disconnected. We spent the following weeks working on developing coping strategies when the emotions felt too big to say in words. Frank loved to run and ride his bicycle. He decided that before he confronted the person he was going to go out for a jog or hop on his bike to give himself a chance to process the feelings. Then Frank came home and grabbed a notebook and started writing. I told him to write down all his feelings without censoring. At first that scared him, too, but he was willing to give it a try. We also worked on some ways to check in with others when he thought they were angry with him. His wife came into a couple of sessions, and we did some work on safe communication and checking in. Sometimes Frank assumed she was mad at him, even though nothing had transpired between them. I suggested he say something like, "I feel like you are mad at me because you haven't wanted to spend time with me." Frank found out that at times she was feeling angry, but it was not about him. She reassured him that if she felt mad at him she would tell him. That provided Frank with relief because when he worried that she was angry, he could do an inventory check. For example, he could ask himself, "Did something happen? Did we get into an argument? Did I intentionally hurt her?"

When survivors explore their anger through therapy or intimate relationships, they do not realize how empowering it can be when expressed appropriately. The longer I worked on my abuse, the more I learned that my anger was part of what was motivating me to fight for my right to live fully. Every time I worked through another big piece of the aftermath of my incest, I channeled those feelings into accomplishing major life goals.

CONQUERING ANGER

How does someone go from spending years or even decades of their life avoiding anger and then find a way to use their anger proactively to create change? I have met several people through the years who have gone through experiences that are enraging and horrific. When patients tell me about their abuse, their combat stories, their losses through illness, their losses from terrorist attacks, or the destruction of their property due to natural disaster, I feel rage. Recently in the news we have been bombarded with stories of mass shootings, and I think about how awful it must be to lose a loved one in such a senseless way. A part of me struggles to understand how patients feel guilty for feeling mad when life hands them such unfair circumstances.

It is difficult for patients to not feel angry when they lose a loved one to an illness, especially when it is a child or partner. Through the years I have met a few patients who have suffered the death of their young child or a parent when they were young children.

Betsy's Story: Lost Her Mom to Cancer as a Teenager

I met Betsy a few years ago when she was in her midforties. She had an extensive history of bulimia and alcohol abuse. On our first session she told me about the awful death of her mom. Betsy said her mom was diagnosed with brain cancer when she was eleven years old. She told me that just months after the diagnosis, her mom died what she described as a horrific death. Betsy had one sister and her father. She said her family fell apart as her mom's condition deteriorated.

When Betsy spoke about her mom's illness, she would burst into tears. It was clear she had not dealt with the loss or her anger about losing her mom at such a young age. Betsy began using symptoms of bulimia during her mom's illness. When I asked her what the role of her eating disorder was as a young teen, she told me it was the only way she could lighten up all the anguish she felt in her body. We talked about how her sister and father continued to function as her mom's health got worse. She told me that no one talked about what was happening to her mom. As the cancer grew in her mom's brain, she became demented and at times did not even know who Betsy was. She told me that at times she talked to her young friends about how sick her mom was, but of course they were way too young to understand Betsy's reactions to the illness. Betsy did not say a word about her eating disorder. She said everyone was so consumed with her mom's cancer that they did not notice the bags under her eyes or the sudden weight loss.

Sadly, Betsy's mom died when she was at school one morning. Betsy never had a chance to say good-bye to her. Family members decided not to allow her or her sister to be present during her final hours of life. At the time, Betsy's family felt like they were acting on her behalf by not including her at her mom's bedside during the vigil.

Betsy told me she was furious with her dad and aunt for not letting her stay home from school that day. We talked about her unfinished feelings about her mom's death and all the anger she felt about losing her mom at a critical time in her own development. Betsy's eating disorder got worse months after her mom's death. She ended up being hospitalized in an eating disorder rehab.

We talked about the family sessions she had while inpatient. She said the therapist tried to help her and her sister and father talk about her mom's death. At the time Betsy said all three of them shut down when the therapist asked about how they were coping with her death. Dad became severely depressed. Betsy's younger sister had nightmares and flashbacks of her mom's illness and ended up being homeschooled due to the severity of her PTSD. I asked Betsy if she ever felt mad at her mom for dying. I thought she was going to explode after I said that. Her face got beet red, and she looked at me and said, "How could you ask me such a dumb question?" I realized Betsy still had not really grieved for mom in all the years she had been without her.

Rather than push Betsy to get in touch with her anger, we decided to spend weeks in session addressing her PTSD and eating disorder symptoms. I asked Betsy to start journaling more when she was experiencing symptoms. She brought her journal into session and would read some of the entries at the beginning of each session. We began to notice a pattern. Anytime a holiday or birthday or anniversary of her mom's death got closer, the bulimia symptoms increased. Her mom died two days after Mother's Day. I knew Betsy was not comfortable addressing her anger toward her mom, so instead I asked her to write about her anger toward her eating disorder.

She came into session one day and began sharing an entry with me. She wrote about how much she hated her bulimia and how it was ruining her life. She went on to talk in her journal about all the medical complications that arose as a result of her frequent purging. She talked about how she was spending thousands of dollars in dental bills and was diagnosed with osteoporosis. Betsy talked about how she could not be close to friends or family because her eating disorder was making her feel like an outsider. Betsy spoke about her relationship with her husband and blamed the eating disorder for their distant connection.

As Betsy became more familiar with her anger, we started finding ways for her to direct it onto things in her life that she wanted to change. Betsy had had it with her eating disorder and the PTSD. She told me about the images of her mom being sick and the memories of watching her mom get eaten away by the cancer. Betsy worked as a nurse for almost fifteen years. She witnessed other people's moms dying. I asked her if that played a role in reliving her mother's death. I would say things like, "Did you ever have flashbacks after work when someone close to your mom's age died?" At the time Betsy did not realize she was having emotional flashbacks. Most people do not understand how PTSD can manifest and how the self-destructive behaviors, such as bulimia, become the vehicle for pushing away the grief and anger. Betsy did not want to own her anger toward her mom because she felt like that would be mean. I explained to her that feeling mad about losing a loved one is normal. I tried to frame it in different ways to help Betsy connect more with her emotions. At the end of one session, I asked Betsy if she would be willing to write her mom a letter. Surprisingly she did not resist.

We sat down the next week, and she read the journal entry. One sentence Betsy wrote several times was, "How could you die on me?" We talked about that question, and again I normalized for her that as humans we can feel angry at anything or anyone, even people like her mom who did not die just to leave her motherless.

Traumatic losses leave people feeling angry, and patients ask how they can be angry at someone for dying. When Betsy and I would talk about her life without her mom, she began to understand how much of an impact it had on her and her whole family. It was not about blaming her mom for dying. It was about having to live life after such unfortunate circumstances. As Betsy began to be more open about her anger, we noticed a shift in her symptoms. The bulimia decreased, and the nightmares and flashbacks quieted down. She talked to me about the death of a young mother while she was at work. Betsy said the kids were around the same age she had been when their mother passed away from ovarian cancer.

We talked about how Betsy felt after leaving her shift the night this young mother died. She told me she was furious. As she was telling me about what happened to this woman, she realized how mad she was. At one point she even said to me, "How could these kids lose their mom to such an awful death?" We took a pause in the session, and I helped Betsy to connect that thought with her mother's death. She allowed herself to think about her younger self and talk back to young teenager Betsy, saying, "I am so sorry you had to lose your mom at such a young age. That just sucks." When Betsy came back to session the next week, I asked her how it felt to be more open with her anger. She admitted she felt relieved. Betsy had been walking around for decades holding on to pent-up anger that was ruining her life. It was bad enough to lose her mother at such a young age without then having to live decades more with nowhere to go with her rage.

We knew that talking about anger in one session was not going to be enough. I sent Betsy home one week with a journal entry that started, "I am going to use my anger to get the following things back in my life." Betsy listed a number of goals she wanted to accomplish. She was ready to use her anger to fight for a better life. She wrote about wanting to get back in connection with her husband, run races to fight for a cancer cure, journal or do something physical to counteract her bulimic urges, and start a grief group for kids who lost their parents.

Using anger to conquer the world is possible, but in order to do that people need to be willing to accept that they feel this emotion. It was not until I started feeling mad at my abusers that my life began to change. For years I cried and went into shame about my story. My therapist used to talk to me about how I could redirect all my grief and use it proactively. Like Betsy, I had many wishes for my life, and I was sick of living life feeling like I was by myself. Everyone deals with trauma differently. Everyone deals with their anger in their own way.

Pat's Story: Abandoned by Mom and Married to an Abusive Drug Addict

Pat was one of my first patients in my private practice. We met when she was in her early fifties. Pat initially presented as mostly happy and reported to me that she had bouts of anxiety and panic attacks. She said she remembered having her first panic attack at around the age of eleven. Pat decided to start therapy because she had a history of dating men who were unavailable physically and emotionally. When we met, she was on the verge of divorcing a man who was emotionally distant and had anger management problems. Pat lived with Brett and his three kids for five years. She told me she was unhappy and felt like she was living with a stranger. Anytime Brett exploded at her, she would blame herself. We started working in therapy to understand why she always felt at fault for emotions Brett was taking out on her.

Pat had a difficult time talking about her childhood. Anytime I would ask her about her relationship with her mom or dad, her eyes would fill up with tears and she would get quiet. Pat's dad passed away when she was in her thirties. Her mom died suddenly a couple of years before she started seeing me for therapy. Pat was unable to admit how abandoned she felt during her childhood. She was protective of her parents and worried too much about what I would think of them if she told me how alone and uncared about she felt.

Rather than push her to talk extensively about her traumatic childhood, I encouraged her to keep talking about her feelings in her current marriage to Brett. She was resistant to making connections between her past and the person she married. I kept that in my mind every time we had a session. Pat's goal was to decrease her anxiety and panic attacks and figure out what to do about her marriage.

One day she came into therapy with Brett. The session did not go well. From the moment we sat down, both of them were defensive. As I started asking them more about their communication, Pat shut down and Brett raised his voice, saying she was not giving him what he needed. I asked Brett to elaborate on what he wanted and how Pat was not meeting his expectations. He focused on their sex life and shamed Pat for never wanting to have sex. I remember feeling a pit in my stomach. When I looked at Pat and asked her to respond, she burst into tears telling Brett she was terrified he was going to leave her. Pat had such an extensive history of being left that all she focused on was Brett's potential to go away. Pat came back for another session two days after she and Brett had come in as a couple. I asked her what made her feel like she did not also have the option to separate if she felt so unhappy.

Then the turning point came. Pat allowed herself to talk more about what had happened when she lived with her parents. Pat looked at me and told me how her mom left their house every week to go be with her boyfriend. She said her mom would be gone for days at a time. When I asked her how she felt about that, she told me she was relieved in a way. She said that when her mom came home the house was tense. Pat said everyone felt like they were walking on eggshells. I asked Pat about her dad and how he dealt with her mom's inability to parent or be present. She told me her dad was gone most of the day at his job. When he got home at night, Pat told me he acted like nothing was happening, as if it was normal to live with a wife and mom who was hardly home. Pat told me her mom had a gambling problem and that she was addicted to her boyfriend. As she got older, her mom would actually pick Pat up sometimes and take her to her boyfriend's house.

I asked her how it made her feel to carry such a big secret. Pat started expressing her anger the more we spoke about her mom and dad. We learned that her anxiety and panic attacks were triggered when she felt abandoned. For example, when Brett did not listen to her, she would become very anxious. A part of her knew she was feeling very familiar feelings. She was mad at her mom and mad at Brett. Often people will feel anxiety when they are unable to hold their anger. Feeling anxious can mask feelings of anger.

A couple of years before we met, Pat's mom became gravely ill. She was rushed to the intensive care unit after suffering a stroke. Pat had continued to have a distant and unfulfilling relationship with her mom when she became an adult. Pat yearned to be loved by her mom but was not hopeful things would change. She spent major holidays with her mom and dad but rarely spoke to her. I asked Pat if she talked to her mom about her marriage with Brett. She said she tried to tell her mom about his explosive episodes of anger and how alone she felt. Pat said her mom's reaction was poor. One time Pat told her mom she was thinking of divorcing Brett. She said her mom said, "How could you do that to me or Brett?" Pat said she would never forget how awful she felt for days after that. She said she had panic attacks almost every day after she spoke to her mom about leaving Brett.

Pat grew up feeling like everything was her fault. She told me there were times when Pat was a teenager that her mom blamed her for going away. As Pat got older, she challenged her mom, and one time she told her mom not to come home if she was going to keep leaving. She said her dad was standing right next to her, and all he said was, "Pat, don't talk to your mom like that." Of course Pat felt furious, but she had no way of working through that at the time. No one was listening to her. She and her dad never had a chance to talk about how let down she felt during her childhood. They never had a chance to talk about what made her dad so complacent with her mom's poor and unhealthy choices.

We spoke about the final week before her mom passed away. Pat received a phone call from the hospital while she was at work. Pat said she was totally thrown off guard, as she hardly spoke to her mom and had never heard that her health was in jeopardy. The hospital staff member told Pat to come to the intensive care unit and that her mom might not make it out of the hospital. She had suffered a severe stroke.

Pat said her heart was racing on the drive to see her mom. She said she felt a combination of anger and fear. Pat had never really thought about how she would feel if and when something happened to her mom. When she walked into her mom's hospital room, she told me her mom looked terrible. She was barely awake and was hooked up to all kinds of machines. Her mom had signed a do-not-resuscitate waiver. Pat said they spent a couple of hours talking, and at times they even laughed. Pat told me that was the most they had ever talked her entire life. Then suddenly her mom went into cardiac arrest. Pat was asked to leave the room while the doctors examined her. Pat said she would never forget the look on the doctor's face as he walked toward her in the family waiting area. She knew her mom had died.

After her mom passed away, Pat said her marriage to Brett got worse. By the time she started therapy, she knew she could not stay married to him unless things changed between the two of them.

We were in therapy for about a year when Pat decided it was time to take the leap. She came to session and announced she was moving into her own place and began the separation process. During the initial weeks of their separation, Pat said Brett was acting out more. He was calling her and texting her very angry messages. He called her names and told her their marriage ending was all her fault.

Pat got tired of being treated like her feelings did not matter. She learned in therapy that she had married someone with similar pathology to her mother. What changed was that she realized she was not the cause of Brett's limitations. Pat wanted to be happy. She wanted to make changes in her life professionally, and she wanted to work through her abandonment issues.

As Pat and Brett went through the divorce process, she got more in touch with her anger. She cried and screamed in session as she played some of the messages he was leaving on her phone. She was enraged. I asked Pat, "How can we help you take some of that anger and direct it in positive ways? What are your goals for your life personally and professionally?" Pat came into a session and told me about an incident that was happening at work. At this point Pat had already been promoted and was the director of an English studies program at a local university. When Pat and I met, she was teaching part-time as an adjunct professor. As she and Brett were splitting up, the administrators at her job promoted her a couple of times, first to a full-time professor. Then she was offered a job as the director of the program. Staff and students raved about her as a teacher and a leader.

As Pat was getting ready to sign the divorce papers, we talked about how she was using her anger to conquer her world. It was amazing to me that someone who was barely parented could find a way to become a leader and direct a program. Pat confronted many challenges with staff and students. Rather than stay in the panic and avoid possible conflict, Pat took ownership of her position and did what she needed to deal with issues. When Pat would get depressed about her divorce or when her abandonment issues from childhood were triggered, we kept reminding her of her incredible ability to run the program. As Pat got more in touch with her anger, she developed better boundaries. When staff members did not meet expectations, she spoke to them. When students were acting out or trying to blame others for their poor performance, Pat sat down with them and held them accountable. Pat had decided she was sick of being blamed for other people's issues.

We helped Pat use what she was feeling in her body when she felt angry. She said that as soon as she felt those knots in her stomach, she knew her boundaries were being tested. We also worked on bringing her anger into her personal relationships. When she felt like her friends were taking more than they were giving, she would pull back. We worked on helping her match so she did not have to keep reexperiencing feeling abandoned or stranded. One day we celebrated her ability to set limits after she said no to another friend who demanded a lot. Pat said she was terrified her friend would leave just like everyone else did. We talked about how using her anger to take care of herself was more important because she was already feeling left by her friend.

Our sessions had much more energy after she and Brett parted ways. Pat was on a roll, and she was working hard not to let her traumatic past stop her from getting what she needed in the present. We spent hours in session helping Pat find ways to embrace her anger. She learned that owning her anger gave her the choice to use it in ways that was going to make her life better!

HEALING STRATEGIES TO GREET ANGER

1. Grab a journal and describe what your anger feels like physically and emotionally. What do you feel in your body when you are angry? What are some thoughts you have when you think you are mad?
2. If writing is not an option, try to find a way to release the emotion: Let yourself cry, exercise, or implement some mindfulness strategies. Go to a yoga class and just be with the feelings in the present. Picture the anger releasing physically and say kind words to yourself.
3. Call a friend or empathetic family member and talk about what made you mad.
4. Scream into a pillow or hit a punching bag. Scribble on a piece of paper.
5. Wait until the anger subsides before confronting the person you are upset with. If you are unsure where your anger is coming from, do some inventory. Ask yourself questions like, "Where is this coming from?" Or check in to see, "Am I angry with my abusive father or am I mad at my partner?"

HEALING STRATEGIES FOR USING ANGER TO CONQUER YOUR WORLD

1. Imagine what it would mean to embrace your anger. For example, if you are a childhood abuse or domestic violence survivor, how would using your anger create positive change in your world?

2. Think about ways you can use your anger to create change in the environment in your community. Would volunteering at a women's shelter or protesting for equal rights provide you with an outlet to your rage?

3. Talk with close friends or your therapist about some goals you want to accomplish and how you can use your anger to make that happen. For example, are you working in a job where you are being disrespected or devalued? Talk with people about what you can do to change that. Does it mean looking for a new job or asserting yourself with supervisors to improve conditions at your current job?

4. If you are an athlete, think about running in a race or competing in a triathlon. If you are a hard worker, think about working toward a promotion or asking for a raise.

5. If you are in a connection with someone who hurt you badly during your childhood, consider confronting that person. Look for a therapist who specializes in reconciliation and talk with that person about doing some therapy to voice your rage and hold that person accountable.

6. If someone you loved died suddenly, write that person a letter. Say how mad you are that he or she died. It is perfectly normal and human to be mad at people for leaving us through illness. You will not hurt them if you get mad. It does not make you a bad person. Think about what that person would say to you. If you lost a spouse, tell your partner how enraged you are that they died. But also think about what he or she would say back to you. Would they want you to live the rest of your life feeling mad and alone,

or would they want you to be open to being in a new relationship?

5

STAYING PRESENT

What does it mean to let go? Is it possible to let go of trauma after surviving abuse, illness, sudden loss, a terrorist attack, or combat? Most trauma survivors yearn for a life where they can live in the present. They talk in therapy about wanting the triggers to go away, the flashbacks to stop, and the emotional pain to stop. Throughout the book, I have talked about how to make sense of experiences that are incomprehensible. I have talked about different ways patients can face their trauma, work past the shame, and eventually find ways to use their anger to reclaim a full life.

People living with abusive partners or spouses have a difficult time accepting that being loved should not also mean accepting harm or mistreatment. How does someone who has been married to a man for over twenty years come to terms with the fact that she is in an abusive relationship? How does she find a way to let go of her abuser, even if it means ending a marriage and starting a new life? It is possible.

KAREN: LETTING GO OF HER ABUSER

About ten years ago I began working with a patient who had been in an abusive marriage for over twenty-five years. I met her when she was still married to her abuser. Our first four or five sessions were set up as couple's therapy so that I could counsel her and her husband on figuring out how to help their youngest daughter deal with developmental delays and learning disabilities. I had no idea then that abuse had been occurring between them. In fact, Karen's husband was the one who made the initial call to start therapy.

During those first few sessions the tension in the room was so powerful I felt as if I wanted to open all the windows and scream once they left the room. This couple would sit on opposite sides of my sofa and would not look at each other. I could feel the rage coming from Karen's husband. He clenched his jaw and acted hostile during most of the session. I could feel Karen shrinking up whenever we spoke of general things such as setting up an individualized education program (IEP) for their daughter. She looked at the floor and hardly spoke. No love existed in that room, only anger and fear. I thought, "Something does not feel right in this room." I also asked, "If I felt that way, how would it feel to be a child living under those circumstances?"

One day after our fourth or fifth session, Karen called me and asked if we could have a session alone. I sensed that she was reaching out for help. When Karen came in for that session, she sat down, breathed a huge sigh, and began revealing episodes of when her husband acted abusively, mostly after he became intoxicated. She recounted multiple times when she hid in the basement to avoid her husband. Karen reported a tremendous amount of guilt when she spoke about how the abuse stopped her from doing the right thing and being able to protect her children. She knew her husband was abusive toward her son and two daughters, but her sense of self was so small that she did not even know how she could do something to get herself and the kids to safety.

I offered to do some counseling with Karen and her husband to address the abuse, but I knew that most likely her husband would not be open to doing that kind of therapy. Unfortunately I was right. He refused to sit in a room with Karen and me to work on the marriage and learn how the unsafety between them was affecting their children. Karen wanted to move forward in therapy even though her husband refused to attend any more sessions. We spent a few more sessions making space for her to share what life was like with her husband.

Once I had heard enough, I knew I needed to tell her that she was married to someone who had a serious mental pathology. Karen turned red when I said to her, "Your husband sounds like a very sick man." She had been with him for over half of her life and had never considered that he might be an addict and mentally ill. She came from a family where denial was strong. She had a post-doctorate degree and was extremely bright, yet no one had educated her on the signs or symptoms of living in a relationship marred by domestic violence.

Both of our hearts broke during that session. She sobbed, and I felt like I had caused her much hurt. When the session ended, we both went off separately to think about what had occurred and returned to that discussion in the sessions to come. Karen learned that she had tried to make believe that her husband was someone he was not so that she could stay married to him. Karen did not have the strength or self-worth to let herself know the truth. She was taught that once someone gets married, they were supposed to stay married, no matter what.

We began looking at her earlier beliefs about marriage and continued to digest specific incidents of abuse. In order to keep her memories conscious, I suggested she write down times when she felt belittled, unsafe, or in harm's way. I also suggested that she record times when her husband treated her kids with disrespect or disciplined them in inappropriate ways. Eventually she took my advice and purchased a journal. Within weeks of buying it, the pages were full of examples to remind her of what she knew was the truth. Karen stayed with her husband for another few months during our therapy. Most weeks she came to session reporting more times when her husband belittled, mistreated, and abused her.

We had many conversations about what made her stay married to someone who acted so poorly toward her and her children. I asked her, "What are you holding on to?" Karen began to understand that her guilt about leaving kept her stuck. She also realized that her childhood life was empty and that she was attracted to a man who had similar traits to her mother and father. Karen was abused by a boyfriend a couple of years before she got married. She told me about one incident when her boyfriend broke her nose when they had an argument. Karen went to the emergency room and got the medical attention she needed. When she called her parents to tell them what he did, they said and did nothing. Karen remembered feeling forgotten and uncared about that day and many other times when she was growing up.

Karen grew up feeling invisible and unlovable. She had basically raised herself and had no interest in being married to someone that could nurture and love her. As Karen resisted leaving her husband, we talked about how she could feel differently in a marriage. We talked about partnership, respect, boundaries, and intimacy. As we continued therapy while she still lived with her husband, she started to wake up.

That Christmas was the turning point for her. She had had enough. She told me her husband got sloppy drunk and that he berated her and started grabbing at her private parts right in front of her children. She told me that something clicked and she realized how awful it was for her kids to watch a man treat a woman with such disrespect. She came into session with her journal filled with examples of abuse done to her. We sat in session as she read some of the entries aloud. I asked her again what she was holding on to by staying in an abusive relationship. Then she figured out that her main reason for staying was that she felt like she did not deserve any better.

We talked about her hopes for her children, and she told me she would never want them to settle or be treated so badly by another person. I asked her, "Why is it okay for you to accept this kind of behavior when you would never want that for your kids?" At the moment she did not respond. She came back to therapy the next week and told me she was going to do it: "I am leaving Bill."

Karen eventually left her twenty-five-year abusive marriage. Initially, Karen did not know what living a life without abuse would feel like. Rather than fear the unknown, she continued working through her abuse in counseling and began forming relationships outside of her therapy. She joined a trauma therapy group. She began taking yoga classes and making jewelry. She moved into the city and got involved in a few different types of hobbies. Karen became friends with Phyllis, a woman who was older than her mother would have been. She and Phyllis started having weekly coffee dates. Gradually, Karen opened up to her about her marriage. Phyllis was the voice of reason when Karen wanted to rescind and go back to her ex-husband.

Throughout the separation process, Bill used intimidation and bullying to try to get her to go back to him. He wrote scathing emails, which she shared with me. He refused to give her money for the kids. He tried to turn the kids against her by telling them that Karen had abandoned him. At one point he became so abusive that she had to ask her attorney to tell him they could not speak without a third party present. He called her horrible names and told her she was a "piece of shit." While it was enraging to be a witness to such bad behavior, it also helped Karen to let go of him. Every time he acted out, we could affirm the truth about the abuse. Bill showed her repeatedly that he was not going to change or care for her in a healthy, loving way.

Once Karen had finished with the divorce proceedings, I asked her if she wanted to start dating. She had been married to an abuser for over twenty-five years, and I sensed she wanted a partner. When I first asked her if she was interested in dating, she said, "Hell no, not after everything I have been through." Rather than join her in the fear, I validated her and reminded myself that it was her decision when and if she wanted to date. Karen worked in her therapy group on intimacy and trust issues, and she met some other women who had let go of their abusers.

One day Karen came into my office smiling and shaking. She told me she met someone named Dave through one of her children. She came into session talking about this man she had met

through her son, and her eyes sparkled. However, when he asked
her on a date, she was terrified. Hours before Dave was going to
pick her up, she had a panic attack. She reached out to me and
asked if she should cancel the date. While I did not want her to
have to feel so anxious, I knew some of the panic was about her
fear of meeting another abuser. I told Karen she was in charge of
her life and she got to decide if she wanted to go on the date. I
knew she did, but I wanted to remind her that she had choices.
Just knowing she could say yes or no to Dave provided her with
relief. It also paved the way for Karen to forge a new relationship
with the knowledge that she had just as much control as Dave did.
I suggested, "How about if you go? You can always leave the date,
but if you say no, you will never know if it was worth giving it a
try." Very ambivalently, Karen went on the date. She met Dave at
a public place and set up a boundary around her time. She allowed
two hours to spend time and then told Dave she would need to go
pick up one of her children.

She called me after the date ended and told me, "Dave is
actually such a nice guy and he asked me on a second date." The
next session we celebrated Karen's willingness to live the life she
wanted by discussing her being open to spending another evening
with this nice man. From that point forward, the relationship blossomed. On countless occasions Karen came into session talking
about all the differences between Dave and her ex-husband. She
would say, "He listens to me, he respects me, he values me, and I
am not afraid of him." After one session, Karen went home and
wrote in her journal all the differences between being in an abusive marriage versus spending time with Dave. The list of examples went on for pages. I suggested she do this to remind herself
where she came from and also so she could recognize how Dave
was different when she had urges to flee from the relationship. On
occasion, Dave's anger triggered her memories of abuse. There
were times when Karen would have a panic attack when Dave
expressed displeasure or disappointment with her. Her expectation was that if she hit Dave's buttons somehow or made a mis-
take, she would be shamed and "thrown to the curb." We devel-

oped techniques for her to communicate these fears so that she could move past the memory and stay in the present moment with Dave. For example, when Karen sensed that she had disappointed Dave, I suggested that she check it out by asking him, "Are you angry or disappointed with me?" Most times Dave would reassure her that his feelings or reactions were more about him and that she should not feel responsible for something he responded to. For example, Dave would say, "My reaction to you was more about stuff with my own ex-wife."

Remarkably, Karen and Dave continued in their relationship, even though on many occasions Karen would try to push him away out of fear of re-creating her abuse. Eventually she shared more details with Dave about her childhood and her first marriage. Dave responded with empathy and compassion. She would tell me, "When I opened up to Dave about my abuse, he just sat, listened, and had a look of concern on his face." Rather than mistreat her as her abusers had, Karen said, "almost every day Dave tells me I am beautiful." After a year of dating, they got engaged. Around Karen's sixtieth birthday, they got married.

MARY: LETTING GO OF THE LOSS OF HER YOUNGEST BROTHER WHEN SHE WAS A KID

Through the years I have met several people who have lost family members due to a tragic illness or sudden death after being in plane crashes or car accidents. I have counseled a few people whose husbands had died unexpectedly. I have worked with people who lost a child from sudden infant death syndrome or car crashes. I met one woman who had to bury her youngest brother after he was hit by a drunk driver at the age of thirteen. She was seventeen at the time.

Mary started seeing me for therapy because she had a long history of severe depression and anxiety. She was hospitalized in her early forties for a month because she could not function at work or in her relationships. Mary did not tell me about her brother's death when we met. She focused on symptom management and trust issues in her relationships. After about six months, Mary told me about her brother. I had no idea she had suffered such a tremendous loss. I nearly fell off my chair when she told me. I could not believe she lived with such a tragic event and had no idea how much it affected her. For over twenty years, Mary was reliving images of her brother's body after she arrived at the scene of the accident. A drunk driver had allegedly blown through a red light and hit her brother when he was riding his bicycle. Mary told me she was the first of her family members to arrive at the scene.

Mary remembered the image of her brother lying on the side of the road gasping for life. While she knew she was not the cause of his death, she could not get past the what-ifs. For example, she would say to me over and over, if only he had waited a second longer to start riding his bicycle, or if only he had biked down a different street, he could still be alive. Mary had a close bond with him, and in some ways she felt like his mother. She was almost five years older than he was and had spent years watching him when her mother was at work.

We talked about how other people in the family reacted to her brother's death. She told me her family disintegrated from the moment it happened. I asked her to explain what that meant. Mary told me her mother grew more depressed over time. She had many memories of her mother lying in her bed crying with all the blinds closed. She told me her parents got divorced within months of the funeral. As more time went by, her mother developed an addiction to alcohol. Her mother's mood was either depressed or angry. Mary told me she always felt like she was walking on eggshells. She also explained that she became her mother's caretaker. She felt responsible for her and never wanted to make her mad. So when Mary was upset or mad, she kept it bottled up inside of her. Mary told me she would do anything to make her mother happy.

During our therapy, we worked on her need for approval and how most of that came from her relationship with her mother after her brother died. She continued to repeat that pattern with boyfriends, coworkers, and friends. She had such a hard time putting herself first. When she went through a rough patch, she would feel resentful and alone. Mary was putting much more energy into others, and when it came time for her to receive support, she felt alone and abandoned. Part of her process of letting go meant finding a way to come to terms with the family loss she felt as a result of her brother's death.

Mary had never been diagnosed with PTSD. Doctors told her she was suffering from severe depression and anxiety. Mary continued to have flashbacks of the funeral and the day she saw her brother lying lifeless in the middle of the street. She would have panic attacks whenever she thought someone was mad at her. Mary's expectation was that if someone was mad at her, they were going to disappear just like her brother or other family members. She spent days, even weeks, before we met in bed. She became so crippled by her symptoms that she had to take a leave from her job to go to an inpatient facility for mental illness. Mary said she told the doctors at the psychiatric hospital about her brother's death. She was furious that her providers did not acknowledge the trauma. Mary told me that when she went to the hospital they medicated her heavily, and once she was stabilized they sent her home.

Mary and I wanted to do more than just help her feel less depressed. As we processed this part of her life, I helped Mary understand how she was stuck in the loss and grief. She had accepted that her brother was gone, but she never mourned for the loss of her family and how his death affected her. Mary wanted to have relationships that were reciprocal. She wanted to learn how to take in support, not just give it to others. She also wanted to find hobbies or different types of mindfulness to comfort her hurt self.

I was inspired when Mary began training for triathlons. Mary developed a passion for racing on her bicycle and spending time swimming laps in the pool. She also learned how to meditate and to use that strategy whenever she felt overwhelmed. Mary was looking for a place to relieve some of her pent-up sadness and anger. She was also looking for a way to feel a sense of community.

She joined bicycle clubs and hired herself a trainer to prepare for races all over the country.

As Mary got more comfortable connecting with others, she took more time to reconnect with her siblings. She had maintained a relationship with her two brothers, but she told me they never talked about her brother's death or her mother's alcoholism. I suggested she talk with her sister about acknowledging her brother on days like Christmas, his birthday, his death day, and other important annual dates. At first Mary was resistant, but then she opened her mind to the idea that making space to honor her brother's life could provide her with comfort. Letting go does not mean forgetting about people who die. Letting go does not mean turning off feelings when reminders of that person's life are present.

Mary brought me to tears when she talked about how her siblings got together on her brother's birthday. They sat around the table and reminisced about his life. They talked about the times when he made them laugh. They even imagined what he would have become if he had lived into adulthood. Mary told me they also talked about the death of their family unit after their brother passed away. They recognized that this was a death they could reverse. It was not too late for them to be close. It was not too late for them to share their feelings and be there for each other on days like Christmas or his death anniversary.

Most trauma survivors yearn for a different life than the one they are living. They want to be at peace and make good choices in their personal and professional lives. In order to live the life you want, it is crucial to let go of the life you lived before, during, and after the trauma occurred. I struggled with this for years in my recovery. I fought the truth. I denied at times that I was an incest survivor. I would say things to my therapist like, "I do not want to be one of those people." I knew I was not going to be happy if I stayed stuck in the wish that it wasn't so. I needed to accept that I was an incest survivor and also recognize that I was others things too. I was a friend, a therapist, a mentor, and I wanted to have a family. After being diagnosed and treated for thyroid cancer in the midst of my recovery, I decided I wanted to let go! I wanted to accept myself for who I was and continue to go after my dreams.

Not everyone I meet can accept who they are or where they come from. Occasionally I have worked with patients who have left therapy because they are stuck in the past. Survivors of childhood abuse have an especially difficult time because most of them suppress the memories and feelings for years, sometimes decades. When children experience physical, emotional, or sexual abuse, they commonly report feeling numb, losing consciousness, and at times leaving their body. People are born with survival mechanisms, and for children these defense strategies help them get through the trauma and continue functioning.[1] In order to keep living with abusive parents, coaches, religious leaders, or teachers, abused children find ways to bury their rage and fear. Their brains have not developed, and they are unable to process horrific acts done to them. The longer someone tucks away trauma, the harder it is for them to speak about it. It is almost impossible to move beyond trauma without having a way to describe it or understand it.

DEBBIE: THE STRUGGLE TO LET GO OF A LOST CHILDHOOD

I remember the day I met Debbie. She had a long history of being in outpatient therapy. She told me she had symptoms of an eating disorder, severe depression, and PTSD. We met after she got married and had two kids, one boy and one girl. She decided to get back into treatment after giving birth to her daughter. Very soon after her daughter's birth, she developed postpartum depression. I thought that was why she was coming back into therapy.

When we first started meeting, Debbie's affect was depressed. She did not open up much, and her affect was flat. She had married a man she met in middle school. They were the best of friends throughout their teens. As I got to know Debbie better, she was able to talk about the missing pieces in her marriage. She expressed tremendous guilt for not being able to meet Marc's need to be intimate sexually. It was not until the end of our first year in therapy that Debbie told me she was suppressing childhood abuse. Once she opened the door for us to have conversations about her past, it was clear to me she had lost most of her childhood. She lived her childhood in isolation and silence. She told me she often felt like an outsider in school and at times considered suicide to end the feelings of isolation.

She had a decent relationship with her mother when she became an adult, but she told me her mother was different when she was a child. She described feeling unheard, disbelieved, and ignored. Debbie lived with her younger brother. They did not have much of a connection. I did not even know she had a brother until she began opening up about suppressed abuse. She and her brother became estranged as soon as she moved in with Marc.

During the course of our treatment, Debbie suffered some awful illnesses and losses. Her mother passed away suddenly during our second year in therapy. Several aunts and one cousin died from terminal illnesses. Our therapy was disrupted by all her loss because she was grieving and not in a place psychologically where she could deal with the deaths of family members and focus on her childhood. While her eating disorder symptoms decreased significantly, her depression became worse, and she needed to start taking medication. A year after her mother died, she suffered a back injury that took her out of work. She was bedridden for weeks and eventually had to have major surgery.

At times we acknowledged our frustration in looking back at earlier childhood trauma, because we knew it was holding her back from living in the present. The loss of her mother and other family members triggered more feelings of loss, and there were times when Debbie journaled thoughts she had been suppressing. One day Debbie told me a story about a picture she had of her and her father. Debbie had pictures of her kids and husband all over the family room walls. She was proud of them, and once the postpartum depression passed, she developed a wonderful bond with them. Debbie told me she kept many of her childhood photos of herself locked away in a basement closet.

She said there were no pictures of her and her father hanging on her walls. I was curious why, and she told me that anytime she looked at her father's face she felt sick to her stomach. In one session Debbie told me, "Every time I look at that picture I know in my heart that my father did some terrible things to me." We talked more about how Debbie kept those pictures as a way to know, but that she was also locking them up to try and keep her memories in her subconscious. A part of me wanted to tell her she had to stop doing that, but it is not up to me to decide how someone works through their abuse. I wanted more for Debbie, but I also reminded myself that she had several current life situations that were preventing her from doing recovery work. Our therapy took an abrupt halt after she needed to have two major back surgeries. As we were getting ready to take a break, Debbie and I spoke about her wish to work more on her past. She told me every day that she knew something horrible had happened to her when she was a child. She said she had many memories of feeling like a misfit in elementary and middle school and that high school was a disaster for her academically and socially. Rather than give up her quest to work through her undigested childhood, we accepted that her health needed attention. Debbie was about to undergo months of painful physical recovery and therapy. I suggested that Debbie start journaling about feelings that surfaced during and after her surgery and reassured her that when the time felt right we would get back to it.

We also decided that while she was on medical leave from work and treatment we would touch base periodically. I wanted Debbie to know that the work she had done in therapy would not go to waste and to give her an opportunity to continue processing, even if she could not attend sessions. It was not all by choice that Debbie could not find a way to understand and come to terms with her unsettling past. Letting go is a process that can be disrupted by current life situations.

There have been many times over the last several years that I have gotten stuck in my recovery when I was on the verge of coming to terms with my lost childhood. Anytime I went through a transition or took risks in a relationship, I fell back into the shame. My therapist and I worked on understanding how the shame served a purpose. It was one of my main defense mechanisms in response to feeling my anger and letting go. We talked about the part of me that felt guilty for speaking and moving on with my life. There were times when I would sabotage myself because I felt undeserving of accomplishing my goals or making a better life for myself. I realized over time that in order to have healthy relationships and live a fuller life I needed to stop feeling guilty for separating from the people who hurt me and stop feeling unworthy of living a good life.

BRIAN: LETTING GO OF BEING THE RESCUER AFTER GROWING UP WITH LOSS AND POVERTY

I remember the first time Brian walked into my office. He reached out to me after being hospitalized for severe depression and PTSD multiple times in adulthood. We met right after he turned seventy years old. When we started having sessions, our main goal was to get him stabilized so he could begin to explore his trauma history and how that affected him in the present. Brian had done several rounds of electroconvulsive therapy because his depression was crippling him socially, emotionally, and occupationally. The Mayo Clinic defines this procedure, which is done under general anesthesia, as small electric currents that are passed through the brain, intentionally triggering a brief seizure. They claim that ECT changes the chemistry in the brain, which helps reverse the symptoms of depression.[2] Brian and I had sessions between his ECT treatments during our first few months in therapy.

Though his mood was improving, talking about his childhood seemed impossible. The ECT caused some memory loss and confusion. At times Brian came to therapy with his wife. They both expressed frustration at the process of recovery because Brian knew he needed to talk about and let go of his complicated childhood, but he was unable to recall his early life experiences due to the ECT.

After about six months, Brian announced that he was stopping the ECT against the advice of his treating doctors. He had had enough and was eager to move ahead. Brian continued to meet with his psychiatrist monthly, and he was taking different kinds of antidepressants and antianxiety medications. Brian was getting out of bed every day. We implemented more structure, and each morning Brian had something to get out of bed for, whether it was to go to yoga, go grocery shopping, or rake the leaves.

After a couple of months in treatment, we began talking about his current struggles and about feeling responsible for rescuing others. Brian had one child who was diagnosed with some processing and developmental delays as a teenager. When I met Brian, his son, James, had just turned forty-five years old.

Brian talked to me about his son and how he always relied on Brian for financial and emotional security. The biggest fight between Brian and his wife was Brian's enabling in his relationship with his son. At first I did not understand Brian's desire to come to James's aid. I asked him about his childhood and what kind of environment he was raised in.

He blurted out that his father died suddenly when he was two years old. He went on to tell me about how after his father's death his mother suffered from severe depression, which went unnoticed and untreated. From as early as ten years old, Brian became his mother's caretaker. There were weeks when she was unable to parent or go to work because of her mental issues. Their family also had significant money problems. A few years after Brian's father passed away, he and his mother were forced to move into low-income housing in the projects. Brian witnessed violence and was the target of bullying at various points in his childhood. Then he would come home after school and find his mother hiding in her bedroom with the blinds closed. When I asked Brian how he understood what was going on with his mother, he told me he thought all mothers were like that. He had no idea how sick his mother got after his father passed away.

When Brian was ten years old, his mother met a man. Brian hardly knew him, and he told me Jack moved into his house a few months after his mother started dating him. Brian said that initially his mother's depression subsided, but Jack brought a whole new set of problems into their home. Brian said that within weeks of Jack moving in there were episodes of physical abuse. He said that at times Jack hit his mother in front of him as he watched, paralyzed with fear. Brian knew his mother was being abused, and he feared for his mother's life. He told me that when he got to school he looked for a safe teacher to talk to, but then his fear for his and his mother's safety silenced him.

Brian said Jack also hit him. He recalled a couple of incidents when Jack beat the crap out of him for no reason. I asked Brian where his mother was when this happened, and he told me she was usually in the next room. No one was looking out for Brian. No one had his back.

It was not until Brian turned twelve years old that his mother got the courage to kick Jack out of their home. Brian told me it was such a relief, but then days after Jack left, his mother slipped back into a major depression. One day when he got home from school he found his mother unconscious in her bedroom. He had no idea what had happened, but she was not breathing. Brian immediately called 911, and she was taken to the hospital. Luckily his mother survived her suicide attempt.

Brian was taken out of his home, and he lived with another family member for a few months. Though Brian was in a safer environment, the separation from his mother was devastating. I asked Brian if anyone talked to him about what was happening. He said that all he was told was that his mother was sick and could not care for him.

Brian knew his mother had attempted suicide. He assumed he was part of the reason because she was responsible for him. Brian did not realize that his mother had not been taking care of him for years. He had no idea that he was acting more like the parent. Throughout his adulthood Brian continued to feel responsible for others at his own expense.

Brian knew early in his son's life that he was having some issues. He went to James's school after the child-study team had evaluated him and diagnosed him with processing and developmental delays. As James got into his teens, Brian's depression and anxiety got worse. He told me he felt helpless and that he should have done more to help his son. At times Brian wanted to get him help, but finances were tight and Brian was working two jobs to pay the bills. Brian also did not recognize the severity of James's mental illness.

Once James became an adult, Brian began to notice his inability to function occupationally and socially. Brian said his son had very few connections. At this point Brian's financial situation improved, and he offered to get James into therapy. Anytime Brian brought up therapy, James became angry and defensive. Brian talked to his son about the benefits he was getting from treatment, but that did not matter to James.

As I learned more about Brian's past, I began to understand more about his codependent relationship with his son. Brian's wife, Beth, began coming into therapy sessions. They got married when James was in his late twenties. Brian was reluctant to bring up times when James turned to him for money, transportation, or at times a place to live. One day Beth came into session when she was at her wits' end. With tears pouring down her face she told Brian she could not continue to watch Brian put his son ahead of her and everyone else.

James got used to coming to his father for money, and there were many times when Brian did not speak to Beth about it. Brian had no intention of pushing Beth away. We talked about what it meant to Brian to put other people ahead of himself. He did not realize that part of his drive to give handouts to his son was connected to years of living in the projects. Brian was terrified that James would end up on the streets, and his fear took over. Rather than set limits with his son and try to empower him, he just kept saying yes. Brian gave money to his son that he and Beth needed to pay their own bills. Brian also gave James his car, even though he needed it himself to get to doctor's appointments.

Our sessions took a turn as I learned more about the effects of Brian's enabling on his marriage. We talked at length about Brian's fears for his son. We talked many weeks about the hope that would come from setting some boundaries with his son. Brian felt like it was up to him to save his son. Brian was so used to doing everything by himself during his childhood that he projected that James would feel abandoned if he said no. Once we understood the connection from his past of feeling unprotected and overly responsible, we were able to work on helping Brian let go of being the rescuer.

I suggested that Brian get a journal and start writing about what he felt when James asked him for things like money or his car. We developed a list of questions. For example, I asked Brian to journal about what other options his son had besides coming to him for money. Brian realized that James had never learned about living independently and managing his finances. I told Brian that if he set limits with his son, it would help him find other resources, such as talking to a financial advisor about budgeting his income. James did not go to college, but he did have a job. He used his income for his phone, food, and social activities. He did not pay rent, as he still lived in his mother's house. He did not have a car payment.

Brian came to session in tears one day after James asked him for $200. He was frustrated and felt trapped. Beth and I gently confronted him about giving himself the option to say no. Brian was in agony, but the pain he was feeling was linked to the years he had lived in poverty. He remembered many times when he ate Crisco sandwiches because that was all his mother could afford. Brian would tell me he was terrified that if he did not keep giving James money, the same thing would happen to him. There were differences. Brian's son had support. Brian's son was not made to feel responsible for his father's health. Brian's son was a grown adult. While he wanted to keep relying on his father for money, that was not his only option.

Brian fought hard to keep holding on to his role of being the savior. At times he set limits with James, but I later found out he gave in and still gave him money sometimes. Brian blamed himself for James's problems. In order for Brian to let go of his past, we needed to help him understand how it was bringing him down in the present.

Beth had been trying for a long time to help Brian gradually cease enabling his son. Beth came to session at times talking about being near the limit of her endurance. She was sensitive to the emotional traumas Brian had endured. He loved his son and struggled with the best way to be a good father to an adult son who had never been financially independent. Brian's son continued to expect his dad to pick up the pieces when he made unwise choices. The trauma caused by her stepson, Beth believed, triggered a major depression episode for Brian resulting in a month's hospital stay and thirty ECT treatments. She did not want to live her life like that forever. She pleaded with Brian to make substantial progress in therapy so that they could live their lives together.

Months after we started working on Brian's relationship with his son, the two of them decided to take a week's vacation in Florida. Brian's depression and anxiety were getting worse, and he did not want to end up in the hospital or go back for ECT. They decided they would go away partly to see how James would react if Brian was unavailable to come to his aid.

Remarkably, the week in Florida did wonders for both of them. Brian talked in therapy about how different he felt being away from his environment and the stressors he had with his son. Beth told me Brian was like a different person. She described him as carefree, motivated, and much more connected. They took walks together, did yoga together, sat on the beach together, and spent hours every night having conversations about their retirement and the goals they had for that chapter of their lives.

I did not even recognize Brian when he came back for a session after his trip to Florida. He was smiling, and it felt like his depression had lifted. As we talked about his trip, his eyes beamed. He told me, "I felt like I had no one else to worry about in Florida except me." That was such a new experience for Brian. For over sixty years of his life he had focused on others. He spent his childhood taking care of his mother and her mental illness issues. He worked starting in his young teens to help his mother pay their household bills. Once he had his son, that became his priority. He was never taught healthy boundaries in a parent-son relationship. He gave his son whatever he wanted. Brian told me he did not want his son to have to worry about money, his living situation, or any other responsibility that most kids have.

Brian would have done anything to help his son have a different childhood than his own. While he sat on the beach in Florida, he decided he was going to let go of being his son's rescuer. Brian had brought in plenty of examples of when his boundaries were being tested, so he had developed some important strategies to not act on the impulse to bail his son out one more time. When his son called or texted him, Brian gave himself several hours before responding. He looked back on his journals and talked to his wife about how saying no was benefiting his son. It was forcing him to develop more autonomy from Brian and ask appropriate people for help. We talked about the difference between his son wanting money and Brian responding if there was an emergency. Brian was not going to sit by and watch his son end up on the street. He decided he was going to support his son in getting a better-paying job and direct him to resources for financial and psychological support.

Brian struggled with feelings of guilt every time he said no. We talked in session about how hard it is to say good-bye to a part of his identity that took such a strong hold of him. At one point Brian asked me who he would be if he no longer came to his son's aid. We also talked in our session about all the opportunities he could give himself when he decided to put himself first.

Letting go is a process. For trauma survivors, feelings of guilt, fear, and shame can make it even more difficult. There is no quick solution to letting go, whether it comes from abuse, loss, or abandonment. It is more about making a conscious decision to no longer hold on to feelings of distrust, responsibility, or guilt about living even when others cannot. It is also normal to slip and slide through this part of recovery.

Letting go is like grieving. It is not a smooth transition for most patients. The benefit of sliding backward is that people can learn more about themselves and what they are holding on to. Developing awareness about what makes people hold on to their past or hold on to a role that does not serve them well is the most important step to healing in this phase of recovery.

HEALING STRATEGIES TO LET GO OF THE PAST

Five Powerful Practices for Releasing Emotional Pain and Regret[3]

1. Write down at least three unresolved situations that have happened in the past. For example, not being home when your partner made a suicide attempt, allowing another soldier in combat to take the lead in the squad and surviving as a result, enabling a family member at your own expense, or not being able to protect your mother from your abusive father.

2. Write down who you are blaming for the trauma. Are you blaming yourself for your abuse? Are you blaming your parents for not protecting you from your abuser? Are you blaming yourself for the death of someone else that you could not prevent? Are you blaming yourself for being attracted to multiple partners who were abusive?

3. Find a way to forgive without forgetting what happened. Talk with abuse survivors or therapists to better understand the mind-set of your abuser. Think about the perpetrator if you were a victim of abuse, terror attack, or combat. Is it possible that this person had a history that led him or her

down such a destructive path? Find ways to put ownership of the trauma on the person or thing that caused your pain. For example, if you figure out that your abuser was also abused as a child, acknowledge that. Do some research on abusers to find out how many abusers were also hurt or mistreated as kids. That does not make it okay, but it could help you find a way to accept why the person or people hurt you in such a deep way. View forgiveness as something we do for ourselves as much as we may do for others. Think of forgiveness as part of the ongoing process toward recovery. Every time you notice anger or resentment toward yourself, give yourself the choice to notice and then let go of it. Write it down. Tell your therapist. Call a friend or talk to your partner about it.

4. Write down the consequences that come with holding on to the past. For example, if your husband died suddenly, is that holding you back from exploring new relationships after much time has passed? Are the feelings of distrust that come from your childhood abuse generalized with most people you come in contact with? Is that holding you back from forming trusting, nurturing relationships in the present? Are you still blaming yourself for losing a buddy in combat? How is that holding you back from living a happy life today?

5. What opportunities come with letting go? More happiness? More energy? More goals being accomplished? The ability to live a fuller life? Write down how you imagine your life could be different as you move through this part of the process. Look into the future and think about some action you can take to make your life better. For example, take a risk in a relationship by allowing yourself to trust. Have some type of ritual to honor your family member who passed away and imagine him or her blessing your choice to build new relationships.

Another Perspective to Leaving the Past in the Past [4]

1. Journal or talk to a therapist or close friend about what you can do with that experience in the present. Can you find a place to file it away and access it when you need to reflect on it? How will you let it affect you moving forward?
2. Rather than avoiding your past, face it. Look at photos from your childhood, talk about it, and write about the memories to reassure yourself you have not forgotten.
3. Ask yourself how much you want to let what happened to you impact your present. For example, it can feel impossible to trust anyone after being violated. Give yourself a chance to be around people who are trustworthy. Recognize that only some people do not deserve your trust, not all people.

6

TAKING TIME TO GRIEVE

SO LONG EATING DISORDER, ALCOHOL, OR DRUGS

Many of my patients started therapy because they were battling an eating disorder, alcohol, or drug abuse to avoid the emotions connected to their trauma. In the moment it can feel much easier to think about skipping a meal or getting high off a drug than to feel the insurmountable loss that comes with surviving combat, childhood abuse, sudden loss, terror attack, or other traumatic experiences.

Grieving takes place over time, and there is no right way to move through it. Elisabeth Kübler-Ross, a Swiss-born psychiatrist and cofounder of the hospice movement, changed the way we talk about the end of life. She developed the five stages of loss: denial, anger, bargaining, depression, and acceptance.[1] Originally Kübler-Ross designed this process to help people dying from illnesses and their family members. One of the messages she leaves the reader with is that people can shift from stage 1 to stage 5 and then at times go back to the beginning of the cycle. As with any type of recovery, it is normal to move through a process and then slip and slide along the way.

The feelings of loss after trauma are complicated, especially when someone has suffered through something like a parent dying suddenly in childhood or an adult realizing that as a child they were sexually abused by an authority figure. Most patients I meet have never dealt with their losses, such as the loss of their childhood, the loss of a family to death, or loss of life as a result of a terror attack or mass shooting. I have met so many patients who have spent years doing whatever they could to not feel grief because it is scary and painful.

Lori: So Long, Eating Disorder after Multiple Family Deaths

Lori reached out to me after she found out her therapist of over ten years was retiring. She was in her late fifties, and she knew her recovery was not complete. The phone call was very sad as Lori told me about the wonderful connection she had developed with her therapist. She told me she was devastated when she heard her therapist was going to stop seeing patients. Lori's therapist gave her months of notice so they could spend ample time processing all the feelings that were triggered. Lori went into therapy with Susan because she had been struggling with a binge eating disorder and bipolar depression for most of her life. She came from a large family, and throughout her childhood and adulthood many people had died. Lori grew up in a volatile household where her mother had problems with anger management.

In therapy with Susan, she learned more about her issues of trust after growing up in a family where she described walking on eggshells. Everyone in her family did what they could to not piss off their mother. Lori had witnessed her mother's anger toward her father and siblings on several occasions. When someone in the extended family passed away, Lori told Susan the message she got was that people should not talk about their feelings. Lori sat at the dinner table for years feeling seen but not heard.

As Susan and Lori were wrapping up their ten-plus years in treatment, they talked extensively about how therapy had helped Lori find her voice. When we spoke about what she was looking for in a new therapy relationship, she told me she really wanted to stop eating food to push away her grief. She had learned a tremendous amount in therapy with Susan on expressing her feelings. She was also working on making connections with people who could tolerate grief. Lori was very active in her religious organization. She felt a sense of belonging and could turn to the priest and some of the congregants when she was going through a hard time or working through old losses.

When we began meeting, we spent time talking about the loss of her therapist. I also began to understand the role of her eating disorder in coping with her childhood issues. When I met Lori, she was in her forties and had been diagnosed with diabetes and high blood pressure. She had to meet with doctors every three months and was put on medication to manage all of her health issues. Lori knew her relationship with food was the main culprit behind her diabetes and high blood pressure. Lori was ready to say good-bye to her eating disorder.

We started the process by talking about how she would eat sweets as a child when she left the dinner table. I asked her to tell me more about how food became more like her friend. Lori told me that when she ate sweets, she felt like she was giving her hurt self a hug. Lori longed for acceptance and wanted to be heard. She had told me and her prior therapist about many times when she had tried to speak to her family and was made to feel unimportant. Lori said that at times family members would completely ignore her or tell her to shut up. No one spoke on Lori's behalf. She had many memories of walking away from the dinner table feeling defeated. As a young teen, Lori told me that relationships with peers were impossible to maintain. She said the kids made fun of her for how she looked, how she spoke, and how she dressed. Rather than come home and tell someone about the bullying, Lori became a recluse. When people were away from the kitchen, she turned to sweets to try to make the hurt go away. This pattern of emotional eating lasted for decades.

When Lori turned fourteen, her mother gave birth to another child who had major health issues. Lori talked in therapy about how her sister's birth affected the entire family dynamic. Lori grew to love her sister, but she also felt angry and resented that her parents could nurture her sister in ways Lori longed for. She told me that her parents were kind, affectionate, and patient with her sister. Lori could not understand why her parents could treat her sister so differently. Over time Lori decided that she was the cause of her yearning to be loved. She developed a belief system that she was flawed and unlovable. When Lori started doing therapy with her first therapist, she was able to talk about those thoughts and work on different ways to reframe them.

As I got to know Lori better, she was confronted with some serious health issues that became the focus of our therapy. She was diagnosed with melanoma and needed to have several surgeries to contain the cancer. When Lori got the news that she was sick, she was devastated. She was afraid and felt alone. We knew that her relationships with her mom and sisters were not going to give her the emotional support she needed as she went into her cancer recovery.

Sadly, as Lori was getting ready for her second surgery for her melanoma, her younger sister passed away suddenly from a heart attack. Lori was heartbroken. She began eating food whenever she felt anything about her sister's death. She felt guilty for the years of built-up resentment and felt awful that she could not say goodbye to her sister.

As we looked at her relationship with bingeing, we realized that Lori was looking to food as something that would never go away. She told me that if she kept eating sweets or storing her house up with comfort food, it reassured her that food would never go away. We used this analogy to work in therapy on her younger sister's sudden death and Lori's loss issues with her parents' inability to be present when she needed guidance or support. Lori was turning to food to mask her feelings of abandonment.

I admired Lori's determination to kick her eating disorder out of her life. She came into therapy week after week with examples of when she felt the urge to binge. Sometimes she gave in to the urges, and sometimes she did not. We created some coping mechanisms to help Lori contain the urge to binge and replace it with self-love strategies. When Lori wanted to binge, she would go to another room of her house and meditate. I asked her what kind of thoughts she meditated on, and she told me anything that made her feel comfort. Lori imagined holding her younger self by telling herself she was not the reason she felt emotionally left by her family. Sometimes Lori turned to music to soothe herself. She went into the bedroom and put on her favorite radio station. She sat in the room until the impulse to overeat subsided.

When Lori was triggered by work stress, she had a difficult time. Sometimes Lori had insomnia because she would ruminate on whatever had happened with a supervisor or colleague and beat herself up for how she handled it. I talked to Lori about finding people outside of work she could talk to about these conflicts. She had a few friends from her old job that she described as supportive. I challenged her to pick up the phone and call one of them when she was upset by work stress.

As we worked together in therapy over more time, Lori became comfortable reaching out to friends. She had some interactions with them where she hung up the phone feeling heard. I would say to her that one great thing about people is that they can listen and affirm us. Food cannot do that!

Once Lori finished her cancer treatment, we spent more of our sessions working on her eating disorder. I was amazed at Lori's dedication to saying good-bye to her symptoms. About a year after Lori's cancer went into remission, she started noticing major changes with her health. Her weight was very gradually going down, and her blood work was improving.

Lori was becoming more connected with her friends. She felt more comfortable asking for help. She found a way to accept her sisters and her mother for who they were and let go of the wish for something different. Through the meditation, Lori became much kinder and loving to herself. She started feeling attractive, lovable, and respectful toward herself. She acknowledged the role of the binge eating and decided it was no longer the type of love she wanted to give herself.

One day Lori entered session and vibrantly announced that for the first time in over forty years she could shop in regular clothes sizes versus plus sizes. She did not make it about the weight loss. It was a major victory because this opened her up to being able to have more choices when buying clothes. Lori talked extensively about the toll of her health issues and how they prevented her from being comfortable doing things such as sitting on an airplane, walking up a flight of stairs, or even attending a social gathering where she needed to be more physically fit. Early in Lori's life she was able to travel and explore different countries. She had to put that on hold for most of her adult life.

Lori was preparing for her retirement as she went through these recovery strides. While she had suffered multiple losses, some that had felt intolerable for years, she believed that the last act of her life looked amazing. Lori's approach to mindful eating was inspiring because she made all the changes with a lot of self-love. We talked about the part of her that felt restricted as a child. When she sat down to eat a meal at home or at a restaurant, she told me that the choices she made of what to eat did not feel depriving. She was able to have some of her favorite foods in moderation, and she added foods that she had never tried in the past. Rather than have a negative tape playing in her mind, Lori would tell herself that she was a good person and that her body could do many more wonderful things when it got healthy.

Choosing to live life without resorting to self-destruction requires determination, patience, and persistence. I have never met a patient who's been able to stop using symptoms after deciding he or she wants to stop being anorexic, an alcoholic, or a drug abuser. No one chooses to live such an unhealthy life. These coping strategies serve a purpose for trauma survivors who have turned to self-destruction because it is the only way they know how to survive. Ashwood Recovery at Northpoint explains that anyone can experience trauma, and many of them unfortunately turn to alcohol or substance abuse.[2] In their research, Ashwood has found that nearly 75 percent of individuals who receive treatment for substance abuse also have a history of exposure to trauma. People turn to intoxicating substances in an attempt to self-medicate. Some turn to drugs to numb their feelings of pain and grief. Others abuse alcohol to comfort the part of themselves that feels angry or sad.

When trauma survivors rely on substances to manage the long-term consequences of trauma, some take their behaviors to the point of furthering their self-destruction. For example, some addicts may drive under the influence, put themselves in precarious situations while intoxicated, or engage in unsafe sexual behavior. Over the years I have worked with a number of patients who became addicted to drugs or alcohol after experiencing a traumatic event in their early teens.

Laura: Turned to Drug Abuse after Being Sidelined by a Permanent Back Injury

I did not meet Laura until she was in her late thirties. She reached out for therapy after being hospitalized in drug rehabilitation centers since the age of sixteen. Before I met her she worked in therapy with a recovery coach who specialized in addictions. When she called me to request an initial visit, she told me she wanted to start doing therapy on the underlying issues of her extensive drug abuse history. Her last inpatient stay was six years before I met her.

Once Laura committed to sobriety she was able to hold a good job as a high school English teacher and dabbled in having intimate relationships with men who were not addicts. Laura went to twelve-step meetings, mostly Narcotics Anonymous, and had a sponsor. She attended these meetings at least three times a week.

When Laura came to my office for her first appointment, she was smiling from ear to ear and seemed mostly content with her current life. She was relieved about the length of time she had been clean from heroin, but she also told me the urges were still there in her daily life. It terrified Laura to think that she could slip with just one impulse to act on her urges.

Laura did a lot of reading on addiction and trauma before she started therapy with me. She knew that one of the key components to sobriety was understanding what got her into the addiction in the first place. During our first few sessions, we talked about the focus of her inpatient stays and the therapy with her previous therapist. Laura had completed the twelve steps many times. When Laura committed to being sober, she was motivated and dedicated to the programs. Unfortunately, she was not able to stay long enough when she was inpatient to do the therapy work required to look at her core issues. I asked Laura what kinds of groups she went to and what kinds of things she talked about in therapy with her recovery coach. She said there was a lot of emphasis on developing strategies to ward off the urges to use heroin. Some of the treatment facilities used cognitive behavioral and dialectical behavioral therapy methods. The groups focused on symptom management as well as daily living habits. Laura had many opportunities to talk with her therapist and group members in rehab about finding a job and dealing with the politics that come with working within a system.

During part of her thirties, Laura had tried to date, but she found herself attracted to men who were actively using drugs. We talked in our sessions about the familiarity of dating someone who was an addict. Laura told me that while she knew it was not the best thing for her, she was still looking for a sense of belonging and that being around drug abusers felt comfortable.

When Lori called me to start therapy, I had no idea about her childhood history of trauma. She told me right away about her sister's bout with anorexia and her parents' limitations in dealing with emotions. Laura talked about feeling unsupported by her family when she had issues with peers or at school. When Laura was in elementary school, she had a difficult time focusing and containing. Classmates found her amusing, but teachers had little patience for her tendency to call out in class. When Laura tried to prepare for exams or do homework assignments, she often procrastinated and at times did not complete her assignments. In the fifth grade, the child-study team diagnosed her with an attention deficit. Laura told me she felt like an outsider because she felt different from all her peers. We explored that in our sessions to help Laura understand that she was not different but that the problem she was experiencing was different from many of her classmates. No one talked to Laura in school about how to manage her feelings of shame. Laura told me that when she tried to tell her parents how she felt like a misfit, she felt unheard. I asked her what her parents would say when she tried to talk to them. She told me they did not really say anything.

As Laura became an adult and spent an extensive amount of time in therapy and rehabs, she understood that her parents' inability to offer emotional support was not about her. At times Laura told me group members would describe coming from very similar homes as children.

After about four months of meeting weekly, Laura brought up another time in her life when she felt alone. I had no idea that Laura had suffered a life-altering injury that took her out of diving and gymnastics, which she had been very involved in since she was a young child. She casually brought up a time when she was in the hospital after having major surgery and a fight she had with her mother.

I jumped in as she began telling me the story and let her know that an injury that sidelined her from her passions could have played a key role into her extensive drug abuse history. Laura began abusing marijuana when she was fifteen years old. Then she tried heroin and was hooked immediately. I asked Laura to tell me more about her back injury that took her out of school, gymnastics, and diving. The injury occurred when she was fourteen years old. Laura told me she was competing in a diving event and that she suffered a severe back injury after a dive that went wrong. She was rushed to the hospital and had to have major surgery right away. Then she spent three months stuck in a bed with a brace and was not able to go to school.

I asked Laura what that was like for her, and she told me she felt devastated. She said that diving and gymnastics were the only things she was good at, and when that was taken, she felt awful.

Doctors told Laura she would be able to walk and participate in some sports, but not diving or gymnastics. During her recovery, she had several specialists working to get her on her feet and back to school, but no one was talking to her about the emotional impact of the injury. Laura told me there were times when she would sit in her bedroom by herself and just sob. At times her mother was home with her, but Laura did not feel comfortable opening up to her about her grief and devastation. By that age, Laura had figured out that her mother and father were not going to be able to comfort her the way she wanted. While she did not start smoking marijuana right away, as soon as she returned to school she connected with some peers who were heavy into drugs.

For years prior to her injury, Laura had been searching for ways to numb her emotions. She realized through her treatment for her addiction that she wanted to stop feeling because that seemed easier than sitting with emotions and not getting what she needed in return. Weeks after Laura returned to school wearing a bulky back brace under her clothes, she found herself experimenting with drugs. Of course Laura told me her intent was not to become addicted. She wanted to fit in, and she wanted to distract herself from the sadness of losing diving and gymnastics. I asked Laura what it was like to be high on drugs, and Laura told me she was hooked instantly. She knew that being high felt like an escape from her grief, loss, and anger. However, Laura did not know where to place these emotions. At the time of her injury, there was a lot of attention to her physical healing, but Laura said no one was talking to her about the impact of the injury on her diving or gymnastics.

I asked Laura what made her know she would not be able to return to either sport, and she told me the doctors said she would have to quit diving and competing in gymnastic meets. Laura told me she remembered feeling devastated, but at fourteen she was unable to process the long-term effect this would have on her.

I asked Laura what school was like when she went back after being homebound for over three months. She told me it was depressing. She said she had no friends and that she felt inadequate in school. The kids she became friends with on her diving team avoided her. Laura said they did not act mad, but they just did not know what to say. So Laura told me they just stayed away.

We talked in therapy about the multiple losses she suffered as a result of her injury: the loss of her identity, the loss of her confidence, the loss of a sense of community and belonging. When Laura got involved in the drug-abusing teenage crowd, she said that filled some of her void. Laura remembered having nightmares about the moment her dive sidelined her, but she never told anyone. Laura also remembered ruminating on the moments as the doctors stood by her bedside and said no more diving or gymnastics. She told me she was overwhelmed and at one point only saw the mouths of the doctors moving but would not let herself hear their words.

Laura's drug abuse quickly became all-consuming. As she went through her junior year of high school, she got suspended frequently, and she told me she was forced to go into rehab. Throughout her teenage years, Laura was taken to rehab eight times.

She said she would never forget when her dad came into her bedroom in the middle of the night after she had relapsed on heroin at the age of twenty-two. I asked Laura what happened, and she said her dad woke her up, handed her a suitcase, escorted her to a car, and had sobriety coaches drive her hours away from home to another hospital. While the experience felt traumatic, Laura told me it was the first time she realized the awful effects of her addiction. Not only did she lose her sense of purpose and feel lost, but she was also losing her relationships. While Laura did not have a tight connection to her parents emotionally, she loved them and did not want to lose them too. She would tell me that her parents were not mean; they just did not know how to talk to her about what she was going through. Laura did not blame herself for her parents' limitations, but she wished they had been different.

As I understood Laura's history with her injury and her family background, we could talk more about her drug addiction and the role it served. Laura was at a turning point when we met because she was yearning to have more in her life than a job and some good friends. Laura wanted an intimate relationship. Though Laura had worked on her sobriety for years and had been clean for six years when we met, she knew that could change if she acted on an urge.

We started to name some of her underlying issues as we knew her history of loss in her past. Laura told me that whenever she began dating a new guy, within a couple of months she would find a reason to break it off. She was terrified of loss and how she would cope with it. Instead of working through that fear subconsciously, Laura convinced herself, "This is not the guy for me." She told me she would get bored and disinterested as soon as someone showed her caring.

We identified the fear of intimacy as a trigger to going back to her addiction, and we discovered that her fear of loss came from the loss of her dream to be an Olympic diver or gymnast. One day when we were talking about the day she got injured, Laura broke down in tears. She was crying and inconsolable as she told me she felt like she had lost her childhood. I asked Laura what that meant to her. She explained to me that the injury was the thing that drove her over the edge. She said, "It was the only thing I had that made me feel good about myself, and boom, without any warning, in a matter of seconds it disappeared."

More than anything, Laura wanted to be sure she would never go back to her addictions. We talked about the pressure that would put on her to make a promise without any guarantee. However, I explained to Laura that the power of choice and all the work she was doing to understand the role of her drug abuse put her at much less risk of relapsing. I told her some stories of other patients I had worked with who had extensive addiction histories and how they remained sober for decades. We talked about the different types of trauma that led to their addictions, and I shared stories of patients with similar losses.

The most important step to saying good-bye to self-destructive coping strategies is to make a conscious decision to do whatever you can to stay clean. Once someone decides they want to live a life without numbing or avoiding their emotions, they can utilize healthy coping mechanisms. For example, when Laura had urges to get high, she surrounded herself with friends who understood her addiction. Sometimes Laura would go on hikes and reflect on her progress. As she climbed the hills in the woods, Laura told me she would think about what she felt like each time she relapsed. She explained to me that the memories of detoxing off heroin or even spending time in rehab facilities reminded her that she did not want to go back to that place.

GRIEVING WITH OTHERS

Most people who stay stuck in eating disorders, alcoholism, or drug addictions have the most difficult time letting go because of the grief that comes with their trauma history. Certain aspects of horrific experiences are more difficult to manage. For example, sitting with the undigested loss can be hard to tolerate. When I work with patients who have lost family members or partners suddenly, they talk in sessions about how their loss impacts them on a daily basis. As with any trauma, there are reminders of their loved one's absence. Holidays, birthdays, weddings, births of others, and illness are just some of the events that can trigger feelings associated with grieving. People also grapple with unfinished business or with not having an opportunity to have closure, and at times some of my patients hurt themselves the most when these feelings get activated. It is never comfortable to feel grief, especially when the loss is unimaginable or unexpected.

Unfortunately, when people go to a place of hopelessness and despair, they often find themselves disconnecting from their closest relationships. I have talked to many patients who have a decent support network, but they do not allow themselves to reach out to others. I remember many times when I was in the worst of my recovery work and feeling such a tremendous sense of loss for my past and my present. In moments I felt like there was no point in talking to someone else because they could not undo what I was feeling or what had happened to me. I chose to focus on not eating or sitting in a dark bedroom crying my eyes out because I just wanted to be left alone. I was so mad and distrusting of others. I found no comfort in hearing what someone else had to say.

My therapist encouraged me to reach out to her or some of my close friends. After months of living in isolation while working through my trauma, I realized I needed to be connected to others. I spent my whole life going through a multitude of horrible events alone, and in a way I was re-creating that same feeling of aloneness by not giving myself the chance to get support from others. The more I allowed others into my dark world, the less I wanted to starve myself or be alone. Looking back now, I believe that the support of close friends and colleagues kept me sane and moving forward.

Dana: Cancer Ravages Her Body While Her Best Friend Is Fighting Terminal Cancer

The idea of having others on the journey of recovery is something I try and pass on to any patients I am working with who would choose to suffer in their grief alone. Dana started counseling with me eighteen years after her dad died suddenly when she was just seventeen. She was at her senior high school prom. She received a frantic call from her mother during the dance that her father had been rushed to the emergency room and that she needed to come home immediately. Dana jumped into her car and drove over an hour to get to the hospital. She had no idea what had happened to her father since he had not been having any health issues.

Dana arrived at the hospital around midnight and walked into a room full of doctors and nurses while her dad lay unconscious in the intensive care unit. Her mother explained to her that he had suffered a major heart attack and needed to be put on life support. There was little hope as her father had no brain activity. Dana told me the whole experience felt surreal. Sadly, Dana watched her dad through the night and was with him as he took his last breaths.

Even though Dana was seventeen, she told me she acted like the family social worker. Her mother asked her what to do, and Dana told her, "Dad would never want to live life like this. Take him off life support." It was gut wrenching to bear witness to Dana's pain eighteen years after she had lost her father. I met her when she was thirty-six. While she appeared put together and fully functioning, she was barely making it. Dana developed a severe eating disorder months after her father died. She told me that her eating disorder was the only way she could stay in her body without falling apart. Dana resorted to bulimic symptoms, sometimes multiple times a day for years, whenever the feelings about her father were triggered. I asked Dana how her family coped with her dad's death. She told me that after he died it was like he never existed. All of Dana's family members on her father's side left her and her mother's life. They celebrated holidays, birthdays, her wedding, and the birth of Dana's two kids without anyone from her father's side present. I asked Dana how she dealt with the loss of her family on top of the death of her father. She told me she was numb to it. We talked a lot about how as soon as any feelings of grief appeared—anger, sadness, fear, or despair—Dana turned to her bulimia to try to push those emotions away. Dana had a decent relationship with her mother, she told me, but there was not a strong emotional bond between them. Even though they both lost the same person, each of them grieved separately. Dana told me her mother became depressed and never moved on after her husband's sudden passing. Dana said she had no interest in meeting another man and basically lived her life by working and then coming home and hiding in her house. When Dana got married at the age of twenty-six, she told me she lived a similar life.

Dana married her high school sweetheart. Mason knew Dana's father, so for Dana that connection was comforting. I met with Dana and Mason a few times to try to help them talk about her eating disorder and the role it played in dealing with her father's death. Both of them had tremendous insight into the long-term impact this loss had on Dana. However, neither was comfortable sharing feelings that deep.

After being in therapy for about two years, Dana's health took a drastic turn. She went for a routine mammogram at age thirty-eight and found out days later that she had breast cancer. The work we were doing took a sudden halt. Fortunately, Dana's eating disorder symptoms decreased significantly after she was in therapy for about a year. The cancer diagnosis came as a total surprise.

I had worked with other patients in the past who had gone through breast cancer, but this experience felt different. Dana was a young woman with two small children. One of her worst fears when she became a mother was leaving her kids' lives at an early age like her father had. Dana was diagnosed with a serious type of breast cancer. After her bilateral mastectomy, doctors said the pathology showed that she had triple-negative breast cancer.[3] Memorial Sloan Kettering reports that triple-negative breast cancers are harder to treat because they do not respond to drugs that target estrogen, progesterone, or HER2 receptors. Once she was diagnosed with this type of cancer, doctors told her she would need at least six months of chemotherapy. Dana had to take a leave from work and set up all kinds of extra support for her two young children.

Thankfully, Dana had already started attending a weekly therapy group I had formed in my private practice for trauma survivors. I had started this group about a year before Dana got sick. The group was composed of five active females who were recovering from all types of trauma: child abuse, domestic violence, life-threatening illness, abandonment, and loss of a spouse. I started running therapy groups in my private practice the year I started seeing patients individually. I wanted to create a space where survivors could support each other and find ways to manage with the fallout of their history. The conversations we had each week focused on setting boundaries in relationships, facing fears about intimacy, letting go of self-destructive tendencies, mindfulness, and containment of strong emotions.

When Dana found out about her cancer, I remember thinking again about how I had spent way too much of my recovery in isolation. Dana and I talked about all the surgeries and treatment that were ahead for her. But we also spent a significant portion of our sessions after the diagnosis talking about how to keep her connected with support. When Dana was first diagnosed, she was apprehensive of talking about it in group therapy. Another group member had just finished going through treatment for her cancer, and Dana did not want to stir her up. We talked about how Dana was worried too much about others, which at times stopped her from getting what she needed for herself.

It was powerful and very sad when Dana announced her cancer to the group. Sheila, the other group member who had just completed surgery and treatment for her cancer, looked at Dana with tears in her eyes and said, "You *will* be okay." There was silence for what felt like an hour after the two of them had that exchange. All the group members began comforting Dana with their words, and they also talked about their own histories of losing people to cancer. I explained to the group that as we got into our thirties and forties, most of us would have lost someone to this wretched disease. I shared this to connect all of us and to help Dana know that the group could handle her diagnosis.

Dana took a three-month leave from therapy and group to heal from the bilateral mastectomy. She returned to group after she completed her first round of chemotherapy. When Dana entered the room for the first time since her medical leave, her appearance was drastically different. She had lost all of her hair and appeared gray from all the chemotherapy. Initially I felt concerned about how this would affect Dana and the rest of the group members. Within seconds of her return, the group members embraced her. They commented on her very cool-looking hat and celebrated her being back in the group. Sheila asked her some questions about the surgery and offered her support with the side effects of chemotherapy. At one point I asked Dana if thoughts or feelings about her dad had surfaced during her cancer treatment. Dana was able to open up in the group about her fears of dying before her children grew up because of the early death of her father. There was not much the group members could say except to validate this as a normal concern based on her history. We did not dwell on the traumatic loss, but we made space in group for Dana to say when these fears began to take over. We also used this as an opportunity for other group members to talk about their own family members who had gone through a life-threatening illness and how that brought up more issues of abandonment. At times group members held back out of concern for upsetting each other. I took the risk of reminding everyone that we were in the group to speak as honestly as we could, even if it brought up feelings for others in the room. Therapy groups offer people the chance to process thoughts and feelings that most relationships cannot tolerate. The boundaries and safety were established when we first started meeting. For example, anything shared in the group needed to remain confidential. Members were required to attend at least two individual sessions monthly in addition to attending group.

A few months after Dana came back to group therapy she received more bad news. She was about to complete her fourth round of intensive chemotherapy when she found out her best friend of over twenty-five years was diagnosed with cancer. Before coming to group that week, Dana texted me. She told me about Melissa's cancer and said she was diagnosed with stage 3 lung cancer. Initially when I read the text I could not respond. I felt so sad for Dana and thought that no matter what I said it would not make a difference. I knew a lot about Melissa because Dana talked about their friendship and the bond their kids had with each other. Melissa had three small children the same age as Dana's two children. They lived around the corner from each other. They did everything together. They walked to school together, their families ate dinner together every Sunday, they celebrated holidays together, and Melissa took Dana to several chemotherapy and doctor appointments.

Moments after I received the text from Dana about Melissa's lung cancer diagnosis, I reached out to the treating psychiatrist, who was also my friend Heidi, to tell her the news. Heidi and I talked for a few minutes via text, and we discussed different ways we could both help Dana manage her fears and anxiety as she continued her journey through breast cancer recovery.

During the next six months Dana went through a couple of reconstructive surgeries and had to miss many more group sessions. We were able to have our sessions individually, so Dana kept me up to date about her recovery as well as Melissa's prognosis. At different points, group members reached out to her as a unit by sending group text messages and group emails. Dana and I kept talking about how to keep her connected to all of her support system, even when she had no energy to reach out. Dana's depression got much worse after she found out about Melissa getting sick. She was spending a lot of time in bed and would be up most of the night. I asked Dana what kind of thoughts interfered with her sleep, and she told me that the idea of Melissa not being on earth for her children bothered her more than her own cancer. Dana spent so many years after her father died grieving in silence. She did not realize how much pent-up emotion was coming into her consciousness.

As Melissa was completing a clinical trial, Dana's six months of treatment came to an end. Even though Melissa was fighting like hell to beat her cancer, the disease infested other parts of her body. Ironically, Dana and Melissa were receiving most of their treatments at the same hospital. Dana would laugh hysterically as she talked to me about the jokes between them about their terrible disease. They used to say to each other all the time, "We are such a hot stinking mess." While what was happening was not funny at all, their sense of humor kept them connected and kept them sane.

When Dana returned to group for the second time after taking a medical leave, she appeared much healthier. Her hair was growing back, her skin color was coming back to normal, and her weight was more stable. The moment she returned for her first group after missing several due to her surgeries, Sheila looked at her and said she knew something was really wrong. Dana just looked at all of us and started to sob. I knew about Melissa's cancer, but the group did not know.

As the tears continued to roll down Dana's cheeks, group members reached out with their words telling her it was okay to speak. All Dana said was that her best friend was sick too. Everyone in the room looked shocked. One group member said, "Are you actually serious?" They knew about Melissa because Dana talked about her many times before she got sick.

I jumped in and started talking with group members about what to do when we got such devastating news. I explained to Dana that even though she had been with the news for a few months, it might take a little bit of time for the group to process what she had just shared with them. As the weeks went by, group continued and Dana kept coming back. She was very quiet most sessions, and she did not seem present. One week another group member, Katherine, who had also suffered many losses of friends and family due to cancer, looked at Dana and said, "Do you feel guilty for getting better even though Melissa has gotten worse?"

For a moment the room was silent. Then Dana started to sob again, and she told us how devastated she was for Melissa's children. We were able to talk to her about the grief she felt in the present but also to help her talk about all the feelings emerging from losing her dad so suddenly at age seventeen. I also encouraged all the other members to share their undigested grief for loved ones who had passed away or left their lives. For a few weeks the group relied on each other to work through some feelings that had been left unnoticed. I asked the group what it felt like to share with each other so intimately, and everyone agreed it brought them comfort. One member talked about how she felt much less alone. She also talked about feeling less crazy knowing others had such similar experiences after burying their emotions for years.

A week after Christmas break, group reconvened, and Dana told us Melissa had been put on hospice. Her cancer took away her ability to breathe without an oxygen tank. Dana told us that she stopped treatment and planned to spend the rest of her time at home with her two children and her husband. We continued to talk in group about the guilt Dana felt for living in a healthier body as her best friend's life was ending. I wanted to help Dana work through these feelings as much as we could while her friend was still alive. One of the worst parts about her father's death was the guilt and unfinished business she carried around for decades. Other members of the group also talked about losses they had suffered and how they had been left with similar feelings.

Group members were able to connect about their emotions and how they turned to food, drugs, or alcohol to dampen their pain. One of the benefits of being in such an intimate group experience is that it allows people to talk about feelings that they cannot talk about with many others in their lives. When the mood of the group got really depressing, I tried to bring in the hope that comes from speaking about such deep, buried pain.

In May of that year, Melissa passed away. Dana called me on the weekend to tell me that Melissa had taken a turn. She reached out to me and a couple of her close friends who also knew Melissa. When I heard the news, I could not respond right away. Like I did when I found out about Dana's cancer, I reached out to a few colleagues to share feelings that were activated inside me. The thing I struggled with the most was how Dana could be going through so much loss at once, especially with her history of losing a parent as a teenager. It felt so unfair. After Dana and I talked about the funeral plans for Melissa, I walked around with a lump in my stomach. I wished I could change it. I wished I could say something to make Dana feel better about being past the worst of her cancer as she lost her best friend to that dreaded disease. I wished I could tell Melissa's children that they would be okay because they had so many family members, like Dana, who would look out for them.

I decided to go to Melissa's funeral. I asked Dana if that would be okay, and she welcomed my offer. The procession of cars felt like an eternity from the church to the grave site. Different family members spoke at the funeral, and Dana stood holding hands with her younger son the whole time.

I continued to see Dana for individual therapy for a year after Melissa died. The therapy group ended due to scheduling conflicts for many of the members. That stirred up more feelings of loss for Dana, but the group continued to talk via group text and met for lunch a couple of times over that year. As the year went on, Dana started telling me about Melissa's husband, who had reconnected with his high school sweetheart.

About a year after Melissa died, her husband announced that he was involved with a woman named Stacey. At first Dana had a difficult time accepting that he had moved on and was allowing another woman to enter the family's life. He started bringing Stacey to Sunday dinners. Dana's older child had a strong reaction at first. During one of the dinners, she abruptly left the table and Dana followed her up to her bedroom. Janelle, Dana's daughter, began hysterically crying, saying, "How could he be with someone else?" She went on to say, "What, now everyone just forgets Melissa was ever alive?"

Dana amazed me at how she responded to Janelle's grief. I asked Dana what she felt about Melissa's husband dating another woman. She was honest and told me she did not like it at all. But she was also able to accept that Melissa's husband was moving on. Dana told me that Melissa's husband had always been a relationship guy and that his children wanted their father to be happy. Dana also talked about her mother's reaction to her father's sudden death and looked at this as an opportunity to bear witness to another person who was grieving but wanted to keep living. Dana told me she had wished at some point that her mother would start dating. I asked Dana why she thought her mother had not allowed herself to connect with another man intimately. Dana told me it was because she was grieving in isolation. She went on to explain how her mother kept quiet about her pain and fears and made no space to live life in the present. Dana saw the toll it took on her mother and also on their relationship.

As Stacey began showing up more and more at family functions, Dana decided to get to know her better. Dana told me she began texting and having phone calls with Stacey. They talked about everything. They talked about Melissa. They talked about how sad it was that Melissa had died at such a young age. They talked about how it was for Stacey to be integrated into a new family only one year after the family had suffered such a terrible loss. Dana nearly brought me to tears every time she spoke about their strengthening bond. The truth was that Stacey and Dana had a lot in common. Both of them experienced trauma as teenagers, and both of them knew what it felt like to lose something and not have anybody to talk to about their feelings. Dana told me that she and Melissa had spoken about what she wanted for her husband if she were to be taken by the cancer. Melissa told Dana she wanted her husband to date and find a woman who loved her children. She did not want her children to live a depressing and lonely life. When Stacey opened up to Dana about feeling like she was intruding on the family unit, Dana reassured Stacey that Melissa would have been happy for her husband.

I noticed as Dana got closer to Stacey that she was more in touch with her emotions. She was more vulnerable in sessions, and she was talking to friends more about whatever she was thinking and feeling. One day Dana sat down with both of her children to ask them how they felt about Stacey. Dana's older child became upset immediately and started to cry. She had missed Melissa terribly and felt like Melissa was being made to disappear. Dana put her arm around Janelle and told her about the conversations she had had with Stacey about what she wanted if she were to die. That gave Janelle a sense of peace, Dana told me. Once Janelle knew what Melissa wanted, she was better able to accept the changes happening in the family.

While Melissa's death was one of the worst things that could ever happen, Dana and I talked about all the opportunities it gave her to go through this loss differently than ones she had experienced in her past. We talked about her eating disorder and how, through the entire illness, the thoughts of using it were barely present. At one point Dana asked me why I thought her eating disorder had stayed in remission. I told her it was because she was talking, feeling, and grieving with others. I talked to her about all the differences between the stories about her father's death and how she chose to approach this loss so differently. Dana understood the importance of doing the opposite of what she had done when she developed the eating disorder.

MISCONCEPTIONS ABOUT GRIEF AND GRIEVING ACCORDING TO HELPGUIDE.ORG[4]

1. The pain will go away faster if you do not face it.
2. It is important to remain strong while experiencing loss.
3. If you do not cry, it means you do not care about your loss.
4. Grieving should only last at most one year.
5. Moving on with your life means forgetting about your grief.

HEALING STRATEGIES FOR COPING WITH LOSS AND GRIEF AFTER TRAUMA

1. Talk to family and friends. Try not to avoid them, and offer guidance so they know how to best support you.
2. Go to your religious affiliation for support. Use the mourning rituals to comfort yourself. Pray, meditate, or go to services. Talk to the leader of your clergy if you feel betrayed by your faith.
3. Join a support group. Look for groups through hospice if you lost a loved one or a parent. Look for support groups for athletes who have been injured if you suffered a life-changing injury. Go to twelve-step groups such as Al-Anon (help and hope for families and friends of addicts). Find a support group for young teens if your child has lost a parent to an illness like cancer.
4. Find a therapist or counselor who specializes in treating trauma or loss. If your emotions associated with the loss result in you feeling worthless, hopeless, guilty, disconnected, or distrusting of others, it is best to get professional help.

5. Use social media for support. Look for social media sites for cancer survivors, abuse survivors, or loved ones who have lost a family member from sudden death. Find websites for people battling PTSD, depression, anxiety, or obsessive-compulsive disorder.

6. Continue to monitor your physical and psychological health. Nurture the part of you that is grieving by focusing on getting enough sleep, eating mindfully, and exercising. Try to avoid using substances to numb your pain.

NURTURING YOUR HURT SELF

1. Face your feelings. Go to your journal or dictate on a phone what you are feeling. Imagine responding to these feelings like you are talking to your best friend, partner, or child.

2. Find tangible ways to express your grief, such as journaling, scrapbooking, or reading old letters. Get involved in an organization that supports a cause you are recovering from. For example, volunteer or start a fund-raiser for cancer, child abuse, or drunk driving. Channeling some of your grief by taking action may provide you with some relief and comfort.

3. Do not minimize or question what you feel. Be kind to yourself and give yourself permission to feel any of the emotions associated with the five stages of loss (denial, anger, bargaining, depression, and acceptance). It is okay to go from stage 1 to stage 5 and then back to stage 3.

7

REAPING THE BENEFITS OF
YOUR RECOVERY

GREETING INTIMACY

Throughout the course of treatment, I ask patients what motivates them to stay on the path of trauma recovery. There are times during the recovery process that patients want to run away. When patients are uncovering the worst of their fears and feelings, some describe feeling agony like they have never felt before. It is important during these times to help my patients stay connected to their aspirations and dreams.

There were many times when I wanted to quit therapy. Whenever I worked through a new memory or realization about my past, I was overwhelmed with grief and despair. I left sessions sometimes and sat in my car sobbing. I would go back to therapy the next week and want to scream at Dorothy. A part of me felt like she was trying to torture me. Then my intellect kicked in and I could hear her asking me, "Why now are you letting yourself know this part of your past?" Each time she asked me that, the answer would be slightly different. However, the theme was the same. I wanted to live a full life. I wanted to feel love and know I could give it without being taken advantage of. I did not want to be so afraid of people. I wanted to become a mother and be someone's partner. I wanted intimacy physically and emotionally. It was that thought that helped me stay on the path and fight through whatever pain was surfacing as I worked through my abuse.

Amy: The Unexpected Loss of Her Husband

I remember my initial phone call with Amy. As soon as we started talking she started crying hysterically. I was not sure what was behind her pain at first, as she had such a difficult time getting the words out. I asked her why she wanted to start therapy now. She told me her son was worried about her. She went on to tell me that her husband had died suddenly of a heart attack six months before we talked. Rather than get into the details of her trauma, we set up our first appointment so she could tell me the story with me present. Within minutes of entering my office, Amy began sobbing. She described the phone call she received just hours after her husband's death. Amy was at work. Her college-age son came home from class and found his dad unconscious on the floor. He panicked and called 911. When they arrived, Amy's husband was already dead.

Amy went on to tell me that her son had called her screaming and asking her to hurry home: "Dad is dead, I think." We talked about what Amy felt when she first walked into her house and saw her lifeless husband lying on the floor. She told me she was in total shock. They had been married for twenty-two years. Amy said both were in good health. They ate mindfully, and both loved working out.

After her husband's funeral, Amy became a recluse. She stopped going to work. She stopped talking to her friends. She barely spoke to her son. Amy told me she did not want to go to therapy, but her son insisted she get help. He told her he felt like his mother and father had both died and wanted her to come back to the world of the living.

During our first couple of months of therapy, I sat with Amy and made space for her to express her feelings of grief. She came to session each week and cried. Rather than just sit in the sadness, I asked her to tell me about their relationship. She talked to me about several memories she had with him. We talked about her wedding day. We talked about when they found out they were having a baby. We talked about the day she gave birth and how loving her husband was throughout her pregnancy. While I never want someone to stay stuck in the sadness around their loss, I wanted to give Amy an opportunity to share what their life was like together.

After we had met around six times, I talked with Amy about her relationship with her son. She told me it was his anger toward her that made her want to get help and find a way to live with her incredible loss. I asked Amy what her son had said that made her realize she was stuck. Amy told me her son said, "Every single day since Dad died you act the way you did the day I found him dead on the floor." I was not exactly sure what that meant. Amy told me that every day for over six months she stayed in her bed, only got up to clean and make dinner, and then she went back to bed. She went on to tell me that anything would make her cry. She said there were some nights when they sat at the dinner table eating as tears poured into her dinner. Her son did not know what to do, and he was also suffering a huge loss.

Amy told me she realized she was letting her husband's death take her out of the world of the living. Repeatedly Amy would ask me how she was supposed to function with all the pain she was feeling. Then our therapy took a turn. I asked Amy what her husband would want for her if something ever happened to him. Actually, Amy told me they had talked about the possibility that something might happen to either of them. Neither had any health concerns, but they loved each other and wanted to make sure they both expressed their wishes for each other if something out of their control were to happen. Amy's husband had told her he wanted her to find love again if he were no longer on earth. He told Amy how much he loved her and that she should never have to live a lonely or empty life. He told her he believed everyone should have love in their lives, even if it happens more than once. Amy also told her husband she would want the same thing for him.

About four months into our work, I decided to refer Amy to my trauma therapy group. While we were doing the work that we needed, I thought it would help Amy to talk with others who had experienced a significant loss, even if it was not a partner. It was not up to me to tell her to move on and be open to finding love again, but I knew she wanted that. And I knew she took in the wishes of her husband because when we talked about what he said she did not disagree.

When Amy started the therapy group, there were a couple of other women who had lost parents at a young age and one of the patients had lost a child. When Amy came for her first group, she introduced herself and immediately after started to sob. Group members had no idea what she was grieving. With respect and kindness we all encouraged Amy to find words to speak about her loss. She was able to tell the group that her husband had died suddenly. That was all she could say the first night. As the weeks progressed, Amy sat quietly in her seat. She listened intently to other members as they shared, but she was unable to say more about her husband's death. Out of the blue, one of the members began confronting her about her ambivalence to share. Kathleen, the other group member, looked at Amy and told her she did not know why Amy decided to join the group. I supported everyone in the room who wanted to talk about what it was like to sit in group with someone who was not participating, but I felt heartbroken. Members were able to talk about having parents who were absent emotionally and being in relationships with their family members after someone died. Kathleen told Amy she felt like she was sitting in the room with her mother after her dad died. Kathleen talked in group about how her mother stayed alone for years after her father passed away. She told the group her mother never recovered from her father's death.

That seemed to light a fire as Amy realized she was not only missing out on living her life but that her son probably felt like he had lost both of his parents. She did not want that for him. One week the group asked her if she would ever consider dating again. When she joined our group, her husband had been gone for over a year. They were not telling her she had to feel pressure to date at that time, but they wanted to know if she was open to bringing love in when she felt ready. At first Amy got angry and defensive. Her voice got louder as she told the group she was never going to date again. Amy explained that her fear of losing someone else made it impossible to be open to loving again. Of course group members understood that feeling and supported Amy in talking more about that. Amy heard from other group members who got stuck in their grief and then found ways to bring intimacy back into their world.

Debbie spoke to Amy in group about the sudden loss of her father. She talked about her family life after her father passed and told Amy her mother left emotionally from the moment Debbie's father passed away from an aneurism. Group members supported Debbie and Amy as they interacted by listening and nodding in agreement. When Amy and I had our individual session after that group meeting, I noticed a shift. Amy was able to talk about her sadness for Debbie, and she told me she would never want her son to feel left by her again.

At this point in the therapy, Amy's husband had been gone for almost two years. Amy still cried every time someone even mentioned her husband's name. However, she started taking steps to move forward. We talked in our sessions and in group how to bring her husband with her as she took steps forward. I suggested she think about what her husband would say and how he would feel as he noticed Amy coming back into her present world. Amy always said her husband would want that for her, and she imagined him smiling down toward her when she started thinking about meeting men. We laughed in session as she told me about some of her husband's quirks, and we became teary when she talked about his compassionate and caring side.

After spending a couple of months talking in our sessions and group about what she wanted for her life moving forward, there was another shift. Amy came into sessions announcing she was going to start hanging out with some of her single friends. She decided to give herself permission to have some fun. When I asked her how that felt, she smiled. At times Amy talked about feeling guilty, as if she was cheating on her husband. Then we reminded Amy of what she shared in group and with me about how her husband would react if he saw her. She never described him as looking mad. Rather, Amy told me and the group members, "He is probably smiling away up there in heaven."

One day Amy entered session with this enormous smile on her face. I knew she had been going to go out with some friends between our sessions. I commented on how happy she appeared, and she told me she met a guy. We giggled and smiled as she described their first interaction. Amy told me there was an instant connection. She said he noticed her from across the bar and smiled. Then Amy told me he approached her and they talked for over two hours. His name was George. He did not lose his partner to death, but he had an extensive loss history with his parents growing up. Both of his parents had passed away from terminal illnesses when George was in his late teens.

He opened up to Amy about the devastation he felt for years after his parents died. He told Amy he turned to alcohol and became severely depressed for years. George did not have any kids. He was married at one time, but the relationship dissolved less than two years into their marriage. George spent over a decade drinking himself to sleep almost every night. When he turned forty years old, he hit rock bottom and went into rehab. When he and Amy met, he had been clean for eleven years. George embraced his sobriety, and he had committed to living a healthier life. At first Amy was fearful about his drinking history because she thought that if he relapsed she could lose him, too. Rather than stay in the fear, Amy and I talked about how she could talk with him more about her concerns if they decided to be in a committed relationship.

The next few months our sessions felt very different. There was joy in the office. When Amy started talking in group therapy about their connection, they celebrated this new relationship for her. At times Amy told the group members she felt guilty for being with another man. They just continued to remind her of what she had shared about her husband and his wish for her to be happy in life if he was no longer here. As the months went on, Amy and George forged a beautiful bond. They talked extensively about their histories of loss and comforted each other. One day Amy pulled out some pictures of her husband and shared them with George. Amy told him about their wedding, the birth of their son, and other memories that were dear to her. George shared stories about his childhood and his relationships with his mother and father.

Amy continued to attend individual therapy for the first year and a half of her relationship with George. Her depression and anxiety diminished significantly. She told me her son expressed relief as he saw his mother moving on with her life. He also told Amy he felt like he had gotten his mother back. George met Amy's son, and the three of them started spending time together.

I will never forget the day Amy came into my office and announced that she was engaged. Her eyes were sparkling as she proudly told me how he had proposed and she showed me her engagement ring. Once Amy decided she wanted to move forward in her life, intimacy came her way. She spent the next few months in therapy celebrating her newfound love. She talked about times when she and George would talk about Amy's first husband. On several occasions she brought tears to my eyes as she spoke about how George nurtured her through her grief. There were times when Amy was able to give George some of the same love back when he brought up feelings about his prior losses.

It was not until Amy gave herself permission to move on after her husband's death that she could tolerate a close connection with a man. Amy told me she thought that if her son had not pushed her to get some help, her depression would have gotten worse. She also believed she could have lived the next forty-something years of her life in hiding if she did not pick herself up and push through her grief. The loss of her husband changed her life, but Amy did not want it to ruin her remaining years on earth.

NO MORE FEAR

When I am working with patients who are recovering from un-imaginable losses, the fear of what will happen if they recover can hold some of them back. Survivors of childhood abuse, sexual assault, and domestic violence tend to grapple with enormous amounts of fear about speaking, even if the relationship with their abuser ended years or decades ago. The fear of what will happen when an abuse survivor speaks or breaks the silence holds so many people back from trusting others in a similar way.

For many patients I have counseled, their biggest victory comes from knowing they will not continue to replicate their history with their partners or children. Sadly, I have met some patients through the years who have missed their opportunity to have children. I have worked with a few men and women who did not get into counseling until they were in their late forties or fifties, and for them the possibility of having children was no longer an option.

I met one man when he had just turned sixty. He had an extensive therapy background, but he told me he felt like he had never faced his fears of being an abuser and therefore had not had children. He was heartbroken as he came to terms with his age and the chances of having a legacy. He had been abused by a priest for years and did not start speaking about it until he turned fifty. Rather than stay in the sadness and grief of what he was missing, he took his emotions and spoke to other people with similar histories. His advice was always the same. When he met people who had any type of abuse in their childhood, he encouraged them to get help. He was able to find some peace in his life losses by spreading the word to others that facing trauma could prevent them from missing out on having their own families.

Karen: After Extensive Childhood Abuse History, Faces Her Biggest Fear

Karen started therapy with me after she was diagnosed with a raging eating disorder. From early adolescence, Karen had struggled with her weight and with a binge eating disorder. When we met, she was very apprehensive about seeking treatment. I asked her why she chose to get help now. She told me her boyfriend and older sister convinced her to get help. Her health was deteriorating due to the longevity of her bingeing and from untreated depression and anxiety.

It took Karen a few months of attending sessions to begin opening up about her trauma history. When we met, she told me she had one daughter and one son, but she did not talk much about her life as a parent. She told me she left her husband when her kids were in elementary school.

Initially our sessions focused on getting her eating disorder under control. Karen reported that she was bingeing almost every day and that she worried about food almost every second of the day. When she was not bingeing, she was forcing herself to restrict her food intake. Every time she had a binge, she punished herself by skipping the next two or three meals. As our therapy progressed, we learned more about what triggered her depression and eating disorder. Karen began opening up about her marriage to Blake.

Karen met Blake when she was a senior in high school. At that time she was sixteen years old and he was twenty-six. They met at a restaurant he worked at. A year before they met, Karen was sexually assaulted by two boys at a high school party. She never told anyone. When we talked about it in therapy, it felt like it had just happened. She locked away years of shame and fear and had no idea how much it was still affecting her. Her eating disorder got much worse right after the assault. Earlier in her childhood, Karen's mom had died suddenly. Karen came home after school one day and found her mom lying on the bedroom floor. She called for help, and by the time the emergency team arrived at her house her mother had already died. There was no known cause of her mother's death. Karen's father refused to get an autopsy, so the assumption was that she had died from an undiagnosed heart condition.

When Karen and I spoke about her marriage to Blake and what she endured in that relationship, she also shared more with me about her grief after losing her mother. Karen told me she walked around for days in a trance. She said her father was undone by the loss and her older brother developed an addiction to drugs. Less than a year after Karen's mother died, her brother left home. Karen lost contact with him, and she told me her father did very little to try to offer help or any kind of intervention. Karen continued to go to school and was able to keep up with her schoolwork. Her life outside of school was empty. Karen told me she had very few good friends and dealt with inappropriate contact from the boys she was in school with.

When Karen started high school, her self-esteem and trust in others had diminished. At times she tried to reach out to teachers and counselors for some type of guidance. Her father was not talking with her about healthy relationships with men. He was not talking to her about how to protect herself and what consent meant in a sexual relationship. Karen also told me he did not express concern about her self-hatred or inability to take care of her body. Karen attributed his absence to the lack of parenting he had experienced in his own childhood. She also felt like his devastation over losing his wife took hold of him. I asked Karen if he ever went to grief counseling for the loss, and she said that at times she had begged him to get help but he had refused.

We talked about Karen's lack of support after the assault in high school. She told me the fear of telling took over. Karen said the boys told her that if she spoke a word they would come after her and her father. She continued to go to school and do what was expected of her, but she told me she felt like a black cloud was following her everywhere she went. She wanted to trust people and was still interested in having a boyfriend. She was terrified about ever having sexual contact with a male after the rape, but she still wanted a best friend or a person who could be her number one.

One day Karen went to a local restaurant with a couple of acquaintances. The person who was serving them instantly showed Karen attention. When Karen went to pay the bill, Blake had left his phone number for her. She told me this was the first time a guy expressed interest in her without commenting on her physical body. Blake and Karen started dating instantly after they met. Within two months of meeting, Blake started asking Karen if she wanted to move in with him. She was still a minor, and he was twenty-six years old. When I asked Karen what her dad thought about this relationship, she told me he was too busy working to even know they were spending so much time together. Reluctantly Karen started having sexual contact with him within the first couple of weeks of dating. She told me she wanted him to stay in her life, and she assumed that if she said no Blake would leave.

Six months after they started dating, Karen found out she was pregnant. She was devastated. She told me they did not use protection because Blake refused. Karen was unable to use birth control because she was told by her doctor not to take it due to other health issues. For the first few months of her pregnancy, Karen stayed in hiding. She moved in with Blake at the end of her first trimester. She told me her dad had had it, and he told her to go live with Blake. He was fed up with her lack of presence at home and just sent her away. He had no idea she was pregnant.

She went to school and work and told no one about the pregnancy. I asked her how Blake reacted when he found out, and she told me she did not even tell him until her belly popped. I asked her why she kept such a secret from him. Karen began to share with me incidents when he became physically violent. She said that on numerous occasions he hit her, berated her, and threatened her. She knew that eventually she would need to tell Blake she was pregnant. Karen decided to call her dad one day and tell him. From what she told me, it did not go well. Karen said her father was ashamed of her and told her to go figure it out with Blake. Karen walked out of her house feeling stranded and alone.

She had nowhere else to go. I asked her if she thought of talking to a friend or an adult at school. Karen told me she felt scared and figured that everyone would react similarly to her father. She continued to live in silence.

Karen went back to Blake and spent the next four weeks of her pregnancy living with her secret. At one point Karen said Blake commented on her weight gain. At that point she felt she had no option but to tell him. Surprisingly, Karen told me Blake was happy at first. But she said that did not last very long. As the months went on and Karen was more pregnant, Blake made fun of her and told her it was her fault she got "knocked up." Karen said the kids at school began to comment on her belly and that the only people who really showed compassion were a couple of her teachers. At this point Karen had resigned herself to the idea that she was having a baby and that she was going to be raising the child on her own. I asked Karen if she had planned to go to college, and she told me that was one of the worst parts about getting pregnant. Karen was working toward going to college to get a degree in genetic counseling. She had always been interested in that line of work and had some family members who were unable to conceive, even with fertility support.

Karen delivered her son, Douglas, right after she graduated from high school. She stayed home with him and had no outside support. She told me she had a couple of friends who showed concern, but they were too young to give her what she needed emotionally and physically. I asked Karen how things were at home once she had Douglas. She told me that during the first year of Douglas's life the abusive episodes became more frequent.

One day after Blake physically assaulted her, she went home to her father's house, hoping he would be more supportive now that she was also a mother. Unfortunately, her father did not take any steps to get Karen or her baby to safety. He just told her that she needed to go back to Blake's house and work it out with him. Sadly, Karen got pregnant a second time when Douglas was fourteen months old. At that point she had just turned nineteen. I asked her what kept her going back and forth between the abuse and the isolation. Karen told me she loved her son and would do anything for him. She decided it was her job to do whatever she could to protect Douglas from Blake's rage. She explained to me that it seemed better to stay with Blake so that she could make sure he did not hurt her. At that time Karen had no access to family support or domestic violence organizations that may have helped her to safety.

Karen gave birth to her daughter, Allison. Karen told me there was an incident when Blake started to go after Douglas, who was just five years old at the time. She said that was what propelled her to grab her things and get out of the house. She showed up at her father's doorstep with her two children. Karen said her father finally realized how turbulent her home life was, and he told Karen to live with him. Her father did not suggest that Karen take any legal action. Karen spent the next five years living with her father and her two children. She went back to school and took some college classes. She found herself a job at a hospital working in the billing department.

Karen said that while the job was not her career aspiration, it gave her more stability, income, and benefits. She was able to move into an apartment after living with her father for over five years. We spent some time in therapy talking about her life with Blake and the impact that abuse had on her. Karen acknowledged that she had lost her voice before she met him. She told me the rape several months before she met Blake had affected her in more ways than she could ever imagine. She did not know at the time how little she valued herself.

We focused a lot in our work on helping Karen rebuild a sense of self and grieve for all her losses: the loss of her mother, the loss of her adolescence, the loss of hope for her career and future after being a teen mother. I saw Karen in therapy for about four years before she was hit with some more horrific news.

Karen called me one night and told me her daughter had said that she was sexually abused by Blake. It took me a minute to get any words out of my mouth. Tears were coming out of my eyes all over my sofa as Karen sobbed on the phone. Once I found my words, we developed an action plan. For years Karen was terrified to go to the police when she was being abused by Blake. When she did speak up, she felt disbelieved by her father. Her mother was no longer here to talk to her.

When Karen came in for session after that phone call, I could feel the fear in the room. It was like we were sitting in the middle of a war trying to find a place to feel safe. All of Karen's buttons were activated, and she was having flashbacks, panic attacks, and insomnia. Rather than stay stuck in the trauma, I tried to help Karen focus on the hope that was coming out of this tragedy. She had lived years of her life in total fear. She had been shown by many people during her adolescence that people did not care about her or take the appropriate steps to help her recognize the danger she was in every day that she lived with Blake.

I was relieved for Karen that she was able to take action as soon as her daughter revealed the abuse. Karen called the police, and investigators arrived at her house within hours of the report. We talked about the fear she felt after telling, and I suggested she tell everyone she knew at work and at her daughter's school about this man and make sure he went nowhere near her daughter ever again.

The reporting process and investigation went on for months after Karen found out what had happened to her daughter. The idea that fear would no longer stop her from doing what she needed to do to help her daughter was our main focus. Karen finally understood that the fear Blake had instilled in her had paralyzed her for many years. At this point she was taking the steps she needed to protect herself and her family. She realized that the work she had been doing in therapy before she learned about her daughter had helped her find her voice.

At times our sessions were gut wrenching as Karen came in and told me about where she was as the investigation unraveled. One day Karen started hysterically crying the moment she entered my office. She started telling me about the part of her that should have made her get away from Blake and that she felt like this bastard had "ruined the lives of two people." She was referring to herself and her daughter. I sat with Karen and tried to reframe her thoughts by explaining that Blake had ruined *some* of their lives, but she was taking steps now to end the wrath of Blake's wrongdoing. Karen was doing whatever she could to break the cycle of abuse that had followed her generations before she was even born. Before her mother died, she learned about her childhood and that she too had suffered multiple traumas. Karen did not understand the impact of her mother's abuse because she had died long before Karen was ready to have those kinds of conversations.

We continued to talk about the importance of what she was doing for her daughter. She was giving Allison the choice to speak. She believed Allison. She took Allison to therapy every week and also participated in some of the sessions. Karen was giving her daughter things she never had after she was sexually assaulted and lived with an abusive spouse. She was creating a space where Allison could share her fears and be reassured that her mother would be there for her no matter what. Throughout the investigation process, Karen and I worked on finding ways for her to cope with the flashbacks, panic attacks, nightmares, and depression that came with this devastating news about her daughter.

We brought her current boyfriend in for some sessions to help them communicate and find ways to support Karen. We did a lot of cognitive restructuring of her thoughts. For example, when Karen would go into self-loathing, I told her to talk back to that part of herself as she would to her best friend. We helped her find outlets to release some of the emotions in her physical body. Boxing, yoga, and even taking walks with her two dogs provided her with more space to express years of pent-up pain. As soon as Karen told me about Allison's abuse, I suggested that she go out and buy a notepad. She was getting clobbered with flashbacks of her own abuse. Karen also needed to find a way to keep track of all the details and memories Allison was sharing with her.

When someone goes through the process of reporting childhood abuse, it can be extremely stressful and slow. I was determined to help Karen continue functioning in her job and have a somewhat normal daily life as the process unfolded. As she went down this journey with Allison, we constantly evaluated her support system. There is no such thing as too much support. The fear instilled in Karen could surface at any moment. We could not prevent Karen from having that feeling, but there were ways we could combat the emotion so it did not consume her.

TRUSTING LOVE

No matter what kind of trauma someone suffers, the most common struggle my patients report struggling with is trusting love in an intimate relationship. Surviving a sudden loss, being in combat, having a parent walk out in childhood, abuse, and sexual assault all leave people feeling stranded or abandoned. These experiences also result in fear about letting love in. When I work with patients who are trying to have close, intimate relationships with partners or spouses, they talk in therapy about the constant battle of believing that love is real and will stay. When something terrible happens, defense mechanisms kick in from the second it occurs.

Patients talk in therapy about all the memories and feelings that come up when they are trying to connect with a person they have brought into their lives, sometimes years after the trauma occurred. The best part about being a witness and guide to all of these patients is watching them reap the benefits of their recovery. Some have found their way into safe, healthy relationships. One of my patients who worked years to overcome anorexia, sexual assault, and violence found a person she could love and accept the love back.

Cassie: Lived for Years with Anorexia and Sexual Assault by a Boyfriend during Adolescence

I met Cassie when she was sixteen years old. Her father reached out to me after she was discharged from an intensive day program for anorexia and panic disorder. Cassie spent months in a partial hospitalization center after her eating disorder had threatened her life. Her weight dropped rapidly when she was a freshman in high school. Prior to her eating disorder, Cassie was an active all-star athlete. She played basketball and was one of the star high school players in her district.

When we met, Cassie appeared to be happy and acted as if nothing was wrong. She talked about her stay at the partial inpatient facility and claimed that all they did was encourage her to eat and restore her body weight. She said the group therapy was focused on decreasing her anorexic symptoms and helping her learn how to manage her panic attacks. We talked about what kind of thoughts or feelings triggered the onset of her anxiety. She described sports and basketball as her only identity, which put more pressure on her to try to be perfect.

Cassie told me her social network was limited. She had made a couple of really close friends in middle school, but she said that those relationships had dissolved. Her freshman year of high school was a disaster. She told me she felt like she had no friends. She said she put a ton of pressure on herself to be a perfect student. Her home life was lonely and disconnected. Cassie lived with her dad and stepmom from a very early age. She told me she did not feel comfortable talking with her stepmother and that her dad was always at work. They were struggling as a family financially, and Cassie picked up on that from a young age.

During our first year in treatment we talked mostly about her eating disorder thoughts and about reducing the number of panic attack episodes she had. Her body image was out of proportion to who she actually was. Cassie told me she thought she was fat, ugly, and disgusting. The flags immediately went up in my brain as I knew she was describing the thoughts that are behind feeling shame. I had such a difficult time imaging how she could feel this awful about herself. When we spoke about the role of her eating disorder, Cassie was able to identify that she was trying to find a way to numb her shame and insecurities.

Cassie had panic attacks before playing basketball games. She said they became more frequent when she was a freshman in high school because she was the youngest member of the varsity team. The coach focused on her more than some of the other players, which she said also made her feel uncomfortable. College scouts were already expressing interest in her. Cassie's dad wanted her to get a scholarship so he could afford to send her to college. Cassie had dreams of being a pediatric nurse, and she knew that the only way she was going to be able to go to college was if she played basketball for a university. We talked about how she felt about having to decide about continuing a sport years before she was even going to be leaving for college. Cassie figured out that part of her eating disorder also came from feeling like she did not have a choice. While she loved the sport, Cassie told me there were some drawbacks to being a varsity player. She said it limited her from making new friends and getting involved in other extracurricular activities. Cassie wanted to be more than a great basketball player. She said she wanted to be in student government, and she also wanted to work once she was sixteen years old.

At the end of her freshman year of high school, she began dating a high school senior. There were not many boundaries around contact, so Cassie spent several days a week with him when she was not involved in sports. I began feeling concerned, as I noticed her anorexia was getting worse after we had been meeting weekly for about a year. She began dropping weight and seemed more shut down. She was benched from playing basketball because the doctors said her heart rate was low and her weight was not stable. Oddly, Cassie seemed relieved to not be on the court playing with her team. That confirmed for me that this part of her life meant more to others than to her. At one point I asked her if she thought that she needed to be sick to say no to basketball. She adamantly denied that notion, but I knew it was still possible that she felt this was her only out.

Cassie was reserved whenever I asked her how things were going with Brian. She would smile and look embarrassed. I figured she did not want to talk much about that relationship with an adult. Cassie did not have a mother to open up to, and her dad expressed little interest in anything she was doing socially with boys or girls. It struck me that Cassie was struggling with a serious eating disorder while saying she was in a happy relationship. I sensed that she felt stuck but continued to remind myself that all I could do was make myself available to her to tell me her feelings. I could not force her. Rather than put emphasis on her connection with Brian, I just told her she could feel free to talk about anything involving dating whenever she was comfortable.

When I noticed the increase in her symptoms, with her permission I reached out to her father and stepmother. I asked them to come in for a session to discuss what might be causing Cassie's relapse. Cassie was apprehensive about having them involved in our sessions, but because of her age, if her health was in danger, I needed to have communication with them.

When her father and stepmother entered the room for the family session, Cassie chose to sit in the seat farthest away from them. She barely spoke as I talked with them about my concerns and asked them if they had noticed. Cassie's father was defensive and angry. He started berating Cassie in the session, telling her she should be trying harder to get better. At one point he shouted, "Why can't you just knock it off and eat?" I took that opportunity to try and educate him about the complexities of recovery and that we were working on identifying the root to her current symptoms. I also suggested some books that her father and stepmother could read on the recovery process. Cassie's stepmother was very quiet during the session.

When I meet families of eating disorder patients, I try to explore their relationship with food and their bodies. I tried to engage Cassie's stepmother by asking her what she thought about Cassie's decline. She hardly looked at me when I spoke to her. I noticed she glanced over at her husband, Cassie's father, before answering any of my questions. She did admit to having an eating disorder during college but claimed that was in the past and that she was recovered. However, she also spoke about her concern about weight and trying to stay within a certain limit of caloric intake on a given day. I asked Cassie what she felt about her stepmother's rigidity with food, and Cassie just smiled and said, "I am used to it." While we did not make a lot of progress in the family session, I was enlightened by the dynamics. Cassie's father was clearly in charge of this family, and Cassie's stepmother did not seem to have a voice.

Once I better understood the environment Cassie was living in, I felt able to ask Cassie more about how her living situation affected her in her relationships. I asked Cassie if she would be willing to bring Brian in for a session. She jumped at the opportunity. She told me she always wanted Brian to understand her eating disorder, and she told me she did not know how to explain it to him.

I will never forget that session when Brian came with Cassie. They walked into the room and barely looked at each other. I introduced myself to Brian, and he turned away and did not shake my hand. They sat down on my very long green sofa, on opposite ends. Cassie had the pillow over her stomach, and Brian stretched out his legs as if he was sitting at a bar. It was difficult to get started because I could feel the tension in the room. It did not feel that different than when Cassie had her father and stepmother in. I was caught off guard because I never heard Cassie complain about Brian. She did not tell me much about their relationship. I wanted to help Cassie figure out what was causing her to rely more on her anorexia, and I had already learned some about her home environment.

Once we began to have a conversation, Brian started asking me all kinds of questions about Cassie's therapy. He was older than her, but that still struck me as odd. Why would her teenage boyfriend be that concerned about why she was seeing a therapist? Cassie stared at my rug as he asked me why she was coming to see me every week and when she would be done with therapy. I told Brian why people with eating disorders are in treatment long term and that this was normal, especially if someone had a history of being hospitalized for the illness. He looked at me with an angry stare and did not seem open to what I was saying. I gave Cassie an opportunity to respond to Brian's concerns. I asked her, if she had anything she wanted to add after I gave Brian some psychoeducation about recovery. She paused, looked at him with what felt like terror, and said no thank you.

The remainder of the session we spoke about their relationship. Brian spent several minutes complaining about Cassie's lack of interest in being sexually active. Cassie was about to turn seventeen years old, and Brian had just turned twenty. I was shocked that he would bring this up in a session. It felt like he was talking about what he wanted and he had very little regard for her feelings. Rather than lecture Brian about sexuality, I left space in the room for Cassie to try and have a voice. Unfortunately she barely spoke the entire hour. At one point I felt like Cassie was sinking into my sofa. As we went through the session, it felt like she was shrinking into a person who was barely visible. All of my red flags were popping up in my head, and I was relieved I would be seeing her for our next session later in the week.

Cassie came back three days later for an individual session. I started by asking her how she felt the couple's session with Brian had gone. Surprisingly all she said to me was she thought it was fine. I was completely perplexed. Rather than jump on her, I decided to talk with her about what I noticed. I told her I sensed that she felt afraid to speak or be heard. Tears welled up in her eyes, and she started losing eye contact with me. I told Cassie that if there was anything that bothered her about the session or their relationship, she could tell me.

After that session we continued to work on her symptoms with the eating disorder. Cassie's health continued to decline. About six weeks after the session with Brian, I gently confronted Cassie and expressed my concern for her health. I told her we needed to have her parents come back in for a session to start talking about reentering the partial program. She burst into tears as I started explaining to her that sometimes people need to go back for intensive treatment a second, third, or fourth time. Cassie began to sob as she told me she would do anything to stay out of the hospital. I agreed to give her a couple more weeks as long as she complied with my calling her parents and went to see her pediatrician. Cassie chose that option.

She came back to session the next week and announced that she wanted to break up with Brian. She began telling me about some very concerning incidents. While I felt sad for her, I also felt relieved. I sensed she was holding on to some secrets that were contributing to her overall decline. Cassie told me she was afraid to break up with him because she was worried he would get mad. We talked about what was behind her fear of ending a relationship. I talked with her about choices and asked her if she felt like she needed to be sick to tell Brian she wanted to end their relationship. At this point she could not make the connection.

Cassie was able to break off their relationship the following week. We continued to have sessions, and I noticed that her eating disorder urges and anxiety were decreasing. However, her mood seemed depressed. As the first few months went by after the breakup, Cassie was withdrawing in our sessions. She was making less eye contact and talking less about her feelings. I asked her a few times what was bothering her. I did not know if she was grieving or questioning her decision to break up with Brian. Each time I asked her if something was on her mind, her eyes would well up with tears, but she had very few words. My gut told me she was keeping something secret, but I felt like she needed the space to decide when and how to share her thoughts and feelings. By this point we had been in a relationship for three years, so I just told her in different ways she could talk about anything that was bothering her.

A week after I checked in with her again about her apparent sadness, she walked into the office, and before she even sat down she said, "I need to tell you something." I sat quietly as she began reporting incidents when she was mistreated and sexually assaulted by Brian. It was agonizing for Cassie as she told me about times when Brian would force himself inside of her when she was asleep. As she was telling me about one of the episodes, she cut herself off and asked me, "Can you be sexually assaulted by your own boyfriend?" We began to talk about consent and what that meant. I explained to Cassie about respect and boundaries and that even with someone she had been intimate with she had the right to say no.

Our therapy took a turn as over the next several sessions we processed what had happened to her. We talked about her right to report Brian and also about seeking medical attention to rule out any conditions as a result of the assaults. A part of me just wanted to wrap my arms around her and go to Brian's house and blast him. I was trying to imagine what it was like for her to be hurt so badly by someone she loved. I understand the complexity of abuse in an intimate relationship. Part of Cassie felt enraged by his behavior, and another part of her thought Brian had the right to treat her that way because she agreed to be his girlfriend.

As we talked more about the abuse in the relationship, Cassie noticed a pattern. He sexually assaulted her either when she was asleep or after they had been drinking. He found the times when she was the most vulnerable and took advantage of her. I asked her what she would think and feel the next day. Cassie told me she felt physical and emotional pain, and she would often vomit after it ended. Even though her body and mind were sending her a clear message, she slipped into denial and pushed these memories out of her consciousness. She continued to go to class and work and do all the things she had done before they began dating. It was a struggle for Cassie to let go of the guilt and blame she placed on herself. She kept asking herself why she would stay with someone who treated her so badly. I told Cassie this was normal for most sexual assault survivors. She could not comprehend how you could be raped by your own boyfriend.

Over time Cassie got in touch with her rage. I remember during one session she began screaming and crying and saying, "How could he do this to me?" She bumped into him at a college party. Cassie said that when she saw him that night the lightbulb went on. She had flashbacks of several times when he had assaulted her in their dorm room, at his house, and at her house. She allowed herself to reflect on how she felt when it ended. She also remembered how she survived the attacks. Cassie told me she would lie on the floor or wherever they were and close her eyes, praying it would end. She had a recurring thought every time he forced her to do sexual acts she did not want to do. Cassie said she heard her own voice saying to him, "Make him stop." On some occasions Cassie told me she fought back and told him to stop. When she resisted, Brian would restrain her, put his arms around her neck, or hold her head down onto his groin.

Brian did not just abuse her sexually. He also emotionally attacked her when they were in public settings. Cassie said he made fun of her when they were with friends and that he called her derogatory names. She said her friends would just stand there and not know what to do. She told me she lost friends as a result of their relationship. A couple of her girlfriends confronted her about Brian's public humiliation and pleaded with her to break up with him. Cassie said that after a while they pulled back because they could not tolerate someone treating her so poorly. Cassie never spoke in therapy about the loss of these friendships.

Over the course of months we continued to process her experiences with Brian and the impact her relationship with him had on her life. Amazingly, Cassie did not regress into her anorexia as she opened up about the abuse. Rather, she began to understand that her eating disorder was her way of telling herself something was really wrong. At the time, she felt like she needed to hold on to the symptoms because they were the only thing she had control of. I asked her if her father or stepmother ever considered that there might be something going on with Brian that was related to her eating disorder. She told me they never asked her about Brian. She said they did not really like him, but they showed little interest in trying to check for her safety or happiness. Cassie was not only being abused by Brian; she was also feeling abandoned by her family.

In a way, her eating disorder became the voice she did not have. Losing weight causes alarm, and part of Cassie was hoping people would notice if she disappeared. Sadly, that is not what happened. I offered to have a family session to talk with her father and stepmother about their connection, but Cassie declined. She did not feel they would react appropriately or give her the support she needed. Part of her recovery was about setting up a larger support system. She pushed herself to connect with some peers and eventually found her way back to the friends who had left earlier because of how Brian had acted.

Bravely, Cassie reached out to two of her friends and met them for coffee, and she told them everything. Both of them grabbed her and hugged her, and they told her they were so sad she had gone through all of that by herself. They were able to affirm the part of Cassie that lived with the secret.

We continued therapy, and Cassie began feeling close to her friends. She was looking for a job right after graduation. Within weeks of getting her bachelor's degree, she got a job on a pediatric unit in a hospital. She was not talking about dating. She was not interested. Actually, she was terrified. She did not trust herself or anyone else in that type of connection. I reminded Cassie that the more we helped her heal from the sexual assaults, the more likely her feelings would shift.

The longer Cassie was away from Brian, the better she felt about herself and others. She was loving her new job and her sense of independence. She struggled with her body image, so we continued to work on placing those feelings back on earlier experiences of feeling used and abused. It took Cassie several months to work past the shame and place the responsibility of her abuse on Brian. When she got stuck in self-blame, I would ask her if her best friend told her she was being treated like that, would she judge her? Of course Cassie said no. Cassie found her way back to the gym, but she used it for health reasons. During her eating disorder, she forced herself to work out and run, even when she felt too weak to stand up.

Now the gym was about relieving stress, getting back in touch with the athlete from her school days, and making friends. Cassie smiled when she talked about taking classes and getting stronger. When she had flashbacks of Brian hurting her, we would talk about how she could picture taking her strong arms and legs and pushing him to the ground. We created many metaphors to reframe the feelings and shift to the side of her that was enraged.

We worked on boundaries and trust and how she wanted to feel different if she were to begin dating. By total surprise, Cassie entered session one week and told me she had met a guy. I was shocked. Her eyes were glowing. She decided not to talk about David until she had gone on a few dates with him. She wanted to give herself a chance to check in with herself and how she felt before sharing with others.

When she first told me about David, I saw these twinkling lights shine through her eyes. I could feel how happy she felt. We talked about some of the dates they went on. Cassie said she never had been taken on a real date before she met David. We laughed as she told me about how he planned romantic outings and opened doors for her. She was about to celebrate a birthday after they had been seeing each other for almost three months.

As more time went by, Cassie opened up more about the contrast she felt with her ex-boyfriend and David. Once she felt more secure in her relationship with David, she confronted some excruciating memories with Brian. She told me about the times when Brian had forced himself inside of her. She told me about the times when he had forced her to give him oral sex.

As Cassie spoke more about these memories, her body image deteriorated. She slipped back into anorexic thinking. She was having urges to restrict herself of food and do anything she could to lose weight. She expressed fear and frustration about the return of these self-defeating thoughts that had been dissipating for over two years. Rather than stay in the shame, I told Cassie we could use this information to help her understand what part of her abusive past she had not digested.

Cassie rarely cried in session. She came from a family where showing feelings was not acceptable or received well. When we talked about the flashbacks of sexual assault, her eyes filled up with tears. We figured out that she was having eating disordered thoughts because part of her still believed she did not deserve to be in a happy, healthy relationship. Once Cassie was able to put this into words, I responded by teaching her how to talk back to that part of herself. I asked her if her best friend said she did not feel worthy of being treated well, what would Cassie say to her? Of course she told me she would want the best for her friend. I challenged her by asking why she did not feel like she should have just as much happiness as her best friend. That helped Cassie separate from the shame and reframe how she felt about having David in her life.

Our therapy for the next year was a combination of grieving for the younger Cassie who was hurt so deeply and a celebration of her progress. In the time I knew Cassie, I watched her evolve from a scared, safe, frail teenager to an empowered, grown-up, successful woman. She got her first job as a pediatric nurse when she met David. She talked about work and how happy she was to be doing a job that she felt passionate about.

There were a few incidents when family members and colleagues berated and disrespected her. Cassie came into session one day and told me about a fight she had with a family member. She described the argument and told me the names that she was called. In the past, Cassie told me she would hold her head down and wait for the moment when the fight ended. Not this time. Cassie got in his face and told him, "It is not acceptable for you to talk to me like this," and walked away. She told me she was shaking as she left the room, but she felt proud and relieved for knowing she had a voice. There were a few times when our sessions focused on her transformation after giving herself the right to stand up to people who mistreated her.

Cassie also became an advocate for other women who were being abused by their partners. She joined websites online and told her story. She gave advice to other women and helped them find their way out of the situation. Cassie accepted that her recovery was a process and that she had no control over when memories surfaced. She learned how to use the memories to manage her life in the present. She understood that the part of her that was remembering the abuse was to help her continue to digest or work through another part of her history. Cassie also talked with other women about their struggle with eating disorders, and she told them about the connections she made with her anorexia and living in fear and silence. I felt inspired by Cassie and her determination to live a full life. I felt proud to know her and had no doubt that her future was going to be full of many more victories.

HEALING STRATEGIES AS YOU REAP THE BENEFITS OF YOUR RECOVERY

Strategies to Manage Fear, Trust Love, and Use Self-Compassion

1. Validate your fear. It is normal to feel afraid of having intimacy if you were hurt by someone physically or mentally. When you feel fear, place it. Ask yourself if these feelings match the relationship or situation you are currently in. For example, has this person or circumstance proven to you that you are in any type of danger, physically, sexually, or emotionally?
2. Talk about your fears with your partner, your therapist, your therapy group, or your friends. Keep reminding yourself you are not alone in this feeling.
3. Develop a strategy for when the fears take over. If you experience high anxiety or panic attacks when you try to connect with someone or be present in a new situation, implement grounding techniques. If you are doing CBT or DBT, grab your notebook and use the tools of mindfulness for reframing your negative thinking, for example, if you hear yourself saying something like, "He is probably going to be just like my abuser," or, "Once she finds out more about my past she will never want to stay." These are thoughts that lead to feeling fear. Ask yourself if you are with a person who is demonstrating a lack of empathy or who places judgment when you open up to that person.
4. If you are having flashbacks during intimacy, talk with your partner about how to create safety in that setting. Tell him

or her what you need. If there are certain physical sensations that trigger flashbacks, talk about that. Bring that into
your therapy. Journal about it. Meditate on the feeling and
imagine putting it on a bookshelf as a way to place the fear
and remember that it is based on the trauma, not necessarily
what is happening in the present.

5. Use self-compassion when you question your worth. Are
you struggling to feel worthy of the benefits after allowing
yourself to work through your trauma? Think of some ways
you can love the part of yourself that feels the most unworthy. Imagine talking to your younger or hurt self. Talk to
yourself the same as you would to your best friend, daughter, mother, partner, or friend. Grab a journal and write
yourself a letter. Remind yourself of the work you have to
do to get to the point in your life where you feel safe and
happy.

6. Continue to talk with friends about your story and which
parts you are most determined to reclaim. Did the events or
experiences you survived take away your childhood? Did
they make you feel like you could never love another person? Did they make you feel like you would never feel safe
in your environment? Consider the people you are connected to in the present and write down how they are different from the people who hurt or betrayed you.

Quotes of Self-Compassion[1]

1. "If your compassion does not include yourself, it is incom-
plete." Jack Kornfield
2. "Lack of forgiveness causes almost all of our self-sabotaging
behavior." Mark Victor Hansen
3. "Self-acceptance is my refusal to be in an adversarial relationship to myself." Nathaniel Brand
4. "The privilege of a lifetime is being who you are." Joseph
Campbell

5. "There is only one success—to spend your life in your own way." Christopher Morley
6. "It's not your job to like me, it's mine." Byron Katie
7. "To be yourself in a world that is constantly trying to make you something else is the greatest accomplishment." Ralph Waldo Emerson
8. "Accept everything about yourself—I mean everything. You are you and that is the beginning and the end—no apologies, no regrets." Clark Moustakas

Quotes I Have Created throughout My Recovery

1. "Screw trauma; it is not all of who you are."
2. "Treat yourself as if you are your own best friend; do not accept any less."
3. "Take the shame and kick it to the curb."
4. "Life is awesome when we take the bad and turn it into something amazing."
5. "Keep loving yourself, no matter how bad you feel."
6. "Do not give up. It will get better over time."
7. "Recovery is a process. Keep finding ways to manage all the crap feelings and know they will pass."

8

MY LIFE IN RECOVERY

LETTING GO OF THE WISH

My recovery did not start until I was ready to face the truth about the first twenty-two years of my life. I did whatever I could to push away years of secrets from my childhood because I did not want to think that the people who were supposed to love me the most could hurt me so deeply. I became completely independent around the age of twenty-three. I rented an apartment and went back to school for my master's in social work. I had no idea where this degree would take me, but I knew from a very young age that I wanted to help others. I got my master's degree in less than two years from Rutgers University and started working in the mental health field.

Less than a month after I graduated, I got a job at a well-known eating disorder inpatient program. I worked as a counselor and ran different types of therapy groups for patients. The group therapy focused on underlying causes and symptom management for people struggling with all kinds of eating disorders. My second day on the job I listened to a young woman talk about her history of sexual abuse. She was getting ready to be discharged from the program, and she shared in the group how her history of trauma was the main reason she developed anorexia and bulimia. As she was sharing her history and her mother's ritualistic abuse patterns, I could feel my body leaving the room. It was like I was sitting on the chair, but my body and heart were no longer present. I left work that day and I got lost driving home. I had lived in that area for three years and I knew how to get home. The feelings of dread and fear were overpowering, and I lost my sense of reality.

When I got home that day—and many other days after I continued working at that rehab center—I found myself going into a trancelike state each time I returned to my apartment. I had two kittens eagerly awaiting my return, and I remember walking into my bedroom, getting into bed, and falling asleep each day after work. My self-care suffered. I started skipping meals because I felt sick and the idea of eating was repulsive.

After about three months, I realized that something was really wrong in my life. Whenever I went home to visit family, I experienced similar feelings to the day I sat in group with that patient who reported a history of sexual abuse. Pulling into the driveway caused me to freeze. Other times I would walk into my house, go up to my childhood bedroom, and begin to sob. I kept asking myself, "What is wrong with me? Why am I like this?"

I continued working at the center for several more months. I connected with some mentors and began opening up to them about my dread of being near family. I also started talking to them about my history with dating men. I had never had a consensual sexual relationship, and I was almost twenty-four years old. That did not make any sense to me. When I spoke with one of my colleagues about a session I had with two angry parents, she looked at me and told me maybe I should consider seeing a therapist. At first I was furious. "Why is she telling me I need to see a therapist?" I wondered. There was another part of me that knew she was giving me appropriate advice.

I met Dorothy when I was twenty-five years old. I found her after hearing a colleague at my job talk about how wonderful she was and that she had amazing boundaries. She was known for teaching her patients how to set limits and take better care of themselves. Dorothy had a lot of experience working with eating disorder patients and at one point served as a local representative for the New Jersey chapter of ANAD (the National Association of Anorexia Nervosa and Associated Disorders).[1] While I did not identify with having an eating disorder, I knew I had an unhealthy relationship with food, and I had loathed my body ever since early childhood.

I called Dorothy and set up an appointment. I was terrified. I canceled the day before I was supposed to meet her. Then I called her back and said I wanted to meet with her. I walked into her house and knew in my gut this was the place I needed to be. In our first few sessions we spent time getting to know each other, and she asked me some questions about my issues with food and my body image. She asked me about my relationship with my parents and sister. I said, "I have a great relationship with my parents." I told her I did not get along with my sister. I minimized the amount of fighting that went on in my house and did whatever I could to gloss over that topic.

Dorothy asked me what brought me to therapy, and I just told her I needed help managing the feelings that were getting triggered at work. She did ask me about dating relationships and if I ever had a serious boyfriend. I felt shame throughout my entire body when this subject came up. I looked at the floor in her office and I told her I had dated some but had never met the person who was right for me.

I spent the first six months in therapy talking about work, and I opened up a bit about my terrible relationship with my body and food. I told Dorothy I hated my body and would do anything to change it. She tried to help me understand where that was coming from. I just told her that for years the kids at school made fun of me. I had a curvy figure, and the boys especially made comments about my sexual parts.

When I was around fourteen years old, I went on my first diet. I lost several pounds in a couple of months and received compliments from family and friends. The kids at school still found things to bully me about. They made fun of my hair. They made fun of how I danced. They made fun of how I talked. But the positive attention I got for the weight loss drove me to develop restrictive eating habits for several years of my later childhood.

I told Dorothy I could relate to the patients when they talked about their fears of letting go of their eating disorders. I also had a history of bingeing, but that word would never come out of my mouth in Dorothy's office. I thought about it when I sat in session, but the embarrassment kept me silent. A part of me was screaming at myself to let this part of my history out, and at times I had flashbacks of binge eating as a young child when we were having a session.

About a year into my therapy, a close family friend who was a mother figure to me became gravely ill. I told Dorothy about Karen's cancer, and her eyes filled up with tears. As I described the progression of her illness and my grief about her impending death, Dorothy had tears rolling down her face. That was the first time I felt like someone heard me and really cared about what I was saying. I left that session wishing I could make Dorothy my mother. I spent so many years of my life yearning for a compassionate, nurturing woman to hear me, and I felt like I had finally found her.

When Karen passed away, I called Dorothy. She did not try to fix it. She listened. She told me she was so sorry for my loss. All I wanted to do was run to her house and ask her for a hug. I felt guilty for feeling that way, and I continued to keep these thoughts to myself. I had no idea where they were coming from.

A few weeks after Karen died, I went to my childhood home. As soon as I entered the kitchen I burst into tears. I felt like a bomb had just fallen on my head. I felt like I was never going to stop crying. I do not remember how I got back to my apartment that night. I just remember feeling like I could never step foot back in that home. I called Dorothy as I was panic stricken. She was just as confused as I was. I spent the rest of that week sitting with these feelings of dread and shame. Then the floodgates opened.

I called Dorothy when I knew she had left the office. I left her a cryptic voice mail. I said, "Someone went inside of me." As I spoke those words, I could feel in my body what I was saying to her in words. I had never experienced body memories before, and that sent me into a crisis. We began meeting three to four times a week for months. I left my job at the eating disorder rehab.

Once Dorothy and I had spent some time in sessions processing my buried secrets, I was able to tell her who raped me. My earliest memories went back to preschool. I could remember standing on the playground thinking, "I wonder if everyone has people going inside of them when they are trying to sleep." As I spoke more about my abuse, I got more overwhelmed and flooded. Dorothy suggested I start writing down my memories. I kept a pocket-size notebook with me at all times. The flashbacks came at any time and any place. I would write down what I remembered and leave her phone messages starting to speak the memory.

As I let myself explore my feelings and know my truth, I distanced myself from family members. I was not ready to speak to anyone except my therapist. I was heartbroken when my family just let me go away without any concern about what was happening to me. After a couple of months, I told them I was remembering sexual abuse. At one point I confronted each of my family members. My parents just sat on the sofa, clutching onto each other, and said to me on many occasions, "Our memories are not the same as yours." They adamantly denied any type of abuse and questioned my therapist. At one point they insinuated that Dorothy was putting these memories into my head.

For months I questioned myself. I felt like the worst family member for saying such awful things about biological family. I went through a period in therapy after I confronted my family trying to take back all the memories I had shared with her. Sometimes I was so angry and confused that when I got to Dorothy's office I would lash out. I also had a difficult time leaving her office. I would say to her, "How can you let me leave like this?" She offered me the option of going to a more supervised setting to help me feel safe as the feelings and memories resurfaced. Then I felt abandoned by her. I felt like she was giving up on me.

There was another part of me that understood the role she played in my recovery. I reminded myself that even though I was in touch with childhood pain, I was an adult and I had choices about how to move forward. I knew I needed to let go of my wish that I had the perfect family. I knew I needed to accept that by letting myself know the truth I was making space to have a better life moving forward. I wanted to stay in my apartment and continue fighting for myself in my environment. I did not want to go to a hospital.

As the therapy got more intense, I developed more strategies to stay grounded and keep myself out of the denial. I got a dog, a Cavalier King Charles spaniel named Chloe. I needed something besides myself to take care of. I needed to keep the nurturer in me alive. I needed something to keep fighting for. We became the best of friends in an instant. I got a bag for Chloe, and she began coming with me to my therapy sessions. She sat very quietly in her "house," and at the end of each session, I opened the top of her bag so Dorothy and I could greet her and she could help me walk out the door. Chloe would hop out of her bag and wiggle her adorable furry body, wanting some love from us. She actually looked like she was smiling.

When I slipped back into denial about the abuse, I would have flashbacks, stop eating, isolate, and have body memories, which sometimes went on for hours. I could feel the intrusion, ripping pain, and burning in different parts of my body. I knew exactly what my abuser had done to me. At one point I told Dorothy there was not a part of my body he did not violate. The abuse always took place in my bedroom when I was sleeping. Over time I was able to talk to Dorothy about what I did to try to protect myself at night. I would put layers of pajamas on. I would cover my entire body, including my mouth, with a blanket. I would leave the door ajar so I could hear where people were in my house. At times I would try and keep myself awake so I could guard my doorway.

Part of my struggle to trust what I was feeling was that I was never awake when my abuser entered my room. Some of my memories were foggy and unclear. I remembered things out of sequence. Usually I remembered different incidents from the end to the beginning. For example, I would remember what I would feel the day after I was raped, before I remembered the actual violation. I had many memories of finding evidence in my bedroom that I had been assaulted. I recalled the physical pain, the fear, and the shame. If I saw things in my bed or my pajamas, I would try and get rid of the evidence. When I would look in the mirror as I got dressed to go to school, I could see the sadness in my eyes.

As the memories came flooding back into my consciousness, I began feeling more curious about what people thought and if anyone suspected I was being abused. I started with my pediatrician. I called the office almost twelve years after I was discharged from their care and asked for my medical records. In my early childhood through my early adolescence, I was diagnosed with several urinary tract infections. I wanted to see if the doctors ever documented any concern or had suspicion of abuse.

When I was leaving to drive to the pediatrician's office, I grabbed Chloe so I could have her with me. I felt sick to my stomach but was also able to tell myself why I was going back in time. I wanted to know if anyone had known what was happening to me. I was trying to find different ways of staying in the knowing and stop questioning myself. I got a hold of my medical records, which were filled with notes from different visits over the course of eighteen years. Between the ages of four and five, I was diagnosed with three urinary tract infections. I rummaged through those papers hoping someone had questioned why this was happening to my body. It was devastating to see the diagnosis and no documentation of possible abuse.

After I gave myself some time to be with this information, I called a therapist I had seen during seventh grade. I was sent to him because I had attempted suicide. It was the first day back at middle school after Christmas break. I had a terrible day. The kids were bullying me about my weight and my hair. I felt like the world would be a better place without me. When I got home from school, I went into the bathroom and looked at all the pills in the medicine cabinet. A part of me knew I did not want to be dead, but I saw no way out of the pain. The thought of living another day or going back to school seemed impossible. I knew I was not okay and not safe, but I did not allow myself to know about my abuse.

I grabbed the pills and poured a handful of them into my mouth. After a few minutes, I got scared. Did I really want to die, I asked myself. I picked up the phone and called my best friend at the time. Within minutes the ambulance arrived at my house. The first thing I asked the EMT workers was whether they had to call my parents. I was more concerned about getting in trouble than with what kind of damage the pills could do to my body.

The emergency room doctor entered my room and asked me why I took the pills. I told him I hated my life and felt like the world did not need me in it. He gave me a lecture about suicide and told me that if I ever attempted to hurt myself in that way again, I would be sent away for months to a hospital. My family was in the room as the doctor reprimanded me. He advised my parents to get me a therapist.

I saw that therapist for months. Not once did he ask me if there was anything wrong at home. We spoke mostly about the kids at school and how to handle them when they were pushing me around. I talked to Dorothy and told her I wanted to get my records from that therapist. The next day I called his office and asked to have a copy of all my records. My eyes bulged out of my head when I saw he had diagnosed me with dependent personality disorder. DPD is an anxious personality disorder, and the main symptoms are when people need constant reassurance, advice, and support.[2]

I learned about personality disorders in graduate school. I was taught that a patient could not be diagnosed with this type of disorder until the age of eighteen. I was only thirteen. I read through my therapy notes and saw no indication of concern about abuse. I brought these records into my next session with Dorothy. I thought that if my pediatrician and therapist did not suspect abuse, maybe I was making the whole thing up.

After going through a stretch of time feeling hopeless, I decided to take Chloe and myself to the Poconos. I wanted a change of scenery, and I wanted to do something adventurous. We checked into our bed-and-breakfast inn and got back into my car. I found a steep hill a mile from where we were staying. Chloe and I had taken many hikes the few years I had her. We loved to play in the snow. We arrived at the bottom of the hill, and there were layers of snow and ice all around us. I was not equipped with appropriate footgear, but I was determined to take the hike. I wanted to feel strong.

It took us about an hour to get to the top. We would get about ten steps ahead, and then one of us would slip down the hill. Rather than get frustrated, I just laughed at myself. I was building strength, and I wanted to see how I felt once we got to the top. When we arrived at the top of the hill, I turned around and could see views of the sun setting and the mountains all around us. I felt like the universe was giving me a huge hug.

I stood there for several minutes and began imagining all of my mentors and my therapist standing around me and cheering me on. I felt like I had an army behind me. That hike created a shift in my mood and allowed me to develop this strategy of building strength anytime I wanted to give up, which at times was often. Dorothy had tears streaming down her face when I told her the story about my trip with Chloe up the mountain.

I did intense trauma therapy for a couple of years before I allowed myself to dive into horrific memories of my adolescence. I fought with all my might to not allow this part of my history to be so. It was one thing to accept that I was abused as a younger child, but I could not fathom how someone could rape me once I was in an adult body.

I began to put this part of my past into focus as I talked with Dorothy about the gynecological issues I had beginning around the age of fifteen. I was having erratic menstrual cycles, and I would obsess about getting my period. I actually prayed I would get my period. Dorothy and I talked about point in time during my sophomore year of high school when I was in the spring musical,

Grease. It was the first time I had a major role in a play. I fell in love with theater, and I started to pursue a professional acting career around the same time I was in the spring musical.

I started going to New York City and auditioning. I got a talent manager. My thought was that if I booked a movie, I could move out of my house. I was called into producers' offices to read for leading roles with Bette Midler and Cher. Both movies were considering me to play the part of their daughter in these films. While I loved acting, auditioning was a nightmare. I had no confidence, and I put tremendous pressure on myself to book these roles. I was also worried about my body and why my menstrual cycle was so unpredictable. I learned about how people get pregnant in the sixth grade, so I knew if I was not getting my period I might be pregnant. I was not dating. I was a virgin. At the time I convinced myself that I just had a messed-up body. I never allowed myself to consider I might have gotten pregnant as a result of abuse.

One day I walked into session, and I told Dorothy, "That bastard got me pregnant." I gave myself a few weeks to put this memory together before I spoke about it in therapy. I remember pulling into a parking lot to go to a workout class when the light-bulb went on about what happened when I was performing one of the leading roles in *Grease*. I called Dorothy and left her a voice mail. I told her that my perpetrator had gotten me pregnant and just started sobbing. Whenever I left Dorothy messages, I would tell her if I wanted a callback or just to hold on to the message until our next session.

I sat down in our next session and began telling Dorothy how my costumes all got tight on me as we went through production. Some of my costumes had to be replaced. I blamed myself by saying, "You should not have eaten so much, and this is your fault." I had a good friend in the show, and after about eight weeks of not getting my period, feeling tired and sick, and gaining weight, I whispered in her ear, "Do you think there is any chance I might be pregnant?" She laughed and said to me, "How can you be pregnant if you are still a virgin?" I just stared at her and decided I was just being stupid. We talked about my fears about boys and sex.

She was also a virgin, and we felt proud that we were holding out for the right guy.

Two weeks after I said something to my friend Dianna, the show went into production. It was our fourth show, and I was onstage with the entire cast. It was the scene in *Grease* when Danny Zucko and Sandy meet. We performed a joyous chorus number, and a split second after it began I glanced down at my belly. Shock and terror filled my whole being as I saw blood all over my skirt. A big red circle appeared out of nowhere. I continued performing the scene, and the second the song ended I ran backstage and screamed for help. I had thirty seconds to get back onstage before the pajama scene with the pink ladies.

I told Dorothy the story, and we talked about the confusion, the isolation, and the shame I felt for getting pregnant and not knowing it at the time. We talked about my frustration in not having proof. At that age, I did not have a gynecologist, so I was left to figure out what was going on without any medical or adult attention. Many of my family members were in the audience that night. I even asked my parents if anyone noticed what had happened to me. They just looked at me and smiled and gave me flowers.

I opened up more to some of my colleagues in the psychology field after I told Dorothy about the pregnancy and miscarriage while performing onstage. I called two of my colleagues who became very good friends, Beth and Jane. Both of them called me back immediately and left voice mails for me filled with love. I connected with them after attending a workshop they cofacilitated on banishing shame.

My world was growing with more connections. I had opened my private practice for psychotherapy, and I was feeling proud of the work I was doing, even under stressful circumstances. I was seeing patients who were recovering from eating disorders, and some were talking to me about their own history of abuse. I continued to see Dorothy several times a week. We talked about work and how at times patient stories triggered some of my shame and pain. Rather than run from the feelings, I used the situation as another opportunity to process what was going on in my life. I did a lot of journaling, and when I felt lost in my work with patients, I reached out to my colleagues.

Once I talked about the pregnancy and miscarriage, I knew in my heart I could not change my past. Abusive episodes take place over the course of minutes. I was pregnant for weeks. When I was seventeen years old, I remembered announcing at the breakfast table that I had not gotten my period in one hundred days.

After I took the time I needed to work through the memory of having a miscarriage while performing in *Grease*, I started talking with Dorothy about another incident that happened when I was getting ready to leave for college. It was the summer after my senior year of high school. I was running every day and trying to lose weight before I went to college. On a hot July morning I took myself for a run around the block in my neighborhood. I was the only one home at that time. After about fifteen minutes I felt cramping and pain like I had never felt before. I forced myself to keep running, and after about two minutes I became dizzy and fainted onto the sidewalk. I lay there in a curled-up ball trying to figure out what this pain was in my stomach. I kept saying to myself, "Get it out of me." I tried to pick myself up and walk home, but I could not move. I got scared. I started screaming for help. A woman who lived in the house across the street from where I passed out came running toward me. Immediately after I told her I was home alone, she called 911. They arrived, and the first thing they asked me was, "Is there any chance you might be pregnant?" I was adamant that I was a virgin and that that was impossible. As one of the emergency workers was giving me orange juice, I pleaded with her not to call my parents. I was still seventeen, so she explained that she was required by law to call one of my guardians.

When I arrived at the emergency room, the nurses asked me again, "Is there any chance you may be pregnant?" I told them that was not possible. When my mother arrived at the emergency room, the nurses asked both of us if they could give me a pregnancy test, and my mother said no. As I was lying on the table surrounded by emergency room personnel, the pregnancy ended. The doctors cleaned me up and sent me home. There was no discussion of what had just happened. I went home that night and sat in the bathtub for a long time. I comforted myself and my body. Then life went on. I did not give it another thought. I was overwhelmed with what had happened and had no way of framing it because I was not letting myself know about the abuse. I knew I was leaving for college in about six weeks, and I decided that leaving home would make everything better. I was not taking birth control, so I knew that it was certainly possible that I could get pregnant.

There were times in therapy when Dorothy and I took a therapeutic pause. At times I felt inundated with the trauma. I talked to Dorothy about the grief I felt each time I had memories. I explained to her that I was also grieving for not having support as I went through these miscarriages. It was terrible to live through this, and sometimes it felt worse to know as an adult that if I had people who knew about the abuse at the time, these pregnancies might have gotten me rescued. During these pauses, we sat together and focused on my grief. I told her what I wished I had gotten at the time. I remembered feeling alone, confused, and ashamed. I wanted somebody to take care of me and tell me it was not my fault. Rather than stay in these feelings, we worked in therapy to shift back to the present. I described my pregnancies as missed opportunities. I knew that if I had said something at the time, I would have to know how it happened. I expressed my devastation about never being able to go back and prove I was pregnant.

After more months of being in intensive therapy, I allowed myself to talk about another unwanted pregnancy. I was in my early thirties, and I started thinking more about having children in my future. I knew I needed to talk about this experience with Dorothy because the aftermath of this miscarriage took a toll on my physical health.

It was late October during my sophomore year in college. I was getting ready for my midterm exams. It was the first time in my life I felt like I had a group of friends. I became a member of the Delta Phi Epsilon sorority. I was in my dorm room that morning getting ready for class. After a couple of minutes in the shower, I began having painful cramping, broke out in a sweat, and fell down. Somehow I managed to get myself out of the shower and back into my dorm room. I landed facedown on the floor and started screaming out in pain. I was having symptoms of contractions. At the time I had no idea what was happening. My roommate came back from her class, and she found me on the floor. She grabbed some towels and asked me what she should do. I just asked her to stay with me. After what felt like hours of being in excruciating pain, I took myself to the bathroom. The fetus appeared in the toilet as I went to the bathroom. I told Dorothy what I saw and how overwhelmed I felt. I flushed the toilet as fast as I could to try to get rid of the evidence.

I called home to tell my parents something awful had happened. I was still having pain a couple of hours later. Rather than advising me to go to the health center, my parents told me they could not help me and to just go to class. I grabbed hold of my pink Delta Phi Epsilon sorority sweatshirt and went on with the day. I prepared for my midterm and amazingly was able to get an A on that exam. I went on with my life. For a few days after I told Dorothy, I went into a deep depression. I considered suicide. I called the counseling center to make an appointment. When that day arrived, I did not show up for the session. I wanted a mom to wrap her arms around me and get me help. I knew I needed to see a doctor, but it seemed pointless to tell someone that. The ending of that miscarriage stayed in my body for weeks.

I told Dorothy that I drove back home a few times during that semester to see my gynecologist without telling my parents. I fantasized that she was going to tell me I had ovarian cancer. When I went to see Dr. R, she asked me each time, "Is there any chance you might have been pregnant?" I kept telling her no. I told her the same thing I told the emergency room doctors, that I had never had sex before. After my third appointment with Dr. R, she suggested I have a procedure called a laparoscope to figure out why my body was not functioning properly. When I was in the recovery room, she informed me and my parents that she had to do a D and C. It did not make sense to me. At that time I did not know what this procedure was for. I went back to my childhood home to recover from the surgery. I lay in my bedroom by myself and stared at the walls. It felt like the longest week of my life. I wanted to give up.

When the feelings from this memory consumed me and sent me into despair, I said to myself, "Shari Botwin, you made it! If you can get through that miscarriage, you can definitely get through the feelings you buried." I took Chloe on a bunch of hikes, to the beach, and to New York City. I did a ton of journaling. I also found my way to yoga class. I had never done yoga before. I found ways to be in my body and talk back to the body memories when they were consuming me. Over and over I told myself, "You do not need to keep reliving the physical feelings of your abuse to remember."

ON BECOMING A MOM

As more time went by and I was getting older, I began thinking more about the life I wanted. I continued seeing Dorothy two or three times a week for years. I kept seeing patients and learned how to manage the triggers. Right before my thirty-fifth birthday, I was diagnosed with thyroid cancer. It terrified me. I realized my life would not go on forever. A part of me regressed into shame as I was getting ready to have surgery to have my thyroid removed. I decided that the reason I got cancer was because I spoke. I thought I was being punished for breaking my silence. I will never forget when Dorothy said to me, "It is not the speaking itself that is a problem; it is that it happened." It took me several days to digest this statement.

A few weeks after I had the thyroidectomy, I began to shift back into my anger. Rather than blaming myself for getting cancer, I got angry at myself for thinking I caused the cancer. While I never liked feeling angry, I found an energy in the emotion, and I used it to push myself forward.

Around my thirty-sixth birthday I went for my routine gynecological exam and talked to my doctor about fertility. She told me that if I wanted to have a child someday, I was getting close to the time when I needed to think about preserving my right to start a family. When I walked out of her office, I felt very sad because I still had not had a boyfriend, so how was I supposed to start a family?

A couple of months after that appointment, I started dating a guy exclusively. I reclaimed feelings I had never had with a man. I learned how to feel safe during sexual intimacy. I learned how to confront a man when I was upset without fearing for my life. At times the joy I felt took place of all the sadness. I realized how different it would be to be in a safe relationship. I felt hope!

Sadly, our connection did not continue. However, I forged ahead in my life and felt optimistic about dating. At times I felt shame about being single. A lot of my friends were married with children. I kept reminding myself that my path was different. I also learned to accept that my abuse took a huge toll on my adulthood. I lost my childhood to my abuse. I was determined not to lose my whole life to something that happened to me.

I noticed a shift in my private practice after I came back from being treated for thyroid cancer. I started getting more referrals from patients who had some type of trauma in their history. I looked at this as another opportunity to work through parts of my past left undigested. I had several patients open up to me about their trauma history months after they began treatment. Patients were describing feelings I had struggled with for years: denial, shame, rage, and grief. Many of them wanted it not to be so. I felt like I had so much in common with my patients when they talked about the self-hatred and blame as a result of what happened to them. I talked with them about different strategies for overcoming these feelings without disclosing my personal history. I respected the therapy boundary regarding self-disclosure. These sessions were not about me. Many trauma survivors jump at an opportunity to caretake, even in a therapeutic relationship. I took what I had learned from Dorothy and my colleagues and passed it on to patients if I felt it would be helpful.

When I turned thirty-eight years old, I began to panic about my future and starting a family. I was single. I was feeling grounded and had started to reap the benefits of my recovery. Life was getting easier. There were reminders every day about my past, but at this point I had mastered how to combat the feelings. I was still seeing Dorothy at least once a week.

Right after my birthday I went in to meet with a fertility doctor. I did not mention that I was going to see Dr. G to anyone except Dorothy. I gave myself time to build up strength, as I knew I needed to tell her about my abuse and my miscarriage history. I did not know what to expect, but I did not want to meet with Dr. G and walk out feeling like I had kept secrets.

We sat down, and Dr. G gathered my history. I took a deep breath and began sharing with her what had happened to me. I told her I was an incest survivor. I told her I had gotten pregnant at least four times between the ages of fifteen and twenty-two. I told her what happened the day I went running, the time I was performing onstage, and the time I was in my dorm room. She looked at me with sadness and respect. I asked her what she thought of my symptoms. Dr. G told me it sounded like I had had contractions during a couple of the miscarriages. We talked about my options for starting a family as a single woman. Dr. G informed me that she wanted to do a full panel of blood tests to rule out any type of disorders that could affect my fertility or ability to conceive a healthy pregnancy. She did the blood work, and off I went. I left her office and began feeling unfinished. I had just given her a full account of my past, and I realized I did not have any of my medical records from the gynecologist from my late adolescence.

I picked up the phone and made an appointment to consult with my former doctor, Dr. R. I had not seen her in almost twenty years. Dr. R and I sat down, and she pulled out all of my medical records. We went through the file, and I told her what happened to me. She said she had not suspected incest, but she had known I was keeping something from her. I nearly lost it when I read in the reports on different dates, "Patient denies any chance of pregnancy." It was in writing that I knew I was not making my past up.

A week after I met with my old gynecologist, Dr. G called me with the results of my blood work. She told me the blood work showed I had a genetic clotting disorder that caused miscarriages. She explained that the only way I could conceive and keep a pregnancy was if I gave myself daily injections of blood thinners. When I told Dorothy about what Dr. G diagnosed me with, I kept saying to her, "Now I cannot act like this is not so." I finally felt like I had proof.

I did not go back to Dr. G until right before my thirty-ninth birthday. When we met I sat down and told her I was ready to talk with her about my options. Dr. G explained the process of using fertility to conceive as a single woman. She spoke with me about the process and that it could be lengthy, emotional, and did not always work. I talked with Dorothy and a few friends about my plan to become a single-by-choice mother. At first some of my friends expressed concern for me. They asked me about finances. They asked me if I could have a child knowing I had no family members to support me. Dr. G knew about my lack of family support.

I talked with Dorothy for a few weeks about how I could surround myself with family by choice. I could pick the friends whom I wanted to be intimately involved with the process, so I did not have to go through another challenging life event feeling alone. The last thing I wanted to do was set myself up to feel abandoned. I worked for years in therapy learning how to not re-create my trauma. I was driven to have a different experience as I set forth on my path to become a mother.

For about nine months I went to Dr. G to create a miracle. I went through five cycles of fertility, which took place over nine months. Each time I found out I was not pregnant, I had to find ways to not make it my fault. A part of me felt undeserving of having a healthy pregnancy. Part of me blamed myself for the miscarriages. These feelings resurfaced every time the nurse called and said the cycle did not work. One of the worst parts of my abuse was that it led to many layers of shame. Anytime something bad happened to me, like my thyroid cancer, I felt like I deserved it. Anytime I was hit with disappointing news, a part of me felt like I did not deserve to have what I wanted because I spoke up about my abuse.

I remember the day I walked into Dr. G's office for what felt like for the hundredth time. I had been through four failed attempts to conceive. I was taking all kinds of fertility injections and giving myself daily injections of blood thinners. I was getting burned out and had started to feel like I was never going to have a baby. I was almost forty years old.

When I arrived at Dr. G's waiting room for the fifth attempt, a feeling of joy and hope took over me. I was sent back to the doctor's room where Dr. G was going to do the procedure. I spent almost two hours waiting in that room, as she was having an emergency of some kind with the patient next door. There were moments when I felt like I was going to scream because I was nervous and frustrated. I decided to look out the window, which looked out onto the city of Philadelphia. The sun was shining, and the sky did not have a cloud in it. I lay on the table, closed my eyes, and told myself, "Shari, it is going to work this time. You will see." Once Dr. G came into the room, this calm came over me. We spoke about lighter stuff as she did the procedure. I could hear her words, but I was more focused on what she was doing and what could happen as a result. I imagined that Dr. G was creating a life inside of me.

Sure enough, five days later I started showing signs of a pregnancy. I was overjoyed. I told my friend Sandy what I noticed in my body. She giggled and whispered in my ear, "I think it worked."

Two weeks later the miracle was affirmed. I took a home pregnancy test, which came out positive. I jumped up and down and ran to my dog Chloe, shouting, "Mommy is pregnant." Chloe started running all throughout my condo, and I was dancing in my living room. I called Dorothy and told her. I went back to Dr. G's office two days later, and the blood work showed that all the numbers were increasing, which was the sign that conception was successful.

The first five weeks of my pregnancy were amazing. I felt elated. I felt present. I felt nausea. All good signs that I was going to be able to have this baby. Around week eight my mood took a big turn. I began having the same symptoms in this pregnancy as I had when I was impregnated by my abuser. These feelings threw me into some dreadful flashbacks of being a teenager and not knowing what was going on in my body. I remembered the weight gain, the headaches, and trying to cover up my popped-out belly. I talked to Dorothy about these flashbacks and decided that these memories were coming back to help me accept the times when I was pregnant during the abuse.

When I went in for my ultrasound around week thirteen, I saw the fetus in my uterus. Minutes after I left that appointment, I had more flashbacks of what I saw during the miscarriage in my dorm room. I reminded myself that if I could get through those awful miscarriages alone and without any help, I could certainly survive whatever memories or feelings were triggered. It was not easy. I felt my gut wrenching for several days. However, I also made space in my heart and mind to move forward and take care of my body as this beautiful miracle continued to develop within me. I told myself every day I was pregnant, I chose this! I also thought about the injections of the blood thinners I was doing twice a day and thought to myself, "I must really want this."

The last two trimesters of my pregnancy were wonderful. I felt great. I was eating well, sleeping, and still going to the gym. During many of my workout classes I was dancing through them because I felt joy. I celebrated my fortieth birthday when I was twenty weeks pregnant. I loved sharing the news with friends, patients, and colleagues.

I had a great relationship with the doctor who was managing my pregnancy. Every time I went in for a checkup, he did an ultrasound. I got to see my baby boy moving, and I could hear him when he had the hiccups. At times it looked like he was dancing in my belly. I was ecstatic when I found out I was having a boy.

Andrew arrived in the early spring. My friend Sandy was in the operating room with me during the C-section. Before I even saw Andrew, Sandy started dancing all around the room, saying, "Oh my gosh, Shari, I see a baby!" It was one of the best days in my entire life. When the nurses handed him to me, I just cried. I stared at his tiny toes and fingers, and I could not believe this miracle was actually real. When we got home from the hospital, I spent hours talking to him, singing to him, and doing all the things mothers do when babies are infants. Chloe spent a lot of time sitting with us. My goal besides staying sane was to be present. I wanted to remember these precious moments forever.

When I went back to therapy, I talked to Dorothy about the transformation I was beginning to feel after giving birth. It was the first time in my life I embraced my history. I felt like my life was finally making sense. I knew I had found a way to stay hopeful during my abuse, but I did not know it was partly because I wanted to be a parent. I realized this was my opportunity to take my past and break the cycle of abuse. I could parent differently than I was parented. I could prove to myself that I could nurture and love a child, even if that was missing in my childhood. The biggest challenge during Andrew's time as a toddler was when he was diagnosed with viral-induced asthma. He was nearly two and a half years old.

Unfortunately, I was not able to manage his symptoms without the help of a specialist. Andrew needed to have nebulizer treatments, sometimes every four to six hours through the day and night when he was flaring. The thought of going into his bedroom when he was asleep to give him a treatment was terrifying. I did not want to scare him or force him to do something he did not want. I was able to reframe the idea and remind myself that I was going into his bedroom with the medicine to help him, not scare him.

He lay in his crib sound asleep. I had fifteen minutes to process all the feelings that came up as I held the mask to his adorable face. I told myself that what I was doing was helping him as he clutched onto my fingers during the treatment. The middle-of-the-night treatments continued off and on until Andrew was around four years old. The hardest part for me was seeing my very young self in my bed, trying to understand what was going on inside the head of my abuser. When I looked at Andrew asleep, I saw his innocence. I could not imagine how someone, especially a family member, could take advantage of a life so young. Dorothy and I talked about this concept several times, and eventually I realized more about what goes on in the mind of a pedophile. It sickened me. It also helped because I could make sense of this type of pathology. I began to feel bad for my abuser, that he could commit acts of atrocity to me for so many years and not be able to stop.

Having a child also helped me separate from the guilt I felt for being abused. As a parent, I could see how Andrew was helpless and trusting, no matter how I acted. He did not know any different. He needed me just like I needed the people in my family. I also learned from firsthand experience as a parent that small children do not have the words to express when something awful is happening to them.

Some of the best gifts of healing came to me as Andrew became a little older. When he started going to elementary school, his personality blossomed. There is not a day that goes by that I do not have flashbacks of being in elementary school. The second I enter the school building, I think about or remember another feeling from my past. I do not cave in to these memories. I allow myself to have them and ask myself what they have to do with my life today. Over time it has gotten easier for me to accept that the older Andrew gets, the more I will have to face the different aspects of my abuse during my childhood.

I still remember sitting at Back to School Night when Andrew started at his elementary school. The principal, Dr. H, stood at the front of the room with tears of joy in her eyes as she described the staff and her goals for the new school year. When I went into Andrew's first-grade classroom for orientation, I met his teacher,

Mrs. K. She was like a ball of bright energy. She was excited for the new school year, and she was ready to greet Andrew and all the other children as they started the next phase of their lives with her. As I was sitting with Dr. H and Mrs. K, I flashed back to several times when I was in first grade. I remembered sitting on my first-grade teacher's lap and how she would reassure me and make me feel loved.

There were many times when I walked through the hallways of Andrew's school, whether it was for a school event or to pick him up. On many occasions I watched Andrew skip down the hallway as Ms. L, one of the kindergarten teachers, would greet him or the school counselor, Mrs. W, would wrap her arms around him with a big smile on her face. These moments brought me back to the time when Chloe and I climbed up that big icy hill in the Poconos and the image of all my supporters standing around me. I knew Andrew was developing connections with many other safe, loving people, and that brought me tremendous relief. I knew he would confront challenges at times, just like most children. But I never had to worry about how the staff would treat him.

Dr. H was a kind, strong, loving woman who had no tolerance for unkindness or bullying. That also reassured me that Andrew's school environment with his peers would be different from when I was in elementary school. At times when I watched Andrew interact on the playground with the other children, I felt sad. I would remember the children standing around me, pushing me, calling me names, and making me feel like the world hated me. I do not have any memories of teachers or staff telling them to stop.

When Andrew entered the second grade, a whole new level of growth was happening right in front of me. He got a male teacher, Mr. L, whom he was absolutely crazy about even before he got to second grade. We celebrated the news, and in the back of my mind I felt thrilled that he would have an opportunity to be with an adult male for many hours every week. I noticed as he went through the second grade that he was becoming more confident and he was trying many new extracurricular activities. He played baseball in the fall and spring and basketball in the winter.

From the second he met his coaches, he thrived. Andrew did not feel pressure to please them. He was just so happy to be around other men who could teach him how to get a home run or how to make a basket. I will never forget watching him play defense in basketball and going after the tallest player on the other team hoping for a steal. He had no fear, and he smiled the whole game. Whenever the coaches commended him, his eyes sparkled, and at times he would leap through the air because he felt proud of himself. As I watched him feel passionate about a sport, I noticed a shift in my confidence. I remembered many times when I could not compete or perform because I felt insecure and afraid. Rather than feel depressed about more missed opportunities in my childhood, I focused on the joy in Andrew's face and was proud I could be a part of his success.

Many times I have said to my friends and colleagues that having Andrew has made me braver. Before I became a mom, I was working through my abuse and finding different ways to manage the feelings. For years I wanted to speak about what happened to me. I will never forget a day in the fourth grade when I stood on the playground and said to myself, "Someday someone will hear you."

GOING PUBLIC WITH MY STORY

As the years went by being in recovery and counseling other trauma survivors, I felt a stronger desire to speak out about my story. I had already written several articles and gone on air to give testimony as a specialist treating patients who reported abuse, trauma, and eating disorders. I began feeling frustrated because I was commenting on other people's stories, but then I would walk away from those experiences still feeling silent. As Andrew got older, I challenged the part of me that felt like I could only share my story with my therapist, close friends, and colleagues. I asked myself what stopped me from getting out into the public. I thought about the possibility of being disbelieved or shamed for using my voice.

In 2014 I decided to take a big leap. I wrote an op-ed for the *Philadelphia Inquirer* on understanding and surviving abuse.[3] In the article, I wrote about my abuse and explained to the public why survivors stay silent. I received multiple responses from people around the country hours after the article was released online. Men and women in their forties, fifties, and sixties sent me emails sharing their own struggles with overcoming childhood abuse.

I was inspired. I was sad. I was angry. I asked myself again why I chose to stay silent, and I gave myself the choice to speak. One of the women who wrote me asked me to write a book. I sat with that email for a few days. Then the impulse of writing a book became a thought I ruminated over for days. I went back and forth about the benefits and possible disadvantages of going public with my story.

I decided to move forward. I found an editor whom I connected with instantly. Stephanie and I started working a few years ago on developing a book proposal. Right after we got to work, after he was arrested on December 30, 2015, on three counts of sexual misconduct, I watched a *Dateline NBC* episode with Kate Snow interviewing several of the Cosby accusers.[4] I sat on the edge of my sofa after I listened to about ten women share specific details of their alleged assaults. My heart was racing as I thought about their bravery in coming forward and speaking out about a powerful, loved, well-known actor. I could not sleep that night. Each of the women talked about the aftermath of their alleged assaults. It was clear to me that some of them had bottled up their horror for decades and that their lives were deeply affected. They sobbed. They spoke about their fears of intimacy. They described the self-hatred and decades of addictive behaviors that followed the trauma. I could relate to each of them in different ways. I woke up the next morning thinking I needed to do something.

I sat at my computer and wrote another op-ed for the *Philadelphia Inquirer* on how the Cosby case could help many victims.[5] Minutes after that article went online, I received emails from two of the alleged Cosby victims. Both of them shared their story with me and also commended me for sharing some of my own abuse history. I was inspired. I was pumped. I was ready. I checked in with myself again about the possible risks of making myself vulnerable to the public and realized that my fears were holding me back from being authentic to myself.

Over the next several months I developed relationships with some of the main players in the Cosby charges and several of the alleged victims. When I found out the Cosby trial would be held thirty minutes from my house, I decided I needed to go. I wanted to support the women, the Constand family, and all the prosecutors fighting on behalf of the alleged victims. I sat in the back row of the courtroom during the first trial for a week. I also hung around the courthouse over the days that followed, waiting for the verdict to come in. There was media all around us. They began approaching several of the alleged accusers and me after the jury requested a mistrial. I stood next to some of the women as they shared their stories and sadness about the trial's outcome. At the end of the trial, a few of the reporters and journalists confided in me about assaults they had experienced and how triggering it was to listen to the witnesses testify and be cross-examined. I realized that I was not the only one in that courtroom feeling stirred up and at times enraged at the humiliation and disrespect the witnesses had to tolerate in order to be part of the trial.

After the mistrial, I began doing more writing on stories related to all types of trauma, including some of the mass shootings that took place in high schools, nightclubs, religious institutions, and airports. I was commenting on the horror and grief anyone involved in these tragedies had to endure. I was mostly focused on the bravery of all those affected for speaking out in public and fighting to change the laws around gun control. While these types of trauma were very different from what I survived, there were commonalities. They too were trying to find ways to digest and cope with the lives that were taken or the images they continued to see seconds after the shootings occurred. They were grieving. They were speaking out and trying to take something horrific that happened to them and make a difference in the lives of others.

As the second Cosby trial was getting ready to begin, I noticed another shift. I was no longer just writing about my abuse but had started going on podcasts and talking with news outlets about what had happened to me. I was determined to keep speaking, with the hope of empowering the public and those who were living in silence or fear.

I attended the entire Cosby retrial. This experience felt different. Not only was I connected to several of the accusers and the team of prosecutors, but I was also paying more attention to the Constand family and their steadfast support for Andrea Constand and the five other witnesses who testified against Cosby. I had spent years in therapy working on letting go of the wish that I had a perfect family. There was still a part of me that did not want to believe my family could hurt me so deeply. I knew I needed to continue finding ways to know the truth versus beating myself up for wanting to know what happened. I watched Gianna grab on to her husband's hand as we waited for a verdict. I noticed the strength in Andrea's sister Diana as she sat in the courtroom listening to the detailed account of Andrea Constand's alleged assault and drugging. I thought about all the Cosby accusers who had shared with me how many family members had walked away from them when they said they would be coming forward with assault allegations against Bill Cosby. Many of them shared with me that they had lost their marriages and their relationships with parents, close friends, and others because they spoke out. It was the first time in my life I had people who could relate to the part of me that felt banished for saying what had happened to me.

As the trial moved forward, I began writing incessantly about my reactions to watching Cosby and the Constand family and to being part of the support network for all of the Cosby accusers. I began to understand the denial that runs through a predator. There were many times during the court proceedings that I caught a glimpse of Cosby laughing or making jokes when the witnesses were talking about being allegedly drugged and raped by him. There were moments when I felt sick to my stomach. I empathized with the witnesses and respected their courage in facing someone who had hurt them.

I began to think about the missed opportunity for myself and many others who would never have the chance to confront their abuser. I thought about all the family members who had disowned me after I told them I could only be connected to them if they went to therapy and took ownership of what they did to me. I will never forget the day the Constand family got up on the stand during the Cosby sentencing and gave their victim impact statements.[6] Gianna Constand got on the stand first and told the jury about the suffering she and her family had experienced throughout the process. She spoke about the changes in her daughter, Andrea, and how for over a year she had no idea her daughter was sexually assaulted and was having symptoms of PTSD. She broke down in tears but remained strong and stood behind her daughter. Andrea's father, Andrew Constand, took the stand and talked about being the proudest man in the world to have Andrea as his daughter. As Andrew read that sentence, I thought about how wonderful that must feel to have that kind of love from a father. He was genuinely sickened by the hurt done to his daughter, and he expressed the deep pain it caused him.

When I watched Diana Parsons, Andrea's older sister, take the stand to read her victim impact statement, I wanted to grab her hand and bring her home with me and all of my patients who yearned for a devoted, loving big sister. She talked about how close their family was and how the trauma nearly ripped their family apart. She talked about the sister she knew before the alleged assault and that the aftermath of the event would never go away. Diana proudly acknowledged Andrea for her courage in telling her mother what happened to her and wondered how she was able to do that. Diana also talked about how Andrea was robbed of trust after the rape and how deeply that affected Andrea and all her relationships.

Rather than sit in the doom and loss, I kept fighting to find ways to take my grief and use it toward action and change. When the sentencing ended, I sat in my car and sobbed. I got in touch with the part of me that felt bad watching Cosby being taken away in handcuffs. I felt sad that I would never have an opportunity to fight for justice for what was done to me. I felt sad for anyone I had met who would never be able to confront their abusers or perpetrators. I decided to pick up the phone and call several friends. I left voice mails for them and spoke directly with my friend, Karen. I could not understand why I felt bad for Cosby. She explained to me what I have said to many patients: "You feel bad for him because you are a good human being." She affirmed the part of me that struggled to speak and hold my abuser accountable.

Days after the sentencing ended, I was on a mission to speak, write, and continue helping patients recover. I wrote an op-ed for *Thrive Global* after #MeToo turned two.[7] Rather than say I was an abuse survivor or a trauma survivor, I said what I was a survivor of: incest.

I went on a podcast, *One Tough Muther*, and spoke freely about what happened to me.[8] I went on air with Gloria Allred, a women's rights attorney, and Patricia Steuer, one of the Cosby accusers. Throughout the hour, we all talked about what had happened to us and the impact that followed. We talked about the years of living in silence and the fear of speaking. We talked about the shame and self-hatred and how we transformed that into action and empowerment. When the show ended, I realized I had shared details on air I had never talked about before. Rather than feel afraid, I felt free. I was coming into a place of peace. I had found my calling. I dreamed about being heard that day on the playground in the fourth grade. It was like my life was coming full circle.

I felt grateful for my buried voice that was coming to life. While I did lose my childhood and part of my adulthood, I have found a way to reclaim my life and live much more fully these last twenty years. Speaking publicly about trauma is not for everybody, but it is the life I started to create before my abuse ended. I tell patients that there is no such thing as telling your story too many times. Every time patients talk about a different aspect of their trauma, or when I write or speak about my abuse, it gives us another opportunity to digest one more part of our story.

Life after trauma is different for everyone. There is not one way to understand it or one method or strategy that has shown the best results for healing. When I decided to go public, I prepared myself to confront the reality of my story on another level. Every time I have shared my story, I have felt sadness and at times guilt and shame. I remind myself what my therapist told me many times, "It is not *you* that is not normal; it is what happened to you that is not normal."

I have accepted that I may live the rest of my life combating memories, feelings, and fears related to my abuse. There are reminders everywhere I go, whether I stay silent or shout it out at the top of the Empire State Building that I am an incest survivor. They can come in something as simple as getting in the shower, walking down the hallway of Andrew's school, driving by spots where I spent time as a child while going to work, or even getting into bed at night. I may have a respite period when the memories are not as present. Typically, I have some type of flashback or feeling from the past every day.

My father died two years after I began speaking about my abuse. I am not in a relationship with any other family members. My immediate family and several distant family members were not able to accept or take ownership of what happened to me. I tried family therapy. I sat in a room talking directly with them about what happened to me. My family continued to disbelieve me and at times treated me like the crazy one. In order to live a full and safe life, I made the choice to estrange myself from anyone who refused to accept the truth. I was not willing to continue burying my pain to be connected to my biological family.

We are at the tipping point of breaking the silence on taboo subjects such as childhood abuse, sexual assault, domestic violence, shootings, and life after combat and related events. These types of tragedies have occurred for hundreds of years. The difference is that we are becoming a society that is more open to shedding light on the impact of living through the trauma. We are becoming a world that is starting to listen to and believe survivors.

We are becoming a world that is educating our youth and helping to make a difference for generations to come!

HEALING STRATEGIES I USED DURING MY RECOVERY

How I Stay Grounded

1. I did a ton of journaling. I wrote letters to Dorothy and to myself.
2. I went to therapy four times a week to manage the memories and feelings that surfaced.
3. I called Dorothy and other supporters when I felt like I wanted to give up.
4. I went on hikes.
5. I went to yoga class.
6. I spent time with my dog, Chloe.
7. I reminded myself of the benefits of healing from the abuse.
8. I used mindfulness strategies when I was feeling disconnected. I concentrated on whatever was going on in the moment.
9. I imagined taking the memories, digesting them, and then putting them on a bookshelf. I imagined the book being on the front shelf and told myself that whenever I needed to I could grab hold of it.

How I Managed the Shame Attacks

1. I implemented cognitive behavioral strategies, such as reframing my thoughts or kindly telling myself, "Stop," when I fell into name-calling and shaming myself.
2. I did the opposite of the feeling: when I felt ugly, I did things to make me feel pretty; when I felt powerless, I did things that made me feel empowered.

3. I sat in yoga class or in a sunny, quiet spot in my development and talked to the younger part of me that had internalized the shame.

How I Dealt with the Grief of Losing My Childhood and Many Family Members after Speaking Out

1. I wrote in my journals about the limitations of others and that that was not about me.
2. I decided to create a "family by choice" circle of support. I reached out to people who represented the family I was missing.
3. I gave myself time to cry when the grief consumed me. I created healing circles with close friends when the pain became too much.

How I Implement Self-Compassion

1. I remind myself of all the benefits of facing my past.
2. I use mindfulness when I make choices of what kind of food to put in my body.
3. I laugh at myself all the time.
4. I give myself permission to be me, whether I am sad, angry, scared, or excited. I tell myself it is not the feelings themselves but how I choose to express them that matters most.
5. I place the memories. When I feel shame or guilt for setting limits, I give myself permission to take care of myself, even though I was left with the message that I need to put others' needs ahead of my own.

9

SURVIVOR TESTIMONIALS

JENNIFER FOX: EMMY- AND GOLDEN GLOBE–NOMINATED DIRECTOR OF THE FILM *THE TALE*

For the last thirty years I have been producing documentaries. One of the main themes I have always been interested in exploring is that "the personal is political." For me each person's life can be viewed as a microcosm of the bigger system of our world. My main interest has been to explore the intimate parts of people's lives. When I produced *Flying: Confessions of a Dangerous Woman*, I put myself under the lens as the main character. I went on a journey around the world to find out what it means to be a woman today. This was the first time I had ever been in front of the camera.

I shared intimate details of my private life. As I was making this film, I had an epiphany that led me to make *The Tale*. I was completely shocked that close to one out of two women I interviewed revealed to me that they had been raped or sexually assaulted. I was making a film about sexual freedom, but these stories hit me at the core. As I was speaking to these women, my unconscious began to wake up. There was a clear connection between the sexual abuse stories and what happened to me when I was thirteen. There were similarities in the patterns. There was a paradigm of careful grooming, where love and attention was bestowed on a lonely, needy child to gain trust. Suddenly my own private story became universal. The word "abuse" hit me.

The abuse was committed by my running coach, who was a celebrated athlete I referred to as Bill in the film. At the time, I believed Bill cared for me. Looking back, I realized that the bond we formed was complex, confusing, and coercive. As I was trying to find ways to grapple with my new perspective on this relationship, I set out to write the script for *The Tale*. The project was a way for me to explore why and how this event happened to me and how I dealt with it. This was not a story about forgotten memory, but how a person takes certain parts of her memory to create the identity she wanted to have. As the character investigates the nature of this relationship with her running coach as an adult, the shadow memory that got locked in her subconscious emerges.

After I completed the first draft of the film, I realized it was not the events themselves that struck me; it was what I had done with them and how I had constructed this story. It was how I lived with it in my memory and how it formed as an adult. I also wanted to offer a blunt and honest depiction of how young people can become emotionally intertwined with their abusers and the ways in which they can be groomed for the abuse without understanding the long-term effects.

The biggest struggle as I was writing the film was finding a way to talk about the memory of the thirteen-year-old who was reflecting back on her abuse as an adult woman in her late forties. My mother was my biggest supporter for this film. She was a constant in this process, pushing me to move forward and write the script. For my mother, it was a way of processing what had happened to me and also of bringing the adults who had harmed me to justice. My mother wanted me to find my abuser and the enablers and hold them accountable. For me, *The Tale* is just as much a film about a mother-daughter story as it is about memory.

My screenplay very closely mimicked the investigation I had done into my own past. I gathered all my writings and diaries from

1973 and all the letters I saved from my coaches, my friends, and even my brother, looking for clues or indications of the abuse. I never forgot some of the memories I had when I was with Bill and Mrs. G, Bill's mistress at the time the abuse occurred. I wrote down these memories too. I found the other children I had trained with, and after I met with each of them, I wrote up transcripts of our meeting. There was not a time I considered using any name for the film's protagonist other than my own. For *The Tale*, I felt the authenticity was the most essential element in making the film.

After the film was released, men and women of all kinds flocked to me to share their histories of trauma and abuse. I was overwhelmed and touched. It was not until after the film was released that I fully understood the impact of my abuse.

For me the message of the film is that we construct our very own identities without knowing we are doing so. How we construct them very much depends on our character, our circumstances, and the tools we are given, our fantasies. I hope *The Tale* helps others find new ways to talk about the mind and memory and inspires people to tell their stories. Reflecting on and speaking about our deepest and most painful truths in the form of storytelling is just one way to put up a mirror to the things we don't want to see.

To view the movie *The Tale*, visit HBO streaming, Amazon, or iTunes. To contact me, visit www.thetalemovie.com.

Jennifer Fox

KAREN'S STORY: SUICIDE OF HER BOYFRIEND

How do I make sense of the words, *someone I loved committed suicide*?

How do I go forward while violently surging backward? How many times did I relive every moment, retrace every step, replay every conversation, reviewing every sign, hoping to ascertain and identify when I failed someone, the person I loved, so it will never happen again?

Every mind-numbing, stomach-souring, self-blaming second of every single day.

Every sound, every fraction of light, every long, lonely night, I questioned, I blamed, and I f—ed myself up.

You silently suffer so others don't speak of it and sink into a scolding white-hot sentiment of self-doubt. Nothing is the same in my world. Why don't people see that? Why don't they care? I stopped talking about my pain, my confusion, and my fear. I realized no one has the answer to why my boyfriend ended his life.

The fact remains, I was the only one there, the only one present, the only one who saw, heard, and held him in the last seconds. *So, what did I do and still do to move on, to move past it, to move forward? I keep moving!*

I try with everything I have in my soul to stop blaming myself for helping so many people in my world, except for the one closest to me. I try not to imagine what he was thinking, doing, and feeling because I will truly never know, and to me that is maddening. I stop my mind from imaging what I could have done differently in the moments, seconds before, and how I could have changed the outcome. I am well aware that my imagination will bury me, while the cold hard truth is buried with him.

I help as many people as I can, listen to as many stories as I can, stories of deceit, heartbreak, abuse, disease, and death, sharing those real-life lessons for others to learn from—the life lessons of others who have faced devastation and gotten burned, bullied, or buried but dug out to move forward.

I silently fight my fear of another failed relationship, celebrate the little wins, and remind myself that although some people may think they are always in control, they are not.

My life lesson: we are not in control of other people's demons and can only help those who ask for help. Remember, the truest quote in the world is one from Robert Frost, which goes, "In three words I can sum up everything I've learned about life: it goes on." However, I must add, "and so must you."

Fight for your life.

Karen

TAMIE'S TESTIMONIAL: THERAPIST, EATING DISORDER SURVIVOR, LIFE-ALTERING BACK INJURY

I always thought that I was one of the lucky ones, that I wouldn't need to have *that* surgery. At forty-three, I was active, swimming, healthy, working hard in a career that I love, and doing all "the right things." The harsh reality that my body was decompensating and getting weaker and having more pain was a crushing blow. I was so angry with my body for failing me, for not doing what it is supposed to. I wanted to be happy for my triathlon friends, but it hurt that I was not able to run or ride my bike and that I could not even push off of the wall in the pool. I love my job, but sitting in the car, standing at a conference, and smiling through the pain was more than I could bear.

When I was an adolescent and diagnosed with scoliosis, I was told that I had a deformity. I wish doctors could talk about it in a different way because that word stayed with me. I was deformed, different, and ugly. As my curve progressed, I had to wear a back brace. It was a hard plastic nightmare that went from above my breasts to below my hips. At a time in life when so many already struggle with body image and self-esteem, this felt like a life sentence. I isolated, tried to hide my body, and tried to disappear. I don't blame my brace or scoliosis on the development of my eating disorder, but I do believe that it was a contributing factor.

Beginning in adolescence, I struggled with symptoms of anorexia and bulimia. I began to disappear: maybe if I were smaller, no one would notice my hard plastic shell. I asked the doctor if I could have the scoliosis surgery so that my waist and hips would be even and so the hump on the left side of my back would go away. The surgeon said no. I wondered if he was concerned that my drive to have the surgery was a result of my eating disorder. I remember my last visit, when I was graduating from high school and felt that my scoliosis life was behind me. I thought it was over because I was told that a curve typically does not increase once you have stopped growing.

Fast-forward to twenty-five years old—I was now sober for three years, from alcohol, and still struggling with anorexic eating disorder tendencies. I had severe back pain and pain and weakness down my right leg. An MRI and scoliosis study revealed that my curve had increased significantly and that I had some disk herniation as well as degeneration. I struggled to walk, which led me to eat less and less for fear of weight gain.

At my follow-up appointment, my doctor recognized that I had lost weight. I tried to deny it, but he was very straightforward and told me that I might have osteoporosis because I drank coffee, smoked, and was losing weight. A DEXA scan revealed osteopenia, which is early bone loss. My body continued to fail me. I was deformed, ashamed, and terrified, and no amount of weight loss could help that.

Not long after my surgery, I sought treatment for my eating disorder, one last time! I am happy to say that I have been recovered for many years. Part of my long-term recovery was to work on PTSD caused by many different struggles, including this one. My recovery work included individual therapy, art therapy, psychiatry, and attending a weeklong experiential program. My trauma includes other factors in addition to my scoliosis and surgeries, so I needed to do a lot of work on myself.

At thirty years old, I was faced with a similar pain and weakness, which led to the need for another surgery for my L5/S1 disk. The surgeon told me that we would have the scoliosis surgery in nine months. No way! I am one of the lucky ones who did not need *that* surgery. I got all of my medical records and got a second opinion that said that I didn't need the scoliosis surgery. At that time, I was strong and healthy and committed to physical therapy.

In 2014, my sister started to run and do triathlons. She is also a scoliosis warrior and has had many surgeries. It gave me hope that, if she could do it, so could I. I started to run, joined a women's triathlon club, bought a bike, and learned to swim. Competing in a triathlon was physical, but it was more about connecting with other women and challenging myself and my body in a way I never thought possible. I have had physical therapy off and on for over twenty years. Two years ago, I sought a new orthopedic doctor and physical therapist as I was starting to have more pain and weakness. Pain prevented me from continuing to run or ride my bike. I continued to swim and fell in love with open-water swimming. The swimming community is just amazing, and being in open water is mindful and meditative for me. Last summer, I was no longer able to push off the wall of a pool without pain. I had a lot of nerve symptoms, including numbness in my feet. My doctor and I started to have discussions of a life-altering surgery.

Over this past year, I have seen many different types of doctors and had many types of tests. I trust my doctor, so we came up with a plan for a surgery that would take place in three stages over two days. Planning for surgery was scary. It triggered similar feelings to older trauma and underlying issues of my eating disorder. I had to confront fear of the unknown and trust my surgeon to perform a successful surgery. In the past I have questioned authority figures. In the past I doubted my body and its ability to have a positive outcome.

As I write this, I am three months post-op. I have three large scars—on my stomach, ribs, and down my back. I have a lot of numbness in different areas as well as stiffness and discomfort, but no more pain. I have a lot of hope and a lot of fear. I am in a body that is not mine. My hump on my back is gone, but that is the only body I've known, so it does not feel like mine yet. I cannot trim my own toenails, but I can make a cup of coffee and drive without pain. I can swim and cannot wait to relearn how to swim with this new spine.

Prior to surgery, someone asked me if I could remember what my life was like without pain, and I could not. My life was lived with limits and constraints because of the pain I was in and the fear that it would get worse. I have an invisible disability, so I would either push myself or make excuses and rely on my self-destructive tendencies to help me cope with my limitations.

Through this experience, I have become open about my daily struggles and celebrate every little victory. The benefit of having done so much trauma work is that I am very in touch with my body and its pain and sensations. I listen closely, without judgment, and rest when I need to and play when I can. I don't know what the future will hold, but I know that I am not in this alone and will continue to accept myself. I had the surgery that I always dreaded, and I'm grateful I did. I feel like I have been given a second chance, and I intend to care for my body and speak out about my experiences.

Tamie

JANICE'S STORY: SEXUAL ASSAULT SURVIVOR

I was raped. Those are the three most difficult words I have ever said. I was raped in the early 1980s, but I did not say those three words until 2015. I never admitted to being raped because I blamed myself and I knew my rapist, and the term "acquaintance rape" was not part of the common vernacular at the time. I was raped by Bill Cosby. Many of those reading this book will be familiar with the Cosby women, the trial, and his ultimate conviction. I am not writing this to rehash the past but to share what coming forward has done for me and how it has brought strength and hope and light into my life.

Coming forward was difficult because of the thirty-plus years I had denied my assault by blaming myself. I played the self-doubt game as so many seem to do after being sexual assaulted. Through the encouragement of my family and close friends, I found the strength to make a public statement during a press conference held by my attorney, Gloria Allred. It was not easy, that first step, not even close to easy. But the gate had been opened, a toxic chain of silence was broken, and there was no turning back. Admitting that one has been the victim of rape is scary and difficult enough to begin with, but then add national scrutiny from the press (and the trolls) and it becomes overwhelming. I was fortunate to have an incredible support system, especially from my fellow survivor sisters. I had an immediate connection to these women who became my lifeline. I began to learn more about each victim and their truths about their assaults and stopped feeling so alone in my guilt and shame.

My need to feel this connection left a mark on my marriage, though, as I began to shut down my sharing with my husband as I grew closer to my fellow survivors. I had no idea how burying that night way down deep inside of me for so many years would affect me once I finally came forward. This was new territory with so many emotions to deal with. There was still the underlying guilt, shame, and blame, but now I had to actually think about them and admit that I was, in fact, a victim of sexual assault. Luckily I found a wonderful therapist who helped both my husband and me navigate our way back to each other and who encouraged me to communicate my shame and fears to this loving man I had in my corner. It wasn't easy and there were plenty of tears, but my marriage probably would not have survived had it not been for a good therapist and a year or so of counseling.

The following year became a whirlwind of activity surrounding the alleged Cosby victims. In 2015, *Dateline NBC* invited many of the women who had come forward to appear on a special they had regarding the Cosby survivors. *New York* magazine did a cover story on thirty-five of us. I appeared on several local TV and radio news programs over the next year discussing "believing women." My voice and my resolve became stronger with each appearance and with each additional woman who came forward because of us. In 2016, I became involved with a group of survivors to form "End Rape SOL" in California. Our testifying before the state assembly in Sacramento, the relentless lobbying and phone calls to members of several committees, and our perseverance in eliminating the statute of limitations on rape and sexual assault was realized when Governor Jerry Brown signed SB 813, the Justice for Victims Act, into law. I found my voice and felt empowered. I joined the millions of women who marched for justice and equality on

January 21, 2017, and I continue to support those who speak their truth.

If there is anything I've learned these past four years, it is that we survivors must encourage and lift one another up. Then in 2018 I became one of the five witnesses called to testify in the Bill Cosby retrial. I proudly spoke my truth and defiantly stood up to the stereotypical "victim blaming" used shamefully by the defense. The network of support I received only served to reinforce my commitment to helping others and being an advocate for those unable or afraid to speak for themselves. Following the verdict, *Dateline NBC* invited four of the five witnesses back to discuss the trial and verdict, and it felt like I had come full circle. I can't say any of this has been easy, but it has been both empowering and liberating.

There are still days when it is difficult to say those three words: I was raped. There are still those days when I have trouble forgiving myself, even with the knowledge that I am not the one to blame for my assault. That irrational, nagging voice that had been buried for so long is still lurking in the depths of my psyche, telling me I could have done things differently to avoid what happened that night. But I would not change one day of my life since speaking my truth out loud. I know I am not alone, and neither are you. Be gentle and forgiving with yourself. There is light and joy and love out there. I pray that anyone reading this who feels the shame and humiliation I felt knows that you are not alone. I see you. I hear you. And I believe you.

Look into her eyes,
see inside yourself.
Open to the light
streaming to
your heart.
Find what
you can give.
In giving,
you will be healed.
Janice

TYLER

March 7, 2017 . . . the day I lost a piece of my heart forever. However, I was presented with such clarity beyond belief in that moment. On that horrific night, I found out my twenty-two-year-old firstborn son, Tyler Jay Onesty, was found dead from an overdose of heroin laced with fentanyl. I remember praying in that moment of hysterical crying for God to give me strength. God did not disappoint me in that worst moment of my life.

I had an overwhelming feeling of peace and a sense of urgency to go public about my son's story and my journey as a mom trying to help her addicted son. This started immediately for me, deciding we were going to go public in his obituary. I then asked a well-known friend of mine to speak on the statistics of addiction and recovery in the United States and New Jersey (our home state) at my son's celebration of life ceremony (his funeral). My younger son Zach spoke about what it was like living with his older brother and best friend being affected by the disease of addiction. Zach's girlfriend, Amanda (they've been dating since September 2011), spoke about what it was like growing up losing both of her parents to the disease of mental illness, the disease of addiction, and the effects of addiction, plus losing the only real sibling she ever had, my son, Tyler. Then my husband spoke about his recreational drug use when he was younger and his struggle with alcohol.

I spoke and told everyone how Tyler was trying to help people get into detox and recovery until the day he died. I always tell everyone that he believed in the recovery process. He just didn't always know how or have the strength to reach out and stay in recovery. At the end of sharing Tyler's story and my testimony as a mom trying to help her son consumed by the disease of addiction, I put out an offer to anyone in the audience, which was over 1,500 people, that they could reach out to me with no judgment and I would help them get connected with resources that might help them navigate a treatment plan or recovery plan a little easier. We went live on Facebook with his whole celebration of life service, so that really started the Facebook messages coming in to me the very next day.

I've been helping kids, moms, and dads ever since try to navigate the system. Just the fact that they have a friendly person who gets what they are going through makes them open up more and feel more comfortable. That brings me to today where I work with several organizations to try to help people get the assistance they need to become well, to get better, and to live a full life in recovery. I have since become a trained recovery coach so that I can help assist families on an as-needed basis.

My family started the Tyler Jay Onesty Scholarship Fund where we provide scholarships to local kids who are pursuing their education in the mental health field, the recovery field, the medical field, or a trade school. The kids have to write an essay of at least five hundred words explaining how addiction has impacted their life; what ideas they think could be implemented in their school, town, or county that would help in the prevention of drug abuse; or how by choosing the field they're going into they could help the medical profession be more responsible and not contribute to the drug pandemic we are living in right now. We also help scholarship people get into treatment, recovery, or therapy.

I run a Bible study at our church, the Fresh Start Church, in Egg Harbor Township, New Jersey, called the Freedom Loop (living out our purpose). It is a mixed group of people in recovery, people trying to help others still in active use, and people who have lost someone to mental illness, addiction, or both. This kind of group is not typical because most groups deal with just one issue. I felt that the combination in the group would lend itself to a higher level of understanding and support. I believe from the bottom of my heart that I am living out my purpose even though this is an education I never planned on or wanted. I know my son Tyler would support it wholeheartedly and be so proud of me. As a woman of strength from my faith, I am guided by God and my angel Tyler, both of whom send me signs that what I am doing is of value and necessary. Being kind to yourself and compassionate and forgiving of others is the biggest strength there is, in my opinion. Be well and stay blessed.

Sally

NOTES

INTRODUCTION

1. Shari Botwin (2014, November 4), Understanding and surviving child abuse, *Philly News*, accessed January 30, 2019, https://www.philly.com/philly/opinion/inquirer/20141104_Understanding_and_surviving_child_abuse.html

2. Shari Botwin (2016, February 11), Cosby case can help victims, *Philly News*, accessed January 30, 2019, https://www.philly.com/philly/opinion/20160212_Cosby_case_can_help_victims.html

3. *Commonwealth v. William Henry Cosby, Jr.* (2018, September 25), MJ-38102-CR-0000131-201 (Montgomery County, PA).

1. TRAUMA DEFINED

1. American Psychological Association (2019), Trauma, accessed January 31, 2019, https://www.apa.org/topics/trauma

2. History Channel (2018), Columbine High School shootings, accessed February 1, 2019, https://www.history.com/topics/1990s/columbine-high-school-shootings

3. History Channel (2010), 9/11 attacks, accessed February 1, 2019, https://www.history.com/topics/21st-century/9-11-attacks

4. Matt Carroll, Sacha Pfeiffer, and Michael Rezendes (2002, January 6), Church allowed abused by priest for years, *Boston Globe*, accessed February 9, 2019, https://www.bostonglobe.com/news/special-reports/2002/01/06/church-allowed-abuse-priest-for-years/cSHfGkTIrAT25qKGvBuDNM/story.html

5. Henry H. Barnes (2016, January 13), Spotlight: The reporters who uncovered Boston's child abuse scandal, *The Guardian*, accessed February 3, 2019, https://www.theguardian.com/film/2016/jan/13/spotlight-reporters-uncovered-catholic-child-abuse-boston-globe

6. Oliver Milman (2017, September 28), Hurricane Sandy five years later: "No one was ready for what happened after," *The Guardian*, accessed February 3, 2019, https://www.theguardian.com/us-news/2017/oct/27/hurricane-sandy-five-years-later-climate-change

7. Donna Weaver (2013, October 27), Survivors struggle with emotional aftermath of Hurricane Sandy, *Press of Atlantic City*, accessed February 3, 2019, https://www.pressofatlanticcity.com/survivors-struggle-with-emotional-aftermath-of-hurricane-sandy/article_17b57e9a_3fof-11e3-b615-001a4bcf887.a.html

8. Mayo Clinic (2018), Electroconvulsive therapy, accessed December 13, 2018, https://www.mayoclinic.org/tests-procedures/electroconvusive-therapy/about/pac-20393894

9. Mayo Clinic (2018), Electroconvulsive therapy, accessed December 13, 2018, https://www.mayoclinic.org/tests-procedures/electroconvusive-therapy/about/pac-20393894

10. Brian Mastroianni (2018, September 25), 5 myths about PTSD you need to stop believing, Everyday Health, accessed February 3, 2019, https://www.everydayhealth.com/ptsd/common-ptsd-myths-debunked

11. Mayo Clinic (2018), Post-traumatic stress disorder (PTSD), accessed February 3, 2019, https://www.mayoclinic.org/diseases-conditions/post-traumatic-stress-disorder/symptoms-causes/syc-20355967

12. Mayo Clinic (2018), Post-traumatic stress disorder (PTSD), accessed February 3, 2019, https://www.mayoclinic.org/diseases-conditions/post-traumatic-stress-disorder/symptoms-causes/syc-20355967

13. Ashwood Recovery (2015), accessed February 8, 2019, https://www.ashwoodrecovery.com

14. Matthew J. Friedman (2019), PTSD: History and overview, US Department of Veterans Affairs, accessed February 7, 2019, https://www.ptsd.va.gov/professional/treat/essentials/history_ptsd.asp

15. Tessa Stuart (2015, December 3), 2015: The year in mass shootings, *Rolling Stone*, accessed February 9, 2019, https://www.rollingstone.com/politics/politics-news/2015-the-year-in-mass-shootings-34983

16. Carolyn Fagan (2018, November 25), The impact of mass school shootings on the mental health of survivors: What parents need to know, *Psycom*, accessed February 10, 2019, https://www.psycom.net/mental-health-wellbeing/school-shooting-survivor-mental-health

17. Sammy Mack (2018, June 30), Stoneman Douglas staff and therapists get free trauma training for start of school year. WLRN, accessed February 9, 2019, https://www.wlrn.org/post/stoneman-douglas-staff-and-therapists-get-free-trauma-training-start-school-year

18. Alison Gorman (2018, February 28), Expert says students need to return to school after trauma, 6ABC, accessed February 10, 2019, https://6abc.com/health/expert-says-students-need-to-return-to-school-after-trauma/3155256

19. Joyce Chen (2017, October 17), Alyssa Milano wants her "Me Too" campaign to elevate Harvey Weinstein discussion, *Rolling Stone*, accessed February 10, 2019, https://www.rollingstone.com/movies/movie-news/alyssa-milano-wants-her-me-too-campaign-to-elevate-harvey-weinstein-discussion-123610

20. Thorpe, JR (2017, December 1), This is how many people have posted "me too" since October, according to new data, *Bustle*, accessed February 9, 2019, https://www.bustle.com/p/this-is-how-many-people-have-posted-me-too-since-october-according-to-new-data6753697

21. Susan Milligan (2018, December 23), Sexual assault reports spike in #MeToo era, *US News*, accessed February 10, 2019, https://www.usnews.com/news/national-news/articles/2018-12-27/sexual-assault-reports-spike-in-metoo-era

22. Tom McCarthy (2018, April 16), Bill Cosby found guilty in sexual assault trial in milestone for #MeToo era, *The Guardian*, accessed February 9, 2019, https://www.theguardian.com/world/2018/apr/26/bill-cosby-guilty-trial-sexual-assault

23. Callum Borchers (2018, April 26), Bill Cosby's conviction will go down as the first of the #MeToo era, *Washington Post*, accessed Febru-

ary 28, 2019, https://www.washingtonpost.com/news/the-fix/wp/2018/04/26/bill-cosbys-conviction-will-go-down-as-the-first-of-the-metoo-era

24. Yahoo Celebrity Staff (2018, September 26), Bill Cosby sentenced to 3 to 10 years in state prison for sexual assault, deemed a "sexually violent predator," *Yahoo! Entertainment*, accessed February 9, 2019, https://www.yahoo.com/entertainment/bill-cosby-sentenced-3-10-years-state-prison-sexual-assault-deemed-sexually-violent-predator-182219288.html

25. Merrit Kennedy (2016, September 28), California eliminates statute of limitations on rape cases, NPR, accessed February 9, 2019, https://www.npr.org/sections/thetwo-way/2016/09/28/495856974/california-eliminates-statute-of-limitations-on-rape-cases

26. Alanna Vagianos (2019, January 22), Larry Nassar's first known victim is a mother figure to hundreds of young survivors, *Huffington Post*, accessed February 9, 2019, https://m.huffpost.com/us/entry/us_5c3656c3e4b00c33ab5f594d

2. FACING THE TRAUMA

1. Matthew Tull (2019, July 8), Is cognitive processing therapy a fast way to treat PTSD?, *Verywell Mind*, accessed July 13, 2019, https://www.verywellmind.com/cognitive-processing-therapy-2797281.

2. Judith Cohen, Esther Deblinger, and Anthony Mannarino (2014), Trauma-focused cognitive behavioral therapy, *Psychology Today*, accessed January 30, 2019, https://www.psychology.com/us/therapy-types-trauma-focused-cognitive-behavior-therapy

3. American Psychiatric Association (2013), *Diagnostic and statistical manual of mental disorders* (5th Ed.), accessed February 7, 2019, https://www.psychiatry.org/psychiatrists/practice/dsm

4. Bessel van der Kolk (2015), *The body keeps score* (New York: Viking Press).

5. Jocelyn St. Cyr (n.d.), About, accessed November 9, 2018, https://www.jocelynstcyr.com

6. Tom Bunn (2014, August 15), Is what you are feeling a flashback?, *Psychology Today*, accessed November 9, 2018, https://www.psychologytoday.com/us/blog/conquer-fear-flying/201408/is-what-you-are-feeling-flashback

7. Matthew Tull (2018), Verywell Mind, accessed November 9, 2018, https://www.verywellmind.com/matthew-tull-phd-2797109

3. HOW THE ROAD UNRAVELS WHEN A WITNESS IS PRESENT

1. RAINN (1994), *Statistics*, accessed November 6, 2018, http://www.rainn.org/statistics

2. *Commonwealth v. William Henry Cosby, Jr.* (2018, September 25), MJ-38102-CR-0000131-201 (Montgomery County, PA).

3. Jane Shure and Beth Weinstock (2009), Shame, compassion, and the journey to health, in William N. Davis, Jane Shure, and Margo Maine (Eds.), *Effective clinical practice in the treatment of eating disorders* (New York: Routledge).

5. STAYING PRESENT

1. Michael Sky (2002), Emotional suppression causes serious damage to bodies, minds, and spirits, *Inner Self*, accessed December 5, 2018, https://innerself.com/content/personal/happiness-and-self-help/performance/4858-emotional-suppression.html

2. Mayo Clinic (2018), Electroconvulsive therapy, accessed December 13, 2018, https://www.mayoclinic.org/tests-procedures/electroconvulsive-therapy/about/pac-20393894

3. Peter Borten and Briana Borten (n.d.), Letting go of the past: 5 powerful practices for releasing emotional baggage, hurt and regrets, *Conscious Lifestyle*, accessed December 15, 2018, https://www.consciouslifestylemag.com/letting-go-of-the-past-5-practices

4. Jodie Eckleberry-Hunt (2018, January 13), Leave that shit behind: Moving on from trauma #PTSD, *Medium*, accessed December 15, 2018, https://medium.com/@jeckleberryhunt/leave-that-shit-behind-moving-on-from-trauma-ptsd-eeae0e2c5468

6. TAKING TIME TO GRIEVE

1. Elisabeth Kübler-Ross (2014), *On grief and grieving: Finding the meaning of grief through the five stages of loss* (New York: Scribner).
2. Susan Pease Banitt (2015), Ashwood Recovery, accessed December 23, 2018, https://www.ashwoodrecovery.com
3. Memorial Sloan Kettering (2018), accessed February 1, 2019, https://www.mskcc.org
4. Melinda Smith, Lawrence Robinson, and Jeanne Segal (2018), Coping with grief and loss, HelpGuide, accessed January 4, 2019, https://www.helpguide.org/articles/grief/coping-with-grief-and-loss.htm

7. REAPING THE BENEFITS OF
YOUR RECOVERY

1. Habits for Wellbeing (2013), 20 quotes to inspire self-compassion, accessed January 31, 2019, https://www.habitsforwellbeing.com/20-quotes-to-inspire-self-compassion

8. MY LIFE IN RECOVERY

1. ANAD homepage, accessed January 24, 2019, http://www.anad.org
2. April Kahn and Kristeen Cherney (2017), Dependent personality disorder, Healthline, accessed January 20, 2019, https://www.healthline.com
3. Shari Botwin (2019), *Publications*, accessed January 30, 2019, https://www.sharibotwin.com/publications
4. NBC News (2015, October 9), Full episode: The Cosby accusers speak, accessed January 30, 2019, https://www.nbcnews.com/dateline/video/full-episode-the-cosby-accusers-speak-543502915620
5. Shari Botwin (2016, February 11), Cosby case can help victims, *Philly News*, accessed January 30, 2019, www.philly.com/philly/blogs/thinktank/Cosby-case-can-help-victims.html?mobi=true

6. Alanna Vagianos (2018, September 24), Ahead Of Cosby sentencing, Andrea Constand and family read emotional statements, *Huffington Post*, accessed July 13, 2019, https://www.huffpost.com/entry/bill-cosby-andrea-constand-impact-statements_n_5ba93eb9e4b0375f8f9fa08d

7. Shari Botwin (2018, October 15), #MeToo turns two, *Thrive Global*, accessed January 30, 2019, https://www.thriveglobal.com/stories/46721-me-too-turns-two

8. Karen Finocchio (2018), One Tough Muther, accessed January 30, 2019, https://www.theonetoughmuthershow.com

RESOURCES

TREATMENT FACILITIES FOR OVERCOMING EATING DISORDERS, ADDICTIONS, AND TRAUMA

Monte Nido offers eating disorder treatment in a serene natural environment, where clinicians, many recovered themselves, combine clinical wisdom, evidence-based protocols, and mindfulness practices to provide state-of-the-art care for the mind, body, and soul. Their unique-level system facilitates the awareness, skills, and hands-on experience necessary for becoming fully recovered. www.montenido.com.

The Renfrew Center is the country's first residential eating disorder treatment facility, treating more than seventy-five thousand adolescent girls and women with anorexia nervosa, bulimia nervosa, binge eating disorder, and related mental health problems since 1985. Renfrew has locations throughout the United States, and its services include residential, day treatment, intensive outpatient, and outpatient programs. Each treatment level utilizes the Renfrew Center Unified Treatment Model for Eating Disorders. www.renfrewcenter.com.

Sheppard Pratt is one of the nation's leading mental health experts helping patients through every step of the recovery process in a compassionate, comfortable setting for healing. www.sheppardpratt.org.

The Caron Foundation has been restoring lives through proven addiction rehab programs for over sixty years. Caron blends addiction rehab and behavioral health treatment with the latest evidence-based practices and historically proven treatment modalities. www.caron.org.

OUTPATIENT TRAUMA PROGRAMS

The **Princeton House** women's trauma program is an innovative model designed to help women understand the impact of trauma in their lives. In this program, women are encouraged to understand the relationship between their symptoms, their coping strategies, and their trauma history. www.princetonhcs.org.

The Foundations Recovery Network provides integrated treatment for co-occurring mental health and substance use disorders through clinical services, education, and research. They provide inpatient and outpatient recovery settings. www.foundationsrecoverynetwork.com.

Rogers Behavioral Health offers inpatient and outpatient treatment options for adults. Cognitive behavioral therapy is used to reduce anxiety related to the traumatic event. The treatment approach combines psychoeducation, mindfulness skills, DBT-informed groups, and experiential therapy. https://rogersbh.org.

VA Medical Centers offer PTSD treatment for all levels of inpatient and outpatient care. Programs are located in several states throughout the country. www.va.gov.

RESOURCES FOR MORE INFORMATION OR TO FIND A THERAPIST

Childhelp National Child Abuse Hotline: www.childhelp.
org.

Psychology Today: Find a trauma therapist at www.
psychologytoday.com.

RAINN (Rape, Abuse and Incest National Network):
www.rainn.org.

Sidran Organization: More resources for survivors and loved
ones, www.sidran.org.

BIBLIOGRAPHY

American Psychiatric Association. (2013). *Diagnostic and statistical manual of mental disorders* (5th Ed.). Accessed February 7, 2019, https://www.psychiatry.org/psychiatrists/practice/dsm

American Psychological Association. (2019). Trauma. Accessed January 31, 2019, https://www.apa.org/topics/trauma

ANAD homepage. Accessed January 24, 2019. https://www.anad.org

Ashwood Recovery. 2015. Accessed February 8, 2019, https://www.ashwoodrecovery.com

Banitt, Susan Pease. (2015). Ashwood Recovery. Accessed December 23, 2018, https://www.ashwoodrecovery.com

Barnes, Henry H. (2016, January 13). Spotlight: The reporters who uncovered Boston's Catholic child abuse scandal. *The Guardian*. Accessed February 3, 2019, https://www.theguardian.com/film/2016/jan/13/spotlight-reporters-uncovered-catholic-child-abuse-boston-globe

Borchers, Callum. (2018, April 26). Bill Cosby's conviction will go down as the first of the #MeToo era. *Washington Post*. Accessed February 28, 2019, https://www.washingtonpost.com/news/the-fix/wp/2018/04/26/bill-cosbys-conviction-will-go-down-as-the-first-of-the-metoo-era

Borten, Peter, and Briana Borten. (n.d.). Letting go of the past: 5 powerful practices for releasing emotional baggage, hurt and regrets. *Conscious Lifestyle*. Accessed December 15, 2018, https://www.consciouslifestylemag.com/letting-go-of-the-past-5-practices

Botwin, Shari. (2014, November 4). Understanding and surviving child abuse. *Philly News*. Accessed January 30, 2019, https://www.philly.com/philly/opinion/inquirer/20141104_Understanding_and_surviving_child_abuse.html

Botwin, Shari. (2016, February 11). Cosby case can help victims. *Philly News*. Accessed January 30, 2019, https://www.philly.com/philly/opinion/20160212_Cosby_case_can_help_victims.html

Botwin, Shari. (2018, October 15). #MeToo turns two. *Thrive Global*. Accessed January 30, 2019, https://www.thriveglobal.com/stories/46721-metoo-turns-two

Botwin, Shari. (2019). *Publications*. Accessed January 30, 2019, https://www.sharibotwin.com/publications

Bunn, Tom. (2014, August 15). Is what you are feeling a flashback? *Psychology Today.* Accessed November 9, 2018, https://www.psychologytoday.com/us/blog/conquer-fear-flying/201408/is-what-you-are-feeling-flashback

Carroll, Matt, Sacha Pfeiffer, and Michael Rezendes. (2002, January 6). Church allowed abuse by priest for years. *Boston Globe.* Accessed February 3, 2019, https://www.bostonglobe.com/news/special-reports/2002/01/06/church-allowed-abuse-priest-for-years/cSHfGkTIrAT25qKGvBuDNM/story.html

Chen, Joyce. (2017, October 17). Alyssa Milano wants her "Me Too" campaign to elevate Harvey Weinstein discussion. *Rolling Stone.* Accessed February 28, 2019, https://www.rollingstone.com/movies/movie-news/alyssa-milano-wants-her-me-too-campaign-to-elevate-harvey-weinstein-discussion-123610

Cohen, Judith, Esther Deblinger, and Anthony Mannarino. (2014). Trauma-focused cognitive behavioral therapy. *Psychology Today.* Accessed January 30, 2019, https:/www.psychology.com/us/therapy-types-trauma-focused-cognitive-behavior-therapy

Coker Ross, Carolyn. (2018, December). Eating disorders, trauma, and PTSD: What you need to know to get better. National Association of Eating Disorders. Accessed February 8, 2019, https://www.nationaleatingdisorders.org/blog/eating-disorders-trauma-ptsd-recovery

Commonwealth v. William Henry Cosby, Jr. (2018, September 25). MJ-38102-CR-0000131-201 (Montgomery County, PA).

Courtois, Christine. (2014). *It's not you, it's what happened to you: Complex trauma and treatment.* Dublin, OH: Telemachus Press.

Eckleberry-Hunt, Jodie. (2018, January 13). Leave that shit behind: Moving on from trauma #PTSD. *Medium.* Accessed December 15, 2018, https://medium.com/@jeckleberryhunt/leave-that-shit-behind-moving-on-from-trauma-ptsd-eeae0e2c5468

Fagan, Carolyn. (2018, November 25). The impact of mass school shootings on the mental health of survivors: What parents need to know. *Psycom.* Accessed February 10, 2019, https://www.psycom.net/mental-health-wellbeing/school-shooting-survivor-mental-health

Finocchio, Karen. (2018). One Tough Muther. Accessed January 30, 2019, https://www.theonetoughmuthershow.com

Friedman, Matthew J. (2019). PTSD: History and overview. US Department of Veterans Affairs. Accessed February 7, 2019, https://www.ptsd.va.gov/professional/treat/essentials/history_ptsd.asp

Gorman, Alison. (2018, February 28). Expert says students need to return to school after trauma. 6ABC. Accessed February 10, 2019, https://6abc.com/health/expert-says-students-need-to-return-to-school-after-trauma/3155256

Habits for Wellbeing. (2013). 20 quotes to inspire self-compassion. Accessed January 31, 2019, https://www.habitsforwellbeing.com/20-quotes-to-inspire-self-compassion

History Channel. (2010). 9/11 attacks. Accessed February 1, 2019, www.history.com/topics/21st-century/9-11-attacks

History Channel. (2018). Columbine High School shootings. Accessed February 1, 2019, https://www.history.com/topics/1990s/columbine-high-school-shootings

Kahn, April, and Kristeen Cherney. (2017). Dependent personality disorder. Healthline. Accessed January 20, 2019, https://www.healthline.com

Kennedy, Merrit. (2016, September 28). California eliminates statute of limitations on rape cases. NPR. Accessed February 9, 2019, https://www.npr.org/sections/thetwo-way/2016/09/28/495856974/california-eliminates-statute-of-limitations-on-rape-cases

Kübler-Ross, Elisabeth. (2014). *On grief and grieving: Finding the meaning of grief through the five stages of loss.* New York: Scribner.

Mack, Sammy. (2018, July 30). Stoneman Douglas staff and therapists get free trauma training for start of school year. WLRN. Accessed February 9, 2019, https://www.wlrn.org/post/stoneman-douglas-staff-and-therapists-get-free-trauma-training-start-school-year

Mastroianni, Brian. (2018, September 25). 5 myths about PTSD you need to stop believing. Everyday Health. Accessed February 3, 2019, https://www.everydayhealth.com/ptsd/common-ptsd-myths-debunked

Mayo Clinic. (2018). Electroconvulsive therapy. Accessed December 13, 2018, https://www.mayoclinic.org/tests-procedures/electroconvulsive-therapy/about/pac-20393894

Mayo Clinic. (2018). Post-traumatic stress disorder (PTSD). Accessed February 3, 2019, https://www.mayoclinic.org/diseases-conditions/post-traumatic-stress-disorder/symptoms-causes/syc-20355967

McCarthy, Tom. (2018, April 26). Bill Cosby found guilty in sexual assault trial in milestone for #MeToo era. *The Guardian.* Accessed February 9, 2019, https://www.theguardian.com/world/2018/apr/26/bill-cosby-guilty-trial-sexual-assault

Memorial Sloan Kettering. (2018, December 30). Accessed February 1, 2019, www.mskcc.org

Milligan, Susan. (2018, December 23). Sexual assault reports spike in #MeToo era. *US News.* Accessed February 10, 2019, https://www.usnews.com/news/national-news/articles/2018-12-27/sexual-assault-reports-spike-in-metoo-era

Milman, Oliver. (2017, September 28). Hurricane Sandy five years later: "No one was ready for what happened after." *The Guardian.* Accessed February 3, 2019, https://www.theguardian.com/us-news/2017/oct/27/hurricane-sandy-five-years-later-climate-change

NBC News. (2015, October 9). Full episode: The Cosby accusers speak. Accessed January 30, 2019, https://www.nbcnews.com/dateline/video/full-episode-the-cosby-accusers-speak-543502915620

RAINN. (1994). *Statistics.* Accessed November 6, 2018, https://www.rainn.org/statistics

Shure, Jane, and Beth Weinstock. (2009). Shame, compassion, and the journey to health. In William N. Davis, Jane Shure, and Margo Maine (Eds.), *Effective clinical practices in the treatment of eating disorders.* New York: Routledge.

Sky, Michael. (2002). Emotional suppression causes serious damage to bodies, minds, and spirits. *Inner Self.* Accessed December 5, 2018, https://innerself.com/content/personal/happiness-and-self-help/performance/4858-emotional-suppression.html

Smith, Melinda, Lawrence Robinson, and Jeanne Segal. (2018). Coping with grief and loss. HelpGuide. Accessed January 4, 2019, https://www.helpguide.org/articles/grief/coping-with-grief-and-loss.htm

St. Cyr, Jocelyn. (n.d.). About. Accessed November 9, 2018, https://www.jocelynstcyr.com

Stuart, Tessa. (2015, December 3). 2015: The year in mass shootings. *Rolling Stone.* Accessed February 9, 2019, https://www.rollingstone.com/politics/politics-news/2015-the-year-in-mass-shootings-349831

Thorpe, JR. (2017, December 1). This is how many people have posted "me too" since October, according to new data. *Bustle.* Accessed February 9, 2019, https://www.bustle.com/p/this-is-how-many-people-have-posted-me-too-since-october-according-to-new-data-6753697

Tull, Matthew. (2018). Verywell Mind. Accessed November 9, 2018, https://www.verywellmind.com/matthew-tull-phd-2797109

Vagianos, Alanna (2019, January, 22). Larry Nassar's first known victim is a mother figure to hundreds of young survivors. *Huffington Post*. Accessed February 9, 2019, https://m.huffpost.com/us/entry/us_5c3656c3e4b00c33ab5fS94d

van der Kolk, Bessel. (2015). *The body keeps score*. New York: Viking.

Weaver, Donna. (2013, October 27). Survivors struggle with emotional aftermath of Hurricane Sandy. *Press of Atlantic City*. Accessed February 3, 2019, https://www.pressofatlanticcity.com/survivors-struggle-with-emotional-aftermath-of-hurricane-sandy/article_17b57e9a-3f0f-11e3-b615-001a4bcf887a.html

Yahoo Celebrity Staff. (2018, September 26). Bill Cosby sentenced to 3 to 10 years in state prison for sexual assault, deemed a "sexually violent predator." *Yahoo! Entertainment*. Accessed February 9, 2019, https://www.yahoo.com/entertainment/bill-cosby-sentenced-3-10-years-state-prison-sexual-assault-deemed-sexually-violent-predator-182219288.html

INDEX

abandonment, 29, 30; fears of, 39–40, 54; by mother, 77–82; self-worth and, 31, 32–33

abuse: denial about, 170; family environment of, xvii. *See also* child abuse; childhood sexual abuse

abusers, 170; past child abuse of, 106

abusive behavior, alcoholism and, 86, 88

abusive relationships: of Alissa, 25; journal on, 87, 88, 90; of Karen, 85–91

acceptance, as loss stage, 109

acquaintance rape, of Janice, 204

addiction: Ashwood Recovery on trauma and, 7, 114–115; Jonathon trauma story and, 42–45; of Tammy's brother, 65–66; trauma and, 7, 8, 114–115. *See also* alcoholism; drug addiction; substance abuse

adolescence, of Botwin: gynecologist in, 181–182; memories of, 173–174

Al-Anon, 132

Alcoholics Anonymous, 44

alcoholism: abusive behavior and, 86, 88; of Betsy, 73; after death of child, 92; of Jonathon, 42–44

Alissa, trauma story of, 23, 27–28; abusive relationships of, 25; combat experience, 42–43; death of father and, 23–25; older boyfriend relationships in, 24–25; rape of, 24–25; supervisor verbal attack in, 27

Allred, Gloria, 12, 193, 204

American Psychiatric Association, on PTSD, 4–5

American Psychological Association, trauma definition by, 1

Amy, trauma story of: death of husband of, 136–141; new relationship of, 140–141; son response to father death, 136, 137; son therapy encouragement, 136, 137; trauma therapy group of, 138–140

ANAD. *See* National Association of Anorexia Nervosa and Associated Disorders

anger, 63–66, 67–70, 76–77, 80–82, 180; ability to conquer, 72–82; death and, 73, 75–76; defense mechanism of, 25–26; expression of, 67, 70–71; family and, 82; healing strategies for using, 83;

ABOUT THE AUTHOR

Shari Botwin, LCSW, has been counseling survivors of all types of trauma in her Cherry Hill, New Jersey, private practice for more than twenty-two years. She has conducted keynote presentations for universities and professional conferences throughout the country. She has given expert testimony on breaking stories related to trauma on a variety of international media outlets, including NBC News, ABC News, CBS News, CTV News, CP-24 News, CNN, and Radio Europe. Botwin has also published feature articles in several online trade magazines, including *Thrive Global*, *Huffington Post*, *Toronto Star*, *Authority Magazine*, *Medium*, and the *Philadelphia Inquirer*.